M000107438

CINEMATIC
FAITH

CINEMATIC
FAITH

*A Christian Perspective
on Movies and Meaning*

William D. Romanowski

Baker Academic
a division of Baker Publishing Group
Grand Rapids, Michigan

© 2019 by William D. Romanowski

Published by Baker Academic
a division of Baker Publishing Group
PO Box 6287, Grand Rapids, MI 49516-6287
www.bakeracademic.com

Printed in the United States of America

All rights reserved. No part of this publication may be reproduced, stored in a retrieval system, or transmitted in any form or by any means—for example, electronic, photocopy, recording—without the prior written permission of the publisher. The only exception is brief quotations in printed reviews.

Library of Congress Cataloging-in-Publication Data
Names: Romanowski, William D., author.
Title: Cinematic faith : a Christian perspective on movies and meaning / William D. Romanowski.
Description: Grand Rapids : Baker Publishing Group, 2019. | Includes bibliographical references and index.
Identifiers: LCCN 2018036416 | ISBN 9780801098659 (pbk. : alk. paper)
Subjects: LCSH: Religion in motion pictures. | Motion pictures—Religious aspects. | Motion pictures—Moral and ethical aspects.
Classification: LCC PN1995.9.R4 R66 2019 | DDC 791.43/6823—dc23
LC record available at https://lccn.loc.gov/2018036416

ISBN 978-1-5409-6205-8 (casebound)

Scripture quotations are from the Holy Bible, New International Version®. NIV®. Copyright © 1973, 1978, 1984, 2011 by Biblica, Inc.™ Used by permission of Zondervan. All rights reserved worldwide. www.zondervan.com. The "NIV" and "New International Version" are trademarks registered in the United States Patent and Trademark Office by Biblica, Inc.™

In keeping with biblical principles of creation stewardship, Baker Publishing Group advocates the responsible use of our natural resources. As a member of the Green Press Initiative, our company uses recycled paper when possible. The text paper of this book is composed in part of post-consumer waste.

19 20 21 22 23 24 25   7 6 5 4 3 2 1

Contents

Movie Musings

Preface

Cinematic Faith is a primer for navigating the world of film—specifically, American film and culture—from a Christian vantage point. This book is written for moviegoers who are interested in the relationship between faith and the cinema. I have kept in mind educators who might make use of this book for courses in religion, popular culture, film and media studies and production, or in church, ministry, and other educational settings. Although the scope of this study is limited to American Christianity, all people of good will are likely to have similar concerns about film viewing, the effects of film and media, and representations of identity groups.

This book is a sequel of sorts to my *Eyes Wide Open: Looking for God in Popular Culture* (first published 2001, revised edition 2007) with a focus on the American cinema, the subject of my research and teaching interests. There are different kinds of movies, including documentaries and experimental films, but I am focusing on fictional or narrative films—the ones seen by most people. Fictional films intend to tell a story. They draw our interest, focus our attention, and engage our thoughts and emotions by involving us in a process of trying to understand their meaning.

With Hollywood being the dominant film industry worldwide, American movies are easily accessible and broadly discussed. In any given year, about seven hundred films will be released theatrically, according to the Motion Picture Association of America (MPAA, www.mpaa.org). Films move in and out of theaters and come out on Blu-ray/DVD, pay TV, or streaming services in a matter of months. This milieu of constant movement presents a challenge when writing about the cinema; the new becomes old rather quickly, and a movie that scores at the box office this year might well be forgotten in the next. And so, relying on enduring "popular" films as illustrations has an advantage: they are likely to be familiar to readers or, if not, readily available on DVD or streaming services.

The movies treated in these pages are a mix of classic, older, and more recent films (several of which I've used in courses that students have expressed enjoying very much). I consider a variety of films, including award winners, popular releases, and some very good ones that have flown under the radar. This is in accord with the world of popular art and culture, where we cannot necessarily equate artistic excellence with popularity or commercial success. I intend to offer effective and workable illustrations that, along with related tools for analysis, can be used as touchstones in talking about other movies along the same lines. The aesthetic criteria that I take up in a Movie Musing about *Rear Window*, for example, can be applied just as well to any other movie. Then again, there are many other ways to consider this Alfred Hitchcock classic.

And while we're on the subject, the Movie Musings are just that: reflections that take a certain slant on a movie and that illustrate key ideas. These treatments are not meant to be thorough or complete. After teaching for many years, I've discovered that a full-blown film analysis is often of less value in generating discussion than one that introduces an idea and raises questions suggestive of a point of view.

One aim of this study is to heighten enjoyment and aesthetic appreciation with a deeper understanding of the ways that movies express *meaning* and, in doing so, convey life perspectives. A second aim seeks to acquaint readers with the mainstream American cinema, with the way it shapes our imagining of the world, and consequently, with how to think critically about dominant cultural beliefs expressed in movies from the vantage point of Christian assumptions. Making critical engagement a routine part of the movie-going experience is a central concern.

This book highlights the benefits of a faith-informed approach that centers on art and perspective. It aims to offer an accessible and workable approach, one that is consistent with the way we experience movies, becomes easier with practice over time, and produces (ideally) results that make the effort worthwhile. As I will argue, emphasizing the role of faith—and specifically Christian faith—is valuable because perspectives, whether religious or secular, can and do make a vital contribution to the movie-going experience. In offering this approach, I hope to show how to take an interpretive stance without being dogmatic about it. A key feature of this approach is the realization that various perspectives exist that could—and should—foster dialogue leading to a deeper understanding of movies and life. Indeed, considering movies in terms of their veracity to our real-life experience constitutes an important benefit of the cinema; movies give us one way of making and testing discoveries about life.

A few details before moving on. I make a stylistic practice of letting scholars, commentators, and film critics speak for themselves as much as possible. I refer to critics regularly, not only to glean insights but also to show how we can benefit from reading critical reviews. I do the same with scholars and commentators as a way of pointing to the work of others who have shaped the ideas and arguments in this book. It's a way of inviting readers to follow up my sources toward a fuller discussion. I invite you to check out the eSources available at www.bakeracademic.com/CinematicFaith. These eSources contain additional info, such as summary points, sidebars, links to movie clips, and other fun stuff. Box Office Mojo (www.boxofficemojo.com) is the source of production and box-office figures.

Some readers may be more familiar with a different vocabulary for thinking about film in terms of faith. As you'll see, I make use of perspective and culture, concepts that have to do with the creation of symbolic meanings as a way of understanding and acting with purpose in life. I will occasionally use the terms *worldview* and *ideology*. A worldview refers to a basic interpretation of reality. Worldviews tend to be largely static, sweeping models of reality that are available to comprehensive analysis. Moreover, worldviews belong more to the historical period and culture perhaps than to the ordinary folks who live in them. Ideologies typically have to do with power relations in society—social, political, economic—and specifically a ruling group's control over the governing ideas or "official" version of reality. With that in mind, I use the term *ideology* to refer to a specific social platform—propositions and policies—as manifestations of a cultural system. These concepts are obviously related, each offering a different slant on a common concern and describing the context and outlook from which people make sense of life and live meaningfully in the world.

Spoiler Alert

I'm aware that as a matter of journalistic practice, film reviewers are supposed to refrain from revealing story twists, character revelations, and surprise endings. And not all readers will have seen the films considered here. For that reason, I provide some context for those who may not have seen a film, but be forewarned: the sort of analysis done here necessarily involves discussing films in detail, including identifying plot points, conflicts, and their resolutions. In other words, if you've not seen a movie treated here, I'm likely going to ruin any surprises. That's unavoidable. Even so, none of my descriptions are complete enough that they can adequately substitute for viewing the movie itself. And there can be some benefit to reading about a movie before seeing it.

The Calvin College McGregor Summer Research Fellowship program provides opportunities for faculty and students to work together on a research project. Two fine students, Eckhart Chan and Michael Lentz, worked through some of the early chapters with me, offering helpful suggestions; they also did the initial legwork in creating the accompanying eSources. I am appreciative of my colleagues at Calvin College for their ongoing support of my research and specifically for granting me a sabbatical to bring this project to completion.

Finally, my life and work benefit enormously from having a supportive community of family, friends, and colleagues. I'm deeply grateful for each one of you, especially Donna and our children, Michael and Tara.

And with that, let's go to the movies.

> Additional materials—including summary points, sidebars, links to movie clips, and other fun stuff—can be found at www.bakeracademic.com/CinematicFaith.

1

Why a Christian Approach?

Hollywood doesn't necessarily want to make Christian movies. It wants to make movies Christians think are Christian.

—Richard Corliss, *Time*

W hat's your favorite movie?
That's the question I get asked most often when people realize I teach and write about film. Sometimes it's about comparing personal favorites. Occasionally, someone wants to measure my film bona fides against the American Film Institute's 100 Greatest American Movies of All Time. Mostly, it's meant to be a conversation starter. People enjoy talking and even arguing about movies they like or don't like and the reasons why.

I don't have one favorite film actually. There's *Casablanca* (1942), a classic Hollywood melodrama set in World War II, starring Humphrey Bogart and Ingrid Bergman: "We'll always have Paris." *Chinatown* (1974) is a near-perfect neo–film noir that resonates with a Calvinist sense of human depravity— "which is nice," as Carl Spackler (Bill Murray), assistant groundskeeper at Bushwood Country Club, might say. I can't remember being on a golf course without someone reciting dialogue from *Caddyshack* (1980): "This crowd has gone deadly silent." "Oh, it looks good on you though." "It's in the hole! It's in the hole!" The movie is laced with crude and sometimes juvenile humor ("Whoa, did somebody step on a duck?"), but what a hilarious satire of the pretensions of the country-club set.

Bull Durham (1988) upended the conventional sports film not by telling a story about winning the big game but by revealing character in the defining moment. "Most of us will never get a chance to play or win that big game," writer and director Ron Shelton said, "but we can all take a big risk that proves to us something about ourselves."[1] Sometimes there's a simple, straightforward connection between film and life. *Toy Story 3* unleashed my feelings about becoming an empty nester. The wizarding world of Harry Potter helped me to see, while directing a study abroad program in England, the joy and fascination students had for this incredibly popular film franchise; through the eyes of those younger than myself I came to see the value of these books and movies as part of their childhood and adolescence.

I suppose this is all to say that I am not a hoity-toity film buff. There are movies I appreciate for their aesthetic inventiveness, clever narrative, or insightful cultural commentary. Others might lack artistic excitement, but I still enjoy them for the ride. There might not be much character development, but the story has a certain intrigue and the ending is satisfying—even if entirely predictable. I suspect there are many others who have a similar movie palette. And that reminds me: Once, during an interview for a research grant, a committee member pulled me aside and asked expectantly, "What d'ya *really* think of *Animal House*?" There truly is no accounting for taste.

I have friends who are much more passionate about film than I am. Terry, who has a PhD in foundations of education, loves going to the movies. It doesn't matter what the critics say. Sometimes he'll stop by the theater and buy a ticket to the next showing—a habit of more than a quarter of all moviegoers.[2] Terry has developed a keen understanding of film genres, story formulas, and characterizations. He can talk about even the most mundane film as a reflection of cultural beliefs and values. Being an avid moviegoer serves him well in his roles as a campus minister and college professor; he's introduced students—myself included—to cinema's potential as a communicator of life perspectives.

Then there's Peggy. Based on a movie trailer, a friend suggested that as a Friday night outing a group of us see *The Choice* (2016), an adaptation of a Nicholas Sparks novel. Peggy checked her trusty source and emailed us: "What!? The Rotten Tomatometer was at a paltry 11%!!!!!!! I RARELY like a film below 80 percent. And I HATE going to bad or mediocre movies." If that wasn't enough to dissuade us, she included blurbs from the reviews:

"Really, almost anything in theaters right now would be a better alternative." (*Fort Worth Weekly*)

"*The Choice* is the cinematic equivalent of staring at a Hallmark Card for 2 hours." (*The Hollywood Reporter*)

"The only choice is to make sure a barf bag is nearby." (*San Francisco Chronicle*)

"Directed by Ross Katz and filmed like an ad for erectile-dysfunction medication, *The Choice* is almost repellently synthetic." (*New York Times*)

"I understand it's a social event," she wrote, "but I'd rather sit through a Super Bowl game than a bad movie. It really depresses me." (Did I mention that Peg's not much of a sports fan?) We ended up seeing the movie Peggy wanted to see from the start: *Eye in the Sky* (2015), a British production starring Helen Mirren and Alan Rickman (in what was his final role).

Peggy has a PhD in linguistics and developmental psychology. She frequents the local art house cinema, prefers Buster Keaton's deadpan humor to Charlie Chaplin's sentimentality, and has over 170 films in her Netflix queue. She watches all kinds of movies, but with one condition: they have to be excellent. What the top critics think matters a lot to her.

Peggy and Terry are film aficionados and conscientious Christians with different tastes and motivations—which is to say there is no definitive "Christian" way of talking about film. My hope, however, is to cultivate some common ground by investigating film as a popular art form that plays important roles in our lives and culture.

Understanding Christian Views

Since the birth of motion pictures at the turn of the twentieth century, the church has played a significant role in the development of the American cinema as a legitimate art and institution. Motivated by diverse goals and outlooks, Protestant, Catholic, and evangelical leaders advanced different agendas aiming to influence Hollywood productions and practices. At various times and under specific circumstances, church groups launched initiatives that included boycotts, calls for industry reforms, efforts to increase film literacy, and even veiled attempts at censorship.

How are we to make sense of the varying approaches to film and attitudes about Hollywood as an institution? First, Christian perspectives are rooted in religious traditions that represent different ideas about the relation between faith and culture. The rules of cultural engagement create expectations for the cinema regarding its purpose, potential, and standards for evaluation. Are movies entertainment? Popular art? A voice for morality? A means of persuasion? Accordingly, Christians apply different interpretive frameworks to draw conclusions about a movie's meaning that reflect moral, religious, and ideological priorities and opinions.

Second, Christian approaches to film attempt in differing ways to merge moral and religious principles with democratic values and market realities. They pivot on two religiously derived principles that exist in some tension: one stresses freedom of expression and individual conscience, while the other has to do with protecting the church and the moral and religious character of American society.

Two different yet complementary visions for the cinema emerge. Those emphasizing the first principle tend to think of the cinema as an arena for cultural conversation. They reserve their praise for searching stories about the human dilemma and complexity of life. If filmmakers were to take advantage of their First Amendment liberties, that calls for criticism but not censorship. Those emphasizing the second view are inclined to favor movies that teach positive lessons and instill right moral and cultural values, especially in youth. If the first tendency runs the risk of allowing for some exploitation, the second can be faulted for its commitment to the status quo, as it tends to favor movies that rely on prevailing stereotypes and that depict a homogenized world in which all issues are plain and simple.

A persistent notion in both camps is that church patronage ought to be enough to persuade profit-minded film producers to make movies that take seriously the concerns of religious moviegoers. Counter to and frustrating this notion, however, is that most people, religious or not, generally think of Hollywood movies as entertaining and show little concern about their potential impact on spectators and society.

The role of religion in public life continues to be a topic of lively debate. The term *Christian* is complicated because it has acquired various meanings with both positive and negative connotations and multiple uses. *Christian* can be used to describe a theology, a person or community of people, a market, or commercial products. Those familiar at all with the Christian tradition will know that it is as theologically rich as it is diverse. Thus, I'm using *Christian* as an umbrella term referring generally to a religious community made up of an array of theological, moral, and cultural outlooks. That said, I make no presumptions about the extent to which my views represent those of other Christians or communities of faith.

The Fifth Quadrant

Hollywood hit a rough stretch in 2005. Movie attendance was down for the third straight year. A film adaptation of British theologian C. S. Lewis's children's book, *The Chronicles of Narnia: The Lion, the Witch and the Wardrobe*, finished second in the final box-office tallies. It came in right behind

Revenge of the Sith, the latest installment in the celebrated *Star Wars* series, and ahead of *Harry Potter and the Goblet of Fire*. The year before, *The Passion of the Christ* finished third in box-office grosses behind the *Shrek* and *Spider-Man* sequels, dumbfounding industry analysts and critics alike. An R-rated movie steeped in religious controversy, *The Passion* is not exactly a Friday-night date film—or family fare. Yet this extremely violent depiction of the torture and crucifixion of Jesus of Nazareth, in Aramaic and Latin with English subtitles no less, became an astonishing commercial hit driven by churchgoers.

The surprising commercial success of *The Passion* and *The Chronicles of Narnia* put the church market on the film industry's radar in a big way. Film studios, a writer in *USA Today* observed, were hoping "to convert those with little faith in Hollywood fare into permanent moviegoers." Hollywood studios routinely divide their audience into four quadrants: male, female, under 25 years old, and over 25. Their mission now? To make churchgoers the fifth quadrant.[3]

Time film critic Richard Corliss reported that film studios were making a concerted effort to pitch their releases to church folks, "a vast, untapped market," as one Christian promotion executive put it. Those Corliss called "cinevangelists" were finding hitherto-unnoticed theological truths in movies like *Spider-Man* ("We keep looking for radioactive spiders, but really it's God who changes us"). With some bewilderment at how "Christians are increasingly borrowing from movies to drive home theological lessons," Corliss made a curious observation about the emerging church-marketing trend: "Hollywood doesn't necessarily want to make Christian movies. It wants to make movies Christians think are Christian."[4]

Oddly enough, as Hollywood studios began developing strategies to go after religious moviegoers, a leading marketing firm discovered that most Americans identifying themselves as religious watched pretty much what everyone else did. An executive observed, "Tastes don't differ at all," except that the more conservative churchgoers were more "likely to see movies rated R for violence." Surveys showed that "most people, even the very religious, are very happy with their movies."[5] That was in 2005; not much has changed since then. More recent surveys show that, for the most part, practicing Christians see the same movies at the same rate as everyone else.[6]

Overall, it appears that most filmgoers—church folks included—find movies enjoyable enough to buy a ticket, but also largely innocuous and, with occasional exceptions, requiring little thoughtful analysis it seems. According to Barna researchers, "For all the concern about the degradation of cultural values and Hollywood's lack of a moral compass," most people believe that

movies have no real influence on their beliefs and values.[7] Survey results provide evidence for what scholars call the "third-person effect": everyone thinks
he or she is personally immune from what might adversely affect others.[8]

Now, movie attendance is one thing, but the more important concern here
is *how* Christians think about movies they watch at theaters, on DVD, or via
streaming services. Does having a faith perspective matter? Can it provide a
distinct way of thinking about Hollywood releases? And why is investigating
these questions a worthwhile endeavor?

A Framework of Expectations

After inquiring about my favorite films, people will often ask me if thinking
too deeply about a movie ruins the enjoyment of watching it. I suggest that,
to the contrary, developing good critical skills and practices can enhance our
experience and make movie watching (and making) more interesting and
rewarding—especially as we become better at it.

Critical approaches are theories or ways of thinking about film. They
consist of assumptions and principles that explain the nature of film and its
functions and effects. Furthermore, critical approaches offer tools for analyz-
ing and assessing the quality and importance of films. There are many ways to
examine movies and interpret their meanings, including by focusing on things
like the production process, film aesthetics, representation (e.g., race, gender,
and disability), the spectator's experience, how a film reflects reality, and more.
A good approach should be practical, provide reliable insights, and sharpen
our judgments. It will open possibilities for film criticism and production.
Film criticism, which some practitioners argue is an art form itself, suggests
new avenues for interpretation and different ways of thinking about the issues
of life that the film addresses. The best film analysis enhances our experience
by sending viewers back to the film with fresh ways of looking at it.

The critical approach presented in this book is anchored in the movie itself
and its unique capabilities as an audiovisual medium. Moviegoers usually
spend most of their time talking about what the film is about, its *content*,
which is understandable. Most, however, are not well versed in talking about
a film's *form*—the means by which it conveys content. Even professional film
reviewers tend to rely on "a heavy dose of plot synopsis," *New York Times*
critic Manohla Dargis concedes. "They pay very little if any attention to the
specifics of the medium, to how a film makes meaning with images—with
framing, editing, *mise en scène*, with the way an actor moves his body in front
of the camera."[9] The upshot is to attribute a movie's impact almost wholly
to the effect of the story, as if acting, editing, cinematography, production

design, and so forth have little influence on the creation of a film's meaning or a viewer's response.

This book does not propose to replace an emphasis on content with an emphasis on form but rather to treat film as both an aesthetic object and an experience—one that can be exciting, pleasurable, boring, disagreeable, or mind blowing. In other words, a spectator's response cannot be reduced simply to the cinematic techniques and patterns a filmmaker employs to tell a story. Nor can the creation of meaning be so reduced either. Rather, as we'll see, meaning emerges from the interplay of film form and the viewer's interpretive stance. I will suggest that both production and reception demonstrate a close relationship between film and perspective.

We typically don't watch a narrative film purely out of aesthetic interest or with what is known as *disinterested contemplation*. Even so, the extent to which one is cognizant of a film's aesthetics can enrich the viewer's understanding and appreciation. The sound and editing in *Dunkirk* (2017) are amazing, but it is not the entire cinematic experience. Christopher Nolan's World War II drama is a "a tour de force of cinematic craft and technique," Manohla Dargis declares, but just as important, the story "is insistently humanizing despite its monumentality." The filmmaker "cinematically" shrinks the distance between past and present with "visual sweep and emotional intimacy, with images of warfare and huddled, frightened survivors that together with Hans Zimmer's score reverberate through your body," so that by the film's end "you are reminded that the fight against fascism continues."[10] Ultimately, *Dunkirk* is an impressive collision of art, politics, morality, and historical memory.

The foregrounding of matters of form and moviemaking draws attention to *how* films represent beliefs and *how* they create meaning. My approach aims to balance interpretive concerns with the ways and means that convey content and perspective. The main concern is with the essential relationship between *form* (the patterns and techniques used to tell stories), *content* (the film's subject), *style* (the filmmaker's distinctive use of patterns and techniques), and *perspective* (the film or filmmaker's point of view). Film scholars and critics may practice this sort of analysis, but most people interested in relating the worlds of religion and film are more familiar with religion than with the methods by which film communicates. Even so, whether mindful or not, while watching a movie we experience these elements—form, content, style, and perspective—as being of a piece. Much more on this will come. For now, it is enough to make the point that appreciating what makes movies artistically interesting and effective can make us better viewers and more creative storytellers.

The approach advanced in this book is just as interested in film aesthetics as in the many benefits the cinema offers as both popular art and culture.

Together these create a *framework of expectations*, an umbrella term that covers several key concepts that form the basis of this study. A framework of expectations describes the bundle of expectations or assumptions that we have about the cinema in general and that inform the way we think and talk about specific movies or kinds of movies. The concept is relevant to both creating cinematic art and interpreting its meaning. Let me explain.

In one sense, a framework of expectations refers to the ideals, beliefs, and assumptions a person holds about the nature of the cinema itself; we expect movies to foster cultural conversation, impart moral values, or simply provide entertainment. When watching a film and discussing it afterward, viewers activate their own *outlook* or *perspective*, which, as we'll see, is their vantage point in life that harbors assumptions (or expectations) used to understand and think critically about movies. But there's more. Viewers tend to prefer some types of movies over others (comedy, fantasy, or historical fiction) and often measure the quality of a film based on prior experiences that are based on these familiar genres. However formulaic, over and over we anticipate the feats of heroism in action-adventure films or the satisfaction of lovers reuniting in romantic comedies. We gauge these movies in part on how inventive and pleasing they are based on expectations acquired from previous viewings. Other factors might be considered as well: a penchant for certain topics or themes, a desire to be entertained by feel-good movies or challenged by those that probe contemporary issues, the graphic nature of the film's subject, a favorite actor or director, the opinion of critics, and more.

In short, a framework of expectations embraces a variety of factors sometimes loosely rolled together—from aesthetic principles, standards, and tastes, to moral, cultural, ideological, or religious concerns—that viewers apply in moving combinations that make sense to them. As this suggests, we approach the cinema with some flexibility. I can fall for a good melodrama as much as anyone else, which may surprise you when you read chapter 6. Then again, I'm not much for horror films even though writer/director Scott Derrickson (*The Exorcism of Emily Rose, Deliver Us From Evil, Doctor Strange*), a Christian, maintains that horror is "the genre that is most friendly to the subject matter of faith and belief in religion."[11]

Movies are at once imaginative creations and cultural and commercial products. This line of analysis accounts for typical moviegoing habits (and moviemaker tendencies) without shying away from or becoming heavy handed about the significance of religious outlooks in appreciating and thinking critically about the cinema. Moreover, a framework of expectations does not belong solely to individuals but can be shared by like-minded people and held in common in some measure by members of a culture or subculture. Filmmakers and audiences alike share a familiarity with the cinema along with common ideals, values, and assumptions about life and the world; this is the basis of cultural communication.

Imaginative Mapping of Reality

In my view, film is a popular art form that is as entertaining as it is valuable in helping people navigate within and by way of their culture.[12] Movies shape our mental geography, our point of view, our symbolic conceptions that give meaning and purpose to life. One way to analyze narrative films, then, is to think of them as *imaginative maps of reality*—a key concept. A map is not the reality it depicts but a representation of a geographical space. Made to scale, it provides a directional orientation (north/south, east/west) and shows highways, byways, cities, towns, and distances that help a traveler navigate from one destination to another.

By way of analogy, we can think about movies as mapping a cultural space. While every film has a spatial and temporal setting, its fictional universe consists of a set of ideals and assumptions that underlie story and character. Herein lies the film's soul: the depth, the substance, the crux of movie meaning. Charting this value system gives us a compass of sorts, or reference points that help us find our bearings in the world of the film.

Approaching movies in this way serves three purposes. First, it draws attention to a film's constructed character: moviemakers as imaginative mapmakers. A movie is a symbolic re-presentation of reality that integrates filmic techniques and concepts to dramatize a view of life. A second aim follows: to blend the outward audiovisual world of the film—characters, setting, actions, and dialogue—with the film's *cultural landscape* (another key concept) that consists of widely accepted ideals, beliefs, values, attitudes, and assumptions. Movies, as you'll see, communicate in a roundabout way—not by *telling* but by *showing*. Viewers discover cultural meanings that find expression in characterizations and story lines, in symbols, images, patterns of cinematography, design, editing, and so forth.

Finally, using this approach highlights the significant role that cinema plays as a cultural conversation partner. Movies can both affirm dominant beliefs and allow us to explore unfamiliar territory. Experience, however, teaches that some maps are better than others, and so are some movies in their way of envisioning the world and navigating the complexities of life. Still, by offering a viewpoint, a film sets up a possibility that we can accept or criticize, or perhaps affirm some aspects and question others. Film viewing, to put it another way, lends itself to thinking about the stuff of life.

For these reasons, I develop the idea of *perspective*, or *outlook*, as a principled and practical way of talking about movies and meaning. The choice is hardly earthshaking. This central concept is widely used across disciplines in the arts, humanities, and social sciences. The term can be traced to the fourteenth century, its usage related to sight and perception. It also describes the way two-dimensional art represents three-dimensional objects by creating an illusion of space and depth. The idea of perspective—as a way of perceiving and thinking about things—is relevant to both art and life. So, we've got that going for us, "which is nice." The term also has the advantage of its familiarity; simply put, perspective is about having a point of view— and everybody knows they've got one. Also, dictionaries include plenty of synonyms—standpoint, viewpoint, slant, approach, and vantage point—that help a writer avoid some repetitiveness. What's most important to emphasize is that what we believe, our perspectives, are among the dynamics animating the design and reception of narrative films.

The American cinema is a multidimensional phenomenon: movies are protected speech, an influential means of communication, and the product of profit-making corporations. We can enhance our talk about film as popular art and culture by keeping in mind that the production of feature films occurs in a highly commercialized environment. Marketing and demographics are impersonal forces that, along with profit making, have a noticeable impact on film production and content.

This suggests three related motifs: *film as popular art*, *film as culture*, and *film as commercial product*. Throughout this book, I will be describing movie design, how meaning is created, and how we use movies to talk about life, along with industry and commercial influences. I make use of an interdisciplinary approach to look at the cinema "ecologically"—that is, in terms of a wholly interacting environment.

Whether creating comedy, romance, horror, drama, fantasy, action-adventure, or science fiction, filmmakers design movies so that viewers will understand, appreciate, contemplate, and discuss them. After watching *Eye in the Sky*, my friends and I shared some of our own thoughts and opinions on the merits of the film, its depiction of the use of drones, and the geopolitics of warfare in the fight against terrorism. Movies invite such conversation. We do well to ask a number of questions: *What* are the stories about life that movies tell? *Who* tells the stories? *What* is their inspiration? From what *perspectives* do filmmakers approach the issues of life? What are the *means* by which filmmakers suggest *meaning*, and how do viewers interpret their films? These are the kinds of questions explored in the chapters that follow.

MOVIE MUSING

Interpreting Time Loop Fiction in *Groundhog Day* (1993)

I don't want *Groundhog Day* here. I don't want us to go through the same thing we went through last year with no result.

—Senator Susan Collins, on gun control legislation

Democrats are living their own version of *Groundhog Day*. Every day, they wake up and realize they are still in the 2016 presidential primary.

—Bill Scher, *Politico Magazine*

In *Groundhog Day*, comedian Bill Murray plays Phil Connors, an obnoxious Pittsburgh weatherman unhappily assigned—yet again—to cover the annual Groundhog Day celebration in Punxsutawney, Pennsylvania. According to folklore, a cloudy day on February 2 means an early spring; the sight of his shadow sends the groundhog, Punxsutawney Phil, back into his burrow—a predictor of more winter to come. So goes the small-town annual event. But after the ceremony, a winter blizzard traps the dispirited Connors and his TV crew, forcing them to spend another night in Punxsutawney. The next morning, in the same bed, at the same B&B, the clock radio comes on at 6:00 a.m. Connors awakes once again to Sonny and Cher singing "I Got You Babe," and discovers that he is reliving Groundhog Day. This happens again the next day, and the next, as Connors suffers through each one inexplicably playing out exactly as before.

The narrative is designed as a *time loop fiction*, a term one scholar uses to refer to fictional "worlds that end only to begin again." A time loop is characterized by a "tension between constant structure and variable interaction." In *Groundhog Day*, the events that occur on February 2 consistently recur even as Phil Connors interacts variously with the repeated encounters. In effect, the time loop narrative incorporates into the world of the film the "repeatability or replayability" that exists for the viewer/interactor.[13]

Connors is the only one in the world of the film who is aware of the time trap, and it seems there is nothing he can do to escape. But "after going through periods of dismay and bitterness, revolt and despair, suicidal self-destruction and cynical recklessness, he begins to do something that is alien to his nature," the late film critic Roger Ebert observed: "he begins to learn."[14] Connors takes piano and French lessons, starts helping townspeople as part of his daily routine, and eventually acquires a sense of humility, empathy, and acceptance. The completion of his personal transformation brings the story to its climax as the former curmudgeon now wins the heart of his news producer, Rita

Hanson (Andie MacDowell), and with that is "released from the eternal cycle of repetition," as one writer put it. "Of course, this being an American film, he not only attains spiritual release but also gets the producer into bed."[15] Phil's ordeal is over; Groundhog Day is now finally in the past. He and Rita stroll hand-in-hand down a snow-covered street presumably to a life of happily ever after.

Since its release in 1993, *Groundhog Day* has become a contemporary classic. It was added to the National Film Registry in 2006 ("a clever comedy with a philosophical edge to boot"), and in 2016 it had a 100 percent rating among top critics on Rotten Tomatoes.[16] *The Atlantic* celebrated the film's twentieth anniversary, calling it "a profound work of contemporary metaphysics."[17] A theatrical musical production of the film is currently having a successful run on Broadway. *Groundhog Day* also turned out to be one of the favorites at the Museum of Modern Art's 2003 film series, "The Hidden God: Film and Faith." As a writer for the British newspaper the *Independent* discovered, it has become "a crucial teaching tool for various religions and spiritual groups, who see it as a fable of redemption and reincarnation."[18]

Religious leaders of different faiths have all laid claim to *Groundhog Day* as representing their teachings. One scholar said the film "perfectly illustrates the Buddhist notion of samsara, the continuing cycle of rebirth that Buddhists regard as suffering that humans must try to escape." A rabbi saw the film as an allegory finding "Jewish resonance in the fact that Mr. Murray's character is rewarded by being returned to earth to perform more mitzvahs—good deeds—rather than gaining a place in heaven, which is the Christian reward, or achieving nirvana, the Buddhist reward." A Jewish film critic, however, read it differently: "The groundhog is clearly the resurrected Christ, the ever hopeful renewal of life at springtime, at a time of pagan-Christian holidays," he explained. "And when I say that the groundhog is Jesus, I say that with great respect." A Catholic scholar argued that it was "a stunning allegory of moral, intellectual, and even religious excellence in the face of postmodern decay, a sort of Christian-Aristotelian Pilgrim's Progress for those lost in the contemporary cosmos."[19] On the other hand, an evangelical Christian in Punxsutawney (the film's setting and shooting location) said her organization did not use the film as an educational tool: "We stick pretty much to Scripture."[20]

The filmmakers never expected *Groundhog Day* to resonate with the religious community, though they welcomed it. "It really was always intended as a very human story," screenwriter Danny Rubin said, admitting that he "was aware in a general way of Buddhist concepts and reincarnation, but it was more something I noticed after writing the original script than anything I did on purpose."[21] The film's director and cowriter, the late Harold Ramis, was raised in the Jewish tradition, but observed no religion himself. "I am wearing meditation beads on my wrist, but that's because I'm on a Buddhist diet," he said with characteristic humor. "They're supposed to remind me not to eat, but they actually just get in the way when I'm cutting my steak."[22] If people found their own faith in the film, "it really was not faith in a God, because there's no God postulated in

Groundhog Day," Ramis maintained. "It's really faith in humanity. And I'm nothing if not a secular humanist. You don't need religion to be a good person."[23] *Groundhog Day* shows that even if the film was not conceived with a specific religious intent, a viewer's framework of expectations can make for interesting interpretations, here with regard to religious tradition.

2

Culture Communicates

*Biblical Principles for a
Peculiar Means of Expression*

> Art washes away from the soul the dust of everyday life.
> —Pablo Picasso

To determine the 100 Greatest Jewish Films of all time, staff at *Tablet Magazine*, a daily online periodical, had some fun asking, "What the heck is a Jewish film?"[1] The most common survey responses were movies that featured Jewish characters, actors, producers, or themes. Some readers were content with a film exhibiting "a distinctly Jewish sensibility" that could be "over-the-top or subtle or even that impossible-to-define 'I know it when I see it.'"[2] In the end, the list included *Fiddler on the Roof*, *The Graduate*, *The Wedding Singer*, and a top choice for many, *E. T. the Extra-Terrestrial*.

Likewise, most of Catholic Culture's Fifty Best Catholic Movies of All Time were directed by Catholics. The list consists "primarily of films that deal with Catholic characters, Catholic society, and the Bible in ways that are not hostile to the Church."[3] It includes *Going My Way*, of course, but also *Casablanca*, *Chariots of Fire*, and *Groundhog Day*. The slogan for Christian Films.com, an online evangelical distributor, announces, "Every movie on this website has a message for Jesus Christ." The website's founder says that makes it "quite simple when it comes to selecting which films to offer. I'm looking for message first."[4] What I could find of comparable Protestant lists feature movies about church figures like Martin Luther or events like the Protestant Reformation.

As expected, the filmmaker's faith affiliation is a key benchmark, along with a film's subject matter and intended purpose, in cataloging movies broadly by religious tradition. In a good-hearted way, this exercise gives us occasion to explore the idea of faith as a context for thinking about film.

I made the point earlier that how Christians think about film depends largely on their reading of the Bible regarding the relation of faith and culture. And so, as a common point of departure for Christians of all stripes, the first step sketches out central features of a biblical vision. A second and related task considers how these basic biblical realities might inform a Christian framework of expectations for storytelling and interpretation. Being mindful of one's own Christian story is a way of taking notice of a film's imaginary world and bringing it into focus through the lens of a faith perspective. This is key to a discerning and exploratory engagement with film. A third task is eventually to employ this perspective in thinking critically about conventional Hollywood films.

Make no mistake. The point of this analysis is not to disparage movies that don't subscribe to the Heidelberg Catechism; nor is it to create rigid categories with a simplistic equation of "Christian" with good movies and "non-Christian" with bad ones—or for some filmgoers perhaps vice versa. Rather, I want to pursue Richard Corliss's remark about Hollywood-produced "movies Christians think are Christian" by considering how a Christian outlook might affect our understanding of American movies that we enjoy for assorted reasons.

We begin on a dark and stormy night when God "laid the earth's foundation" and made humans "a little lower than the angels and crowned them with glory and honor" (Job 38:4; Ps. 8:5). Readers familiar with Terrence Malick's provocative experimental epic film *Tree of Life* (2011) will probably recognize that first verse as part of the film's opening quotation.

Your Mission, Should You Choose to Accept It

A good place to anchor a Christian framework of expectations is in the essential belief that all persons are created in the image of God. A basic tenet in Reformed theological circles is that God endows humans with the capacity, power, and authority to *cultivate* the creation (Gen. 1:27–28; 2:15). The *cultural mandate*, as it is called, is an enduring directive manifested in the human propensity to fashion culture that invests ordinary life with divine purpose.

In short, to be God's image bearer is to be human, and to be human is to be a cultural agent. This appears in Scripture as an overarching theme: "The highest heavens belong to the LORD, but the earth he has given to mankind" (Ps. 115:16). Humankind begins in a garden, with Genesis recording the introduction of agriculture, industry, music, and the arts, and human destiny leads to the city depicted in the book of Revelation.

Human identity, purpose, culture, and history are ultimately bound up in this call to stewardship or administration of God's creation. Culture is both universal and diverse: a common human endeavor and a historical process carried on from generation to generation by "every nation, tribe, people and language" (Rev. 7:9). Thus, culture is the realm of human thought and activity and its results, both material and nonmaterial products. At its crux, it manifests the endless human search for meaning. It expresses the ways we make sense of the world in order to flourish and live meaningfully in it.

Let there be no illusion: This divine calling does not make us into gods. It is futile to think we can fathom altogether life's deepest secrets. We are finite people trying to comprehend the eternal ways of the God that endures across the ages. Every person, unconditionally, has inherent worth as God's image bearer. And while that inherent value as image bearer demands respect for human dignity, human sin is also real and its effects are inescapable. We cannot ignore the persistence of evil in history. Everywhere we see that we live in a world where human sinfulness divides us and wreaks havoc—and that's putting it mildly. We flourish with ideas, actions, and initiatives that secure human dignity and lead to peace, justice, and freedom. Conversely, abuse, hatred, intolerance, and discrimination can lead to chaos, pain and suffering, madness, tragedy, destruction, and death. In short, the world can be a wonderful place or a living hell.

If all this makes for a complex and ambiguous view of the human condition, the dilemma itself points to the need for a remedy that can only come from beyond ourselves. Our yearning for redemption is satisfied by God's promise and deliverance: "But God demonstrates his own love for us in this: While we were still sinners, Christ died for us" (Rom. 5:8). Believers are justified by God's grace through faith in Christ rather than by human effort (Eph. 2:8–9). The ordinary world that we experience—its joys and hardships—is also God's world, where death has been defeated and eternal life has been declared. Even if we struggle to understand God's presence, we end up with not two worlds but one. God offers redemption, which comes from experiences that make people aware of their own brokenness, insufficiency, and need for forgiveness.

The kingdom of God is not of this world, but it is still present within it. Christians live with a tension between present and future realities, often described as the "now" and the "not yet."[5] This phrase refers to the time between Christ's resurrection and the long-awaited return of the Messiah that will bring about the consummation of God's creation into the new heavens and new earth (Rev. 21–22). "Between the times" the care and cultivation of God's creation engages believers in a struggle against powers and principalities (Eph. 6:12). And like the servants in the parable of the talents, we will have to settle our accounts when the rightful owner returns (Matt. 25:14–30).

Revising a Christian maxim somewhat, being *in* a culture without being *of* it calls for discovery, diligence, and discernment. Faithful living then has to do with redirecting unhealthy and damaging patterns in accord with the basic principle of obeying God and loving our neighbor as ourselves. The imagery Jesus used to describe Christian influence—salt, light, and yeast—suggests having a persuasive effect from within a culture rather than control or dominance (Matt. 5:13–14; 13:33). Salt, a common flavoring and preservative, evokes the idea of conserving and enriching; light signifies having vision and understanding; yeast transforms something for the better.

If not already clear, it is important to stress that culture contains and expresses our full humanity. The Latin root of the word "culture" is *colere*, which "can mean anything from cultivating and inhabiting to worshipping and protecting."[6] Ultimately, humans are utterly accountable to God, to whom the psalmist says, "you perceive my thoughts from afar," and about whom the psalmist reminds us, "his eyes watch the nations" (Pss. 139:2; 66:7). There is no dividing life into *sacred* and *secular* realms—a common practice that has resulted in privatizing religion. Ironically, compartmentalizing religion is itself a result of *secularization*, which involves the diminishing scope of religious influence and authority in public life.

So, I understand the term *secular* as a viewpoint or an orientation in life rather than as a boundary. In addition, I consider faith just as important for public as for personal life. In other words, being salt and light has to do not just with individual perceptions and actions but also with cultural practices and social institutions. These are all ways that we carry out God's command to love our neighbor and care for the creation's well-being. We all have the potential to become corrupt. Racism, sexism, and other harmful attitudes can be held personally, embodied in cultural habits and traditions, and codified in public policies.

In this regard, my colleague philosopher James K. A. Smith thinks of institutions as "spheres of action" that, when functioning rightly, "cultivate all of creation's potential toward what God desires: *shalom*, peace, goodness, justice, flourishing, delight."[7] The prophet sums up instruction for a proper relationship with God: "to act justly and to love mercy and to walk humbly with your God" (Mic. 6:8). This value-laden directive applies to both personal and public affairs. And as we'll see soon enough, these values also provide a reliable guide for thinking discerningly about American culture.

Let's look more carefully now at two key and closely related concepts: culture and perspective.

"Life Is Like This": Cultural Communication

"All the world's a stage, and all the men and women merely players." This familiar line from Shakespeare's *As You Like It* suggests a relation between life and drama. Some theorists argue that life *is* drama, which we can study in terms of the roles we play in the acts and scenes of everyday life. Much as a script or screenplay provides point of view, story direction, and character action, a culture serves as a conceptual guide for people's viewpoints, deeds, and motivations in the theater of life.

People are nurtured into a culture and, it follows, are largely bound by it. We tend to see, feel, think, and act according to established norms. As scholars observe, "All experience is cultural through and through, that we experience our 'world' in such a way that our culture is already present in the very experience itself."[8] In short, we live within and by way of culture. Our culture influences our activities, shapes our experience and expectations, and provides a means for coping with the new and unexpected. It brings order, clarity, and direction out of the complexities and contradictions in life. And in doing so, culture gives us assurance about ourselves and our place in the world.

We can understand culture as a complex pattern of widely shared ideals, beliefs, values, and assumptions. Think of the world—all that is, visible and invisible—as a primary environment; culture is a secondary, *symbolic system* that humans create as a way of interpreting reality.[9] Symbolizing assigns meanings to people, objects, or events that represent a certain attitude and perception. The word *symbol* itself is derived from the Greek *symbolon*, meaning to "throw together." A symbol and what it represents have a closeness like two halves of the same thing; a symbol shares in the reality of what it symbolizes.

Symbolizing has to do with the human imagination, the creative ability to mentally fashion new ideas, images, sensations, or things not immediately present to the senses. Creating a symbolic universe happens as a result of a complex process that involves interaction among people and with their environment. To imagine, then, is to have a power over reality: to determine the value and meaning of people, events, and things.

Since cultural conceptions are metaphorical in nature, scholars treat metaphor making as "essential to human understanding and as a mechanism for creating new meaning and new realities in our lives."[10] The word "metaphor" comes from the Greek *meta* ("across or over") and *pherein* ("carry or bring"). A metaphor works by suggesting a way to understand one thing in terms of another by implied comparison. By juxtaposing two seemingly unrelated things, one invests the properties of the one thing in the other to produce a nuanced rather than a straightforward understanding. Love is (pick one) a rose, a battlefield, a garden, a fine wine, an adventure. The kingdom of heaven is a hidden treasure, yeast, a mustard seed, a pearl, a net. Notice that each metaphor stresses certain features of an experience over others to produce different meanings.

To illustrate, the famed abstract artist Pablo Picasso is credited with the saying: "Art washes away from the soul the dust of everyday life." It is not that art literally scrubs clean a soul. Rather, the saying metaphorically evokes the idea that encounters with art can transform ordinary living. Through art, we come to experience, in new and expressive (soulful) ways, deeper meanings that are often hard to see through the "dust" of mundane existence. A metaphor illuminates; it conveys meaning by pointing beyond itself.

Story consultant Robert McKee works with the premise "*Story is metaphor for life.*" We can think of a movie as "a two-hour metaphor that says: Life is like *this!*"[11] Narrative films point beyond themselves to deeper realities that are disclosed within and through the film. They function like metaphors, drawing implied comparisons between a fictional world and real life. Movies amplify the ordinary by portraying a heightened sense of reality; they cut through the humdrum (dust?) to highlight only what is significant to the story. Such knowledge and awareness—along with the fact that movies are often more about the stuff of dreams and desires than real-life experience—makes them seem to transcend the everyday. It's like having an epiphany, the way movies offer viewers disclosures, criticism, and insight into life and the world. McKee attributes this to the way stories, unlike ordinary incidents in life, fuse ideas and emotions in a way that occurs so rarely that when it does happen "you think you're having a religious experience."[12]

A Bit about Perspective

A *perspective* or *outlook* is a vantage point from which we make sense of reality, regardless of how conscious we are of it functioning in our lives. A perspective can be carefully articulated by scholars, expressed in an artist's slant on a subject, and lived out in the activities of ordinary life.[13] It takes shape as a hanging together of ideas, perceptions, and attitudes with more or less coherence as a pattern of meaning—that is, a conceptual design, however loosely cobbled together, used to define reality and make sense of life experiences.

On the one hand, our outlooks are inescapably based on a hope that what we believe is the truth. We all harbor deep-rooted beliefs that are necessary for meaningful action. No matter what they consist of, whether a belief in absolute human autonomy or divine Providence, we take these as articles of faith, so to speak. We hold them as beyond questioning and as true apart from any discourse or argumentation. Perspectives have a religious character insofar as they have to do finally with bedrock beliefs about ourselves and the world we live in.

Then again, our beliefs and values are constrained by space and time— that is, cultural traditions and historical circumstances. This helps explain inconsistencies in our outlooks and the nature of ensuing conflicts. Claims to absolute truth are countered with arguments that values are culturally conceived and historically relative. We have seen this tension foster lively debate, but we have also seen it be exploited in the public arena when portrayed as a choice between values and ideologies, not as competing ideas.

As expected, human shortcomings and limitations thwart our efforts to interpret reality; our views of life are not nearly as unified and consistent as we might wish to believe. It is hard to imagine, for example, a person being unaffected by living in an American culture that prizes self-sufficiency, competitiveness, and immediate gratification and defines success largely in terms of the accumulation of wealth and power. How are Christians to reconcile such a value system that entwines health and wealth with God's favor and, for instance, the parable of the sheep and the goats? In relating the parable, Jesus does not identify with the rich, powerful, and entrepreneurial but with "the least of these," the hungry, the stranger, and the imprisoned. And he makes their care a condition for eternal life (Matt. 25:31–46).

All this suggests that while religious convictions are undeniably important, they may or may not be the most significant in shaping "Christian" attitudes and actions. One way of understanding the variety of Christian groups today might be in terms of the way they coalesce around different viewpoints that are informed by or, contrariwise, that inform their interpretations of the Bible. As far as storytelling goes, assuming a biblically informed outlook suggests complex characterizations and the creation of fictional worlds marked by a measure of ambiguity—that is, the possibility of multiple meanings, some of which will even be opposing.

Just to be clear: God's creation is knowable in part, if never completely. There is a real world that exists outside and independent of human thought.

In the end, we understand the world partly through our engagement with it. Our faulty perceptions eventually encounter bumps in reality. In some measure, certainty, doubt, and discovery together animate a perspective. Still, our conceptions deeply influence our experience in this world.

Biblical Ideas for Thinking about Film

All things considered, we can draw four basic principles as a guide for a critical and productive engagement with the cinema.

First, the arts are a vital aspect of human life and culture, a legitimate and worthy human endeavor enriched with creativity and curious interpretation. We should understand film, then, as valuable *in and of itself* and ask how we can make the most of its creative potential and unique capacities in service of God and neighbor. Therefore, we start by affirming film's essentially artistic character as the *means* by which it fulfills roles and purposes in human life and culture.

What qualifies as art has changed over time, debated endlessly in a crucible of entangled concerns, including racial, cultural, and social prejudices. For our purposes, we can talk about art simply as creative products of the human imagination. Artworks are the result of human handiwork distinguished by their imaginative quality and allusive, or suggestive, character. Moreover, they are designed to serve many purposes in life. In other words, the arts have always acquired their status in relation to their intended uses and functions. And—let's be clear—they have always had a commercial base, whether patronage, public funding, or the consumer marketplace. Movies are no exception.

A peculiar means of human expression, art enriches by subtle disclosure rather than instant clarity—that is, direct statements or discursive arguments. It's "the difference between documenting and dramatizing," as one writer puts it.[14] We should think of narrative films, then, as artworks that do not *say* so much as they *display*; they *show* rather than *explain*. Moviegoers, for example, might be hard pressed to articulate American values in any systematic way, but they probably know and love movies that represent them. Countless films, for instance, dramatize the American myth of success—the belief that through determination and hard work you can achieve anything.

In sum, film follows artistic norms and fulfills various purposes and, in doing so, displays a capacity to both entertain and provide occasion for us to reflect upon and think critically about our lives and society. Movies can address critical issues and communal concerns, offering accessible artistic interpretations of our lives and times.

Second, created to love and worship God, human beings are incurably religious. That is to say that everyone has a *sensus deitatis* (sense of deity) and is endowed with the capacity to know and to respond to God. Researchers have found that religion is "so deep-rooted in human nature, thwarting it is in some sense not enabling humans to fulfill their basic interests."[15] People can live their lives directed in service of God or other things they might take to be of supreme importance, or of "ultimate concern," to use theologian Paul Tillich's recognized phrase.[16] All perspectives of life then are "religious" in the sense that they affirm fundamental beliefs about life's deepest questions and profound mysteries.

This suggests a way of looking at artworks to see how form, style, and perspective come together to reveal in whose service the artist stands. "Art is a symbolically significant expression of what drives a human heart, with what vision the artist views the world, how the artist adores whom," philosopher Calvin Seerveld explains. "Art itself is always a consecrated offering, a disconcertingly undogmatic yet terribly moving attempt to bring honor and glory and power to something."[17] Human sinfulness does not dispel our urge to worship God but misdirects it. With a lively rhetorical flourish, Bono, lead singer of the band U2, expresses this notion in describing the purpose of music making: "Whether it's worship of women or their designer, the world or its destroyer, whether it comes from that ancient place we call soul or simply the spinal cortex, whether the prayers are on fire with a dumb rage or dove-like desire, the smoke goes upwards, to God or something you replace God with—usually yourself."[18] In their own way, these writers are pointing to the religious dimension of art.

To say that all movies are in a sense religious is not to infer that filmmakers, consciously or not, are reflecting on the divine. Indeed, most Hollywood releases are not conceived as such. Rather, I want to highlight how movies function *religiously* by conveying life visions.[19] By creating a world that metaphorically points beyond itself, a movie offers a revelatory kind of experience, one that hinges to some extent on the nature of willing suspension of disbelief in its call for active imaginative engagement. The way spectators make discoveries in dramatic ways can help them make sense of life and the way the world works. McKee even gives this advice to aspiring writers. "The audience must not just understand; it must believe," he insists. "You want the world to leave your story convinced that yours is a truthful metaphor for life."[20] The bottom line for storytellers is to provide us with tales to believe in, narratives that play a part in shaping the way we imagine the world and our place in it.

This is no simple matter. Many factors influence filmmaking, not least of which is crass commercialism, as well as the many considerations related to viewer reception, including moral and ideological positions. Even so, the point is that film is one of the ways we envision life in the world, which relates it to faith.

Third, since faith is universal and encompasses all of life, we should expect movies to deal with our full humanity. That a film is about God, the Bible, or Christian characters makes it no more religious than one treating any of life's eventualities. This view shifts the emphasis away from a focus on explicitly religious content and puts the accent instead on assessing a film's artistic quality together with its manner of treatment—the way it brings a certain perspective to bear on *whatever* subject is portrayed. Seen as such, all movies merit religious reflection in the sense that they represent certain values and a vision of life. To put it another way, instead of making faith the *issue*—that is, the qualifying factor for Christian interest or concern—we allow faith to provide a *context* for thinking about film.

All of this raises several interesting questions: To what extent does the filmmaker's intentions create parameters for possible interpretations and valuation? On what basis are Christians to think about movies that can hardly be seen as having any explicitly theological concerns? Lastly, and perhaps most importantly, how do we remain mindful of our own beliefs in thinking about movies and still accord value to those representing different, even contrary, views?

A fourth principle comes from the idea of common grace—a Reformed theological concept referring to God's general provision for humankind.[21] God restrains evil in human affairs and gifts believers and unbelievers alike with technical skills and talents in art, science, and so forth in pursuit of re-creating the world to reflect God's glory. The biblical imperative charges us to live in light of our faith convictions. It is important, then, to maintain a critical posture without losing sight of the fact that all people have the capacity for creativity and truthfulness. As a popular paraphrase of Saint Augustine goes, "All truth is God's truth."

Regarding film, whatever the filmmakers' faith convictions, they can tell stories that enrich our understanding of the human condition. Many movies explore the shared human desire to understand the nature of evil, sin, and temptation and our yearning for forgiveness and redemption; some delve into our endless hope of living in a world without pain, anguish, and death. Likewise, movies that affirm biblical principles such as love, justice, stewardship, truthfulness, courage, and responsibility to one's neighbor have redemptive value.

The Golden Rule for Film Critique

Together, these four principles lay the groundwork for a two-pronged approach that is both discerning and exploratory, characterized by encounter and dialogue. With this approach comes a certain attitude. This way of doing film analysis recognizes and values diverse perspectives, while also maintaining the importance of one's own perspective in thinking critically about the cinema.

In one sense, awareness of perspective brings into sharper focus what seems clear enough: all films are value laden, which is crucial to their popular appeal. For that very reason, they merit critical reflection. Even comic-book adventures like *Marvel's The Avengers*—just to make the point—dabble in "Big Themes," *New York Times* film critic A. O. Scott notes, "among them honor, friendship, revenge, and the problem of evil in a lawful universe."[22] The tendency of most moviegoers may well be to unthinkingly accept the dominant cultural ideals and values as a "truthful" depiction of life. It's something like rooting for the home team. But that does not make the movies affirming the prevailing viewpoints immune to criticism.

Indeed, research suggests that the persuasive power of the cinema results from the cumulative effect of seeing many movies over time that all portray the world according to the dominant value system.[23] For this reason alone, people of good will ought to be concerned with a steady diet of Hollywood releases that exalt self-interest as the supreme human value, glorify violent resolutions to problems, treat finding the perfect mate as one's primary vocation and highest destiny, and offer material prosperity as the most reliable source of meaning and satisfaction in this life. This value system arguably runs against the grain of most religious traditions. It also draws attention to the importance of being able to discern and think critically about bedrock themes in the American cinema.

In another sense, movies can expose viewers to the lives of others and to cultures different than their own. With regard to the framework of expectations, we can think of these as cinematic encounters with the unexpected or the unlooked for. This may be a view, an attitude, or an eventuality that is new, different, or somehow inconsistent with a spectator's own outlook. Engaging films like these helps us realize that we do indeed perceive things from a certain vantage point. Movies that run counter to our presupposed beliefs can be jolting, enough to make us aware of our unquestioned prejudices and assumptions. Moreover, learning new things or taking up inconsistencies between values and lived experience can become occasions for people to revise or even change their viewpoints. In other words, there is value in engaging contrary views in both life and the movies as a way of learning about our own outlooks and those of others.

There are studies, for example, showing that "stereotyping results from long-term cumulative exposure to portrayals of minority groups in the media." Moreover, it appears that "particularly strong and memorable portrayals of minority characters may create more lasting impressions on viewers than cumulative exposure to portrayals that are more frequent but less significant."[24] Another analysis demonstrates that media depictions of racial minorities are "more likely to exert influence" on people who have little or no interracial interactions in real life.[25] This research highlights the power of art and the importance of the cinema in our cultural conversation. It shows that movies can play a part in how we imagine others, on the one hand, and give voice to those who are marginalized, on the other. It also calls attention to the commingling of art and life among the dynamics of movie watching.

"Movies change us," *Los Angeles Times* film critic Justin Chang writes. "They get into our heads. They get under our skin in all sorts of ways, and they're not always pleasant. You can hate something, but even to have come away hating something is a really useful experience; it tells you something about yourself."[26] We can benefit, in other words, from an honest dialogue with movies that probe the affairs of life, even unpleasant or disturbing events and conditions. And we become better critics with deeper self-awareness through spirited post-movie discussions that make us consider our values and refine our point of view, and even sometimes challenge us to think differently.

These realities lead to a thorny question: How can we critically engage film in imaginative ways that are mindful of and consistent with a faith perspective while also respecting the filmmaker's vision and artistic expression? Or to give it a slightly different twist, how are we to engage movies that are artistically praiseworthy and culturally significant but contain ideals and assumptions that might run against the grain of our own? Becoming impartial critics—fair and just in our judgments, and rising above our prejudices—is easier said than done. Who would deny adhering to one's own agenda when thinking about a film? The risk, of course, is that we might fail or refuse to give a filmmaker's viewpoint a fair appraisal, or we may find it difficult to even appreciate an honest artistic effort.

To engage a film on its own terms means to resist the temptation to unfairly impose your own point of view, while adhering to your own vantage point as a place of reference to understand and think critically about the film. This calls for an approach that plays itself out along the border between conviction and humility—at once critical, while also respectful of diversity of opinion. Think of this approach along the lines of a Golden Rule for film critique: treat the film preferences of others (and the values they represent) as you would have others treat your own film preferences (and the ideals they stand for). Here the principle of *common grace* serves us well.

In the ongoing search for truth, all of us face questions about God, human nature, and the meaning of life. We make moral choices. We deal with sin, temptation, and guilt. And we are confronted with pain, suffering, and injustice. We might have our share of success and enjoyment along with disappointments, moments of disillusion, and failures. Some contend with desperation and despair. We long for love, intimacy, a sense of belonging, and experience of forgiveness. All of us at some point will face death and have to ponder the possibility of redemption and whether there is life in a world to come.

Washington Post film critic Ann Hornaday uses three basic questions as a guide for film reviewing: What was the artist trying to achieve? Did he or she achieve it? And was it worth achieving? "The beauty of that framework is that it allows me to set pure subjectivity aside, the better to judge every film on its merits," she explains, whether reviewing "a mass-market spectacle" or a faith-based film that "preaches to the choir."[27] Hornaday's guidelines offer a thoughtful way of taking a film on its own terms and weighing the value of the questions it attempts to address. It gets beyond simply applauding movies that affirm our own views and rejecting those that do not and moves toward appreciating artistic encounters with various perspectives as a way of enriching our understanding of the human dilemma.

The film-viewing Golden Rule and Hornaday's guide also help us to respect artistic freedom and integrity, recognizing the interests and opinions of other groups and people. This is a necessary first step toward encouraging dialogue and fostering mutual understanding in service of the common good. The larger aim seeks a pluralistic cinema: an arena for discourse with room for diverse viewpoints, including Christian ones, on the universal search for human meaning in God's world.

Frame 1. In *Arrival*, communication with visiting aliens (heptapods) drives the narrative and compels the main characters to consider what it means to be human.

MOVIE MUSING

Manipulating Space and Time in *Arrival* (2016)

> The Sapir-Whorf hypothesis, yes. The theory that the language you speak determines how you think.
>
> —Louise Banks, *Arrival* (2016)

In the science-fiction film *Arrival*, aliens (heptapods) travel to earth in twelve huge spacecraft called "shells." These vessels are strategically located in countries around the globe, hovering about twenty feet above the ground. The aliens' unexpected arrival and unknown purpose (peace or conflict?) triggers a worldwide crisis.

US Army Intelligence officer Colonel Weber (Forest Whitaker) assembles a team whose mission is to clarify the aliens' intentions. He solicits the help of renowned linguist Dr. Louise Banks (Amy Adams) and theoretical physicist Ian Donnelly (Jeremy Renner) to decipher sounds that may be alien attempts to communicate. Weber instructs them: "Priority one: What do they want? Where are they from?" Getting answers to those questions is a slow process that drives the main action. As they are unable to communicate with the aliens, fear of a potential invasion spreads. Time starts running out for Banks as countries prepare for a global nuclear confrontation with the alien visitors.

When introduced to the serious-minded Banks, Donnelly reads from her book: "Language is the foundation of civilization. It is the glue that holds a people together, and it is the first weapon drawn in a conflict." She's got it wrong, he says: "The cornerstone of civilization isn't language, it's science." Their brief introductory conversation highlights the main conflict and theme: real communication—within Weber's team, among nations, and with the aliens—compels the main characters to think about what it truly means to be human (frame 1).

Slowly, in bits and pieces, language experts around the world begin deciphering the alien communications. Pakistani analysts figure out that, unlike human languages, the language of the heptapods—long-legged, squid-like creatures—is written in "logograms," a shorthand that uses characters to represent a word or phrase. A logogram is "free of time," Donnelly explains in a voice-over during a montage sequence. "Their written language has no forward or backward direction . . . which raises the question, 'Is this how they think?'"

Communicating with the heptapods proves difficult and laborious; the process of symbolizing itself becomes an obstacle that Banks and the others have to overcome to prevent the imminent global attack. As tensions mount, nations drop off the communication grid and begin mobilizing their forces. When a heptapod message is translated as "use weapon," she urges caution ("offer weapon"?), but uncertainty over its meaning triggers worldwide panic. "We don't know if they understand the difference between a weapon and a tool," Banks explains. "Our language, like our culture, is messy. In many cases one thing can be both."

Arrival is "an imaginative, escapist what-if scenario overlaid with semi-profound questions about fate, loss and the meaning of love," Ann Hornaday writes. A movie that is not "philosophically deep, exactly," but one that also does not "sacrifice worthy ideas on the altar of pure entertainment."[28] The film has an intriguing story premise and features a strong performance by Amy Adams and impressive production design. What also helps to make *Arrival* a top-tier sci-fi film is the way the narrative manipulates cinematic space and time as a way of mimicking the story's central idea. "The philosophy at the heart of the film is nonlinear time," film editor Joe Walker said, explaining that his method was "to crosscut a kaleidoscope of different moments from a life."[29]

The complex plot is organized in a nonlinear way—the events are not presented in sequential order. While encounters with the aliens happen chronologically with one event leading to the next, there are short sequences inserted with Banks and an unknown little girl: episodes that show the girl's birth, childhood, and eventual illness and death. We discover, along with Banks, that these are personal (subjective) visions she is having and that the girl is her daughter; the sequences, then, are not flashbacks but flash-forwards. These emotionally laden scenes are snippets of what's yet to come that increasingly affect Banks's actions in the present and that eventually merge with and bring resolution to the central story line. Acquiring the aliens' concept of time allows her to grasp the real meaning of their message to humanity.

In sci-fi films, the earthlings find a way to either defeat the aliens (*Independence Day, War of the Worlds*) or negotiate with them (*E. T., The Day the Earth Stood Still*). Either way, the main protagonists are left with a more enlightened understanding of human nature and the universe. Louise's encounter with the aliens affirms a theory she adheres to: "The language you speak determines how you think." As she gains fluency in the heptapods' language, realizing they know at once both the past and future, she begins thinking and even dreaming nonlinearly. Signifying her discovery, she names her daughter Hannah. "It's a palindrome," Banks explains. "That means you can read it both forwards and backwards, and it's still the same." The realization deepens the emotional drama of the main character while playing philosophically with the nature of time and human self-determination. Louise starts wondering, "If you could see your whole life from start to finish, would you change things?"

The nonlinear narrative works on other levels as well. First, it causes viewers to experience *cinematically* the main characters' bewilderment in trying to sort out the aliens' cryptic mode of communication. And second, its nonlinear structure gives a sense, via the narrative itself, of how acquiring the alien language helps create a new concept of the nature of time.

Arrival shows how movies can *cinematically* delve into the nature of reality and the human condition, asking deeply religious questions: Who are humans? What is the nature of reality? Discerning the ways movies probe and represent beliefs about such fundamental issues is a key plank in any framework of expectations.

3

Moviemaking Magic

Poetic Portals and the Power of Perspective

Hugo is specifically about those observers of life who, perhaps out of loneliness and with desire, explore reality through its moving images, which is why it's also about the creation of a cinematic imagination—Hugo's, Méliès's, Mr. Scorsese's, ours.

—Manohla Dargis, *New York Times*

Renowned director Martin Scorsese's *Hugo* (2011) is based on a historical fiction book, *The Invention of Hugo Cabret*, inspired by the true story of Georges Méliès, a turn-of-the-twentieth-century French filmmaker. Méliès began his career as a magician and brought his fascination with creating staged illusions to moviemaking. He became legendary for exploiting cinematic trickery to make delightful fantasy films that were immensely popular worldwide. "Leave it to Scorsese to make his first 3-D movie about the man who invented special effects," Roger Ebert remarks.[1]

Scorsese assembled a top-notch production team who filled the film with audiovisual wonder. The movie opens with a breathtaking digital tracking shot. The camera swoops across the cityscape of 1931 Paris, down into the Montparnasse railway station, along a platform between two trains, across a crowded concourse, and up to a close-up of Hugo (Asa Butterfield) peering wistfully out through the number 4 on a huge clock face. As one reviewer puts it, Hugo is "a crafty Dickensian orphan, a benign phantom of the opera, a

Hugo © 2011 GK FILMS, LLC; *Safety Last* © 1923 Harold Lloyd Entertainment; and *Back to the Future* © 1985 Universal City Studios, Inc.

Frames 2a, 2b, 2c. *Hugo* (top) brims with intertextual references like this symbolic image that appears in the silent classic *Safety Last* (bottom left) and in *Back to the Future* (bottom right).

blood brother of Quasimodo, a cinematic voyeur looking out on the world like the photographer in Hitchcock's *Rear Window*"—all rolled into one.[2] When his widowed father dies, twelve-year-old Hugo moves in with his alcoholic uncle, who goes missing after teaching Hugo to do his job tending the train station's clocks. Hugo performs the work diligently, and in secret, to cover his uncle's disappearance—and avoid the fate of the orphanage. He survives by stealing food and mechanical parts hoping to repair and then receive a message from an automaton his father built—a robot that is supposed to be able to write.

A celebration of moviemaking magic, *Hugo* includes occasions to show movies made by the Lumière brothers, the great silent comedians Buster Keaton and Charlie Chaplin, and of course Méliès. Indeed, the movie brims with intertextual references to the early cinema—many reworked in recent films (frames 2a, 2b, 2c). Hugo dangles from the hand of a giant clock, which evokes comedian Harold Lloyd's iconic clock-hanging sequence in *Safety*

Last (1923) that *Back to the Future* (1985) alludes to. The automaton Hugo's father built recalls the Maria robot created by Rotwang, the evil inventor in Fritz Lang's classic sci-fi futuristic *Metropolis* (1926); both resemble C3PO of the *Star Wars* films. And, as critics point out, the movie itself serves as an allusion to Scorsese's own campaign for film restoration and preservation. A despondent Méliès recounts having to sell nearly all his movies to a company that melted the celluloid into chemicals used to make women's shoe heels. It's a painfully touching scene depicting the destruction of these cinematic treasures as a profound loss.

Throughout the story, Hugo develops a relationship with Isabelle (Chloë Grace Moretz)—Méliès is her godfather—while evading capture by the dogged Station Inspector (Sacha Baron Cohen) and his Doberman pinscher. Hugo manages to find refuge in the clockwork's interior that is crowded with cogs, gears, and wheels, which recalls the original technology invented to make motion pictures possible.

The film finds its emotional core in the second half in the backstory of Méliès. We discover that the grumpy old guy, who is not taking kindly to Hugo's stealing at his toy store, was once a successful silent film producer. In the aftermath of the First World War, escapist fantasies no longer appealed to audiences. Bad fortune and poor business decisions forced Méliès from filmmaking; he disappeared from public life and makes a living now selling toys and candy at the shop in the Montparnasse train station.

The Magic of the Movies

It is not too much of a stretch to go from magician to moviemaker; both are producers of entertaining illusions. The magician's boasted "extraordinary feats of magic" are only stage tricks that give the illusionist the appearance of having special reality-defying powers. We marvel nonetheless at how it all happens right before our very eyes—the sleight of hand, misdirection, and rigged props. As Kingsley's character says in *Hugo*, "Magic tricks and illusion became my specialty. The world of imagination."

The "magic of the movies" refers to the way that moviemakers likewise create an illusion that can have a powerful effect on audiences. Images projected on screen can make us laugh, move us to tears, deliver visceral thrills, comfort, inspire, and provoke us. Rod Dreher, senior editor at *The American Conservative*, recalls how excited he was as a ten-year-old to see *Star Wars* in 1977. He remembers vividly how "the experience was so overwhelming, so hyperrealistic, that I lost myself in the story." As he left the darkened theater and entered "the brightness of the lobby," he says, "nothing looked the same.

Nothing. It was as if I had come down the mountain with my face shining from having seen God."[3]

I'm sure most moviegoers have had something similar happen to them at least occasionally. You're lost in the story, the movie ends, the credits roll, and you just sit there not wanting to leave that fictional world. It's hard bidding farewell to the characters whose experiences you've just shared; we want the adventure or romance to go on. And in some ways, it does, finding a lasting place in our conversations, dreams, and desires.

While watching a film, we put aside for a time the fact that we are sitting in seats with popcorn and drink in hand, staring at moving images projected on a screen. We allow the illusion these images present to transport us to another world. We can find the experience everything from fun and pleasurable to shocking and disgusting. We might feel happy, sad, angry, frustrated, bewildered, upset, or offended. Our hearts race during a suspenseful moment. We cringe when an innocent victim is struck. We might feel dizzy during a fast-paced car chase. We cover our eyes when things get scary. We breathe a sigh of relief when the heroine prevails. We laugh out loud, cry, or startle when we're frightened.

Why? How can we be so immersed in a movie (in one sense) all the while aware (in another) that what we are hearing and seeing never actually happened and is not actually happening right now?

Under normal circumstances, viewers are obviously mindful of the fact that "it's only a movie." Even so, it is common for us to experience a sense of losing ourselves for a while, of being swept away by the story—to be lifted out or temporarily relieved of reality. We want to be "kidnapped by the movie," as cultural analyst Susan Sontag puts it, by allowing ourselves to be drawn into the world of the film.[4] To be sure, the anticipation of having just such an experience is a big reason people go to the theater. We purchase a ticket and enter a darkened theater fully expecting the movie to carry us away into an imaginative world filled with love, mystery, and adventure. The magic of the movies.

Poetic Faith

Writers and philosophers have long contemplated the captivating effect of art. Samuel Taylor Coleridge, a nineteenth-century English poet and critic, famously described the reader of poetry as entering into a "willing suspension of disbelief for the moment, which constitutes poetic faith."[5] Coleridge's idea is widely understood to refer to a reader (and viewer) granting a creative work—whether fiction, theater, or film—its status as *imaginative reality*. We are willing to overlook the margins of the medium—page, stage, or screen—letting ourselves believe enough to voluntarily enter a world of someone else's imagination.

Suspending disbelief is a state of mind, a process of engaging the imagination that involves reasoning, perception, remembering, emotions, and desires. We accept as "believable" (in poetic, or cinematic, faith) that characters have superpowers or the ability to travel back in time or through a wormhole across universes. We believe that aliens, angels, wizards, or Santa Claus exist. We accept the notion that someone can infiltrate and implant an idea in another person's subconscious. It doesn't matter how mundane, whimsical, incredible, or fantastic fictive worlds are, or whether they are set in the past, present, or future. "It is in the mind of the audience that stories and characters become real," as one scholar writes about Coleridge's concept.[6]

I witnessed something of the power of suspending disbelief while watching a 3-D short, *Honey, I Shrunk the Audience* (1995), at EPCOT, one of the Walt Disney World parks. As I sat in the theater with the rest of the audience, Wayne Szalinski (Rick Moranis) arrived at the Inventor of the Year Award ceremony on a hovercraft that went haywire. He crashed through a glass sign, and the 3-D effect sent particles of shattered glass flying at the audience. People reacted by ducking and putting their arms up to shield themselves. The 3-D effect made it look like Szalinski was in the air right above us. And what did people in the audience do? They reached up and tried to touch the hovercraft. Uh, think about that. They know it's just an image, and yet could not resist trying to make physical contact. That's the power of suspending disbelief: we readily accept the invitation to enter into the world of the film.

If you've not seen Pixar's *Get a Horse!*, the 3-D animated comedy short that accompanied the theatrical release of Walt Disney Pictures' *Frozen* (2013), check it out on YouTube. It's a very creative and entertaining film. The story is premised on the idea of the movie screen working like the theatrical convention of a *fourth wall*, an imagined, invisible divider or partition that the audience can see through, but the actors act as if they cannot. Think of the movie screen as a conceptual threshold between one space and another that "simultaneously connects and separates," as film scholars describe it. The screen acts like a "material border between spectator and film," functioning at once to hide, display, protect, and filter while "keeping a safe distance."[7] Let me explain.

In one sense, the screen separates the audience from the world the film portrays, making us invisible in that world; characters don't seem to be aware that we're watching their every move closely. It also shields the audience from the filmic world. We might find ourselves amid the ferocious, bloody battle at

Omaha Beach during World War II (*Saving Private Ryan*), but we don't have to worry about being gunned down by a Nazi machine gun. The film-viewing experience allows for anonymity and safety; you feel no responsibility for what takes place in that world, even though you may be affected emotionally and have opinions about it. Watching a movie, then, is like passing through a *poetic portal* and arriving in another world, one fashioned with an artistic license and allusive finish, one that is different from and yet resembles our own.

The idea of the movie screen as doorway or passageway to an imagined place and time highlights the way movies invite audiences to enter fictional worlds. We willingly immerse ourselves in a captive black man's hopeful yearning for freedom while enduring the brutality of slavery in the antebellum South (*12 Years a Slave*, 2013), a young woman's emotional and physical battle to survive a televised fight-to-the-death (*The Hunger Games*, 2012), and a space pioneer's ordeal against extraordinary odds of being stranded alone on a faraway planet (*The Martian*, 2015). We're made privy to the prayers of a conflicted Pentecostal preacher in *The Apostle* (1997), a heart-wrenching conversation filled with remorse in *Manchester by the Sea* (2016), and an underrated actor's desperate need to overcome the fear of failure and display his real talent (*Birdman*, 2014).

Then there's Christopher Nolan's *Inception* (2010). This mind-boggling movie has viewers bouncing between "concentric layers of dreams" while following a team of "extractors" who infiltrate people's minds in order to plant or steal ideas. "Set in the world of dreams, and dreams within dreams, the movie is the narrative equivalent of a set of Russian nesting dolls," one writer explains. "Every time you think you've reached the center, Nolan pulls the film apart and shows us another world hiding within."[8] These movies and so many more transport us elsewhere, to other places, times, and points of view. They transform the screen into an imaginary space and allow us to artistically inhabit worlds of make-believe.

Aesthetic Emotions in Two Takes

Film viewing is a complex phenomenon. You read a novel at your own pace, pausing to think, turning back a few pages to find an overlooked detail, or even putting the book down for a time. You can do something similar with a movie on DVD or a streaming service. But film is a temporal art form: movies are designed to be watched uninterrupted during a fixed time span. In practice, viewing and analysis require a bit of a balancing act.

While a movie is "happening," viewers respond to what's taking place on screen. All at once, we gather what's going on, connect the dots, make quick judgments, and respond emotionally. The experience has immediacy. Whether a film covers hours, days, weeks, or years, the narrative discloses hidden secrets and makes the truth plain in the here and now, which gives the film a revelatory power. "In life, experiences become meaningful *with reflection in time*," Robert McKee explains. "In art, they are meaningful *now, at the instant they happen.*" A film elicits thoughts and references, blending them into a "meaningful emotional experience" known as *aesthetic emotion*, "the simultaneous encounter of thought and feeling." In effect, McKee explains, "aesthetic emotion harmonizes what you know with what you feel to give you a heightened awareness and a sureness of your place in reality."[9]

Carl Plantinga, my colleague film scholar, describes three types of emotions that characterize movie watching. *Direct emotions* like suspense, surprise, or excitement arise from the development of the story, occurring in response to what is happening on the screen. *Sympathetic* or *antipathetic emotions* have to do with a viewer's feelings *for* a character, like happiness, sadness, anger, or fear. *Meta-emotions* come after some reflection. They result from the spectator responding "emotionally to his or her own prior responses, thoughts or desires while viewing a film."[10] For example, with some afterthought a viewer might be embarrassed at having cried during a sentimental scene or feel guilty about having hoped for a character's demise.

To offer a quick illustration, if in real life the leg brace of a man standing on a railway platform got caught in the door of a train pulling away from the station, most bystanders would be alarmed and rush to help. When the same happens to the Station Inspector in *Hugo*, however, it's funny. Even though spectators understand it as a moment of slapstick comedy, some might feel a bit uncomfortable for having laughed at the momentary predicament of the poor inspector, who wears a leg brace because of an injury incurred during World War I.

In a sense, there are two "takes," to use a production term, in film interpretation. Both happen more or less while we're watching the film, but continue later as we step back, go over the movie in our minds, and reflect on it and our experience in the theater. This might involve talking with others and reading critical reviews, which can make a repeat viewing a very different experience than the first one. These two "takes" eventually become one piece: a process of discovery, analysis, interpretation, and re-interpretation that necessarily activates a viewer's perspective in one way or another.

Think about it. To some extent, viewers go to a movie with preexisting beliefs and emotions that condition their understanding of the film *during* the viewing—one feature of a framework of expectations. Most patrons of *42*

(2013) are already aware that racism is immoral and dehumanizing—seeing the hate and cruelty that baseball player Jackie Robinson endures only reinforces this belief. Audiences likewise go to the theater already rooting for Indiana Jones and fully expecting to see him outsmart the despicable Nazis. Can you imagine it ending any other way? And we've seen enough rags-to-riches stories to know that against all odds the down-and-out Erin Brockovich is going to win in a head-to-head battle with giant corporate executives. And so, as film scholar Nöel Carroll concludes, "Most of the beliefs that we might be said to acquire from art are things we already know and which, in fact, we must bring to the text in order to understand it."[11]

Viewers will also admire characters who demonstrate values and behaviors they already approve. Jones, archaeologist and adventurer, is the quintessential American hero: fearless, resourceful, confident, good-humored, with an abiding integrity—and fear of snakes. Robinson is savvy and tenacious, exhibiting courage, patience, and passion in breaking the color line in professional baseball. Erin Brockovich is the "total package," as they say, an attractive mother of three, and a legal clerk with street smarts, intuitiveness, determination, and a fighting spirit. How we respond emotionally, whether we sympathize with a character or not, and what judgments we make about a character, are complex and depend on a variety of factors based on our preexisting outlooks.[12]

Carroll argues that while narratives play off already existing moral beliefs and emotions, "in *exercising* these preexisting moral powers in response to texts, the texts may become opportunities for enhancing our already existing moral understanding." He calls this *clarificationism* and explains that mass artworks "can deepen our moral understanding by, among other things, encouraging us to apply our moral knowledge and emotions to specific cases."[13] To some extent, we can understand moviegoing as participating in a ritual that has less to do with the acquisition of knowledge than with the processing of cultural values and perspectives that might result in different interpretive readings.

Movies function, then, as "imaginative orderings of experience," to borrow a phrase that scholar John Cawelti uses to explain a culture and its literary formulas. Stories consist of cultural patterns—symbols, images, and myths—that become "modes of perception as well as simple reflections of reality." According to Cawelti, "Formula stories affirm existing interests and attitudes by presenting an imaginary world that is aligned with these interests and attitudes."[14] They function not only to maintain cultural consensus but also to resolve tensions and ambiguities, explore cultural boundaries, and help in the process of assimilating change.

Creating and Sustaining the Viewer's Belief

Clearly, we don't experience film in a vacuum. How we interpret movies and whatever effects they might have are mediated by many factors in differing combinations. We might have different reactions to a movie based on our age, viewing skills, gender identity, sexual orientation, race and ethnicity, education, political views, social and economic status, and religious outlooks. Moreover, these all represent different viewpoints and highlight the significance of perspective in film analysis. Though complex, filmmaking and criticism are animated by what people believe and how they perceive the world they inhabit.

Recall that movies are cultural artifacts. Filmmakers interpret reality and invite audiences to share their vision of life. Movies are designed to elicit emotional responses and deeply felt value judgments. They guide a spectator's pattern of responses by depicting ideals, values, and attitudes, suggesting approval and disapproval, directing point of view, creating an allegiance with a character, and so forth. Stories present events in ways that invite us to think about why they occur, how they affect characters, and how we might respond emotionally or in terms of our viewpoints. And so, if a character impresses us as being "real," eliciting empathy or allegiance, asking *why* and *how* this happens in the context of viewing the film helps us understand our own ideals and values and the craft of moviemaking as well.

Moviemakers go to great lengths to give a movie *verisimilitude*, the appearance of reality. Audience believability rests largely on the collaborative skills of moviemakers to capture and sustain a viewer's interest and curiosity. In one sense, we find a fictional world to be "true" and credible insofar as it remains internally consistent with the nature of its own imagined reality. "You therefore believe it, while you are, as it were, inside," said J. R. R. Tolkien, author of *The Lord of the Rings* trilogy, writing about literary fiction. "The moment disbelief arises, the spell is broken; the magic, or rather art, has failed."[15]

In another sense, we can argue that a film's believability depends on its truthfulness to actuality—or at least a spectator's view of its truthfulness. Is what a character lives or dies for worthwhile and meaningful in our judgment? How believable are the story's underlying assumptions about the nature of good and evil or its portrayal of truth, justice, and social order? How believably does it handle events of historical significance? In other words, the ideals and values that frame the story, provide character motivation, and endow the film itself with meaning must be persuasive in some measure.

Keep in mind that we all tend to compare a film's vision with our own. Narrative meaning occurs as a function of viewers' negotiating the relationship between the fictional world, their own perspectives, and real-life experience. In some measure, then, as a literary scholar puts it, "When we say we 'understand' a narrative we mean that we have found a satisfactory relationship or set of relationships between these two worlds."[16] A film's perspective thus influences how we might invest the movie with personal or cultural meaning, if not also the artistic value we give the film and our own experience in having seen it.

MOVIE MUSING

Blade Runner (1982) and The Imitation Game (2014) as Movie Metaphors

Even in the murkiest reaches of science-fiction lore, a man's gotta do what a man's gotta do.

—Janet Maslin, New York Times

Do Replicants Have Memories?

Based on a novel by Philip K. Dick (Do Androids Dream of Electric Sheep?), the movie Blade Runner is set in a futuristic Los Angeles (2019). The LA police pressure Rick Deckard (Harrison Ford) back into service to hunt and kill ("retire") four replicants—genetically engineered androids. They committed a bloody mutiny, escaped from an off-world colony, and in violation of law returned to Earth to find a way to extend their life span.

The film probes the nature of humanity in a futuristic world engulfed by globalization, advanced technology, and environmental decay. Blade Runner blends the themes and the conventions of film noir and science fiction, as well as their visual styles. From the detective's trench coat and the dark, rain-soaked urban streets of Chinatown to the use of Venetian blinds, low-key lighting, and claustrophobic framing, it clearly evokes the film noir landscape. The androids, police hover cars, high-tech gadgets, and futuristic setting provide a science-fiction context. The film noir universe is dark and cynical. Confronting the meaninglessness of life, its existential heroes harbor self-doubts, lack clear priorities, and try to survive one day at a time while dreading what lies ahead. The future is of course the setting of science fiction, which focuses on humanity's relationship to advancing technology and change. Both types of movies, then, center thematically on the human condition and the nature of reality.

Blade Runner © 1982 The Blade Runner Partnership

Frame 3. The interrogation scene in *Blade Runner* is a superb mixture of sci–fi and film noir.

Replicants have superior physical abilities, and some models, intelligence. Otherwise, they are virtually indistinguishable from humans, except for lacking cognitive empathy, the ability to know how another person feels or thinks. In the film's opening scene, a detective administers the Voight-Kampff test, a reliable psychological profiling exam that exposes replicants by measuring empathy. The room is sparse, with two high-backed chairs on opposite sides of a table laden with sophisticated electronic equipment. A large, slow-moving ceiling fan turns overhead. The blue hue with high-contrast, low-key lighting, and its source, an elongated window high on the back wall, makes the scene feel uncomfortably cold—a superb mixture of sci-fi and film noir (frame 3).

Mr. Holden, a blade runner who tracks down replicants, starts questioning a new employee, Leon Kowalski, an engineer in waste disposal who says he gets "kind of nervous when I take tests." Holden instructs him: "Reaction time is a factor in this, so please pay attention. Answer as quickly as you can." He asks Leon a hypothetical question about finding a tortoise in a desert. "What desert?" Leon asks, becoming antagonistic. "How come I'd be there?" "What's a tortoise?" Same thing as a turtle, Holden tells him. When Leon says, "I've never seen a turtle," Holden gives a look of realization. He continues, his voice made to sound like it is echoing, the tension escalating. "The tortoise lays on its back, its belly baking in the hot sun, beating its legs trying to turn itself over. But it can't. Not without your help. But you're not helping," Holden says. "Why is that, Leon?" Leon is visibly agitated. Both realize the obvious: Holden knows Leon is not human but a replicant. The scene does not end well for Holden.

Blade Runner's central theme—what it means to be human and to love—unfolds as the story increasingly juxtaposes the human and android characters. Ironically, while all the human characters exist in isolation, the replicants demonstrate genuine concern for one another. "Deckard becomes progressively dehumanized" as a result of destroying replicants, Philip K. Dick explains. "At the same time, the replicants are being perceived as becoming more human. Finally, Deckard must question what he is doing, and really what is the essential difference between him and them?"[17] At least that's how the novelist envisioned it. He saw Deckard as a human; so did screenwriter Hampton Fancher, who added some ambiguity in the film adaptation. Director Ridley Scott, however, conceived Deckard as a replicant.[18]

After poor test screenings, and over Scott's objections, Warner Bros. executives insisted on adding Harrison Ford's voice-over narration and an upbeat ending for the film's theatrical release. The director was not happy. When given sway over the Final Cut DVD version, Scott had the voice-over and ending deleted, and he edited a key scene to intensify questions about Deckard's humanity. In a scene from the original film, shots of a unicorn running in a dreamlike world are intercut with close-ups of Deckard at a piano. The reedited scene in the Final Cut version makes a stronger suggestion that Deckard is a replicant. Now, Rachael (Sean Young), a replicant and Deckard's love interest, looks at pictures on Deckard's piano that signify memories, which we know have to be implanted in replicants by Tyrell Corporation engineers. Rachael plays the piano while an exhausted Deckard rests on the couch. A dissolve—where one shot "dissolves" as the next one appears, overlapping and temporarily superimposed—shows a white unicorn running in slow motion, implying that Deckard is daydreaming this image.

At several moments in the film, the mysterious cop Gaff leaves an origami figure (a chicken and a matchstick man) as an indirect way of taunting Deckard, who for some reason Gaff clearly does not like. It establishes a pattern. What purpose do the origamis serve?

In the last scene in the Final Cut version, Deckard finds a unicorn origami on the tile floor outside his apartment—Gaff's trademark. Deckard picks it up, and as he inspects it, it's as if he's reminded of a cryptic statement Gaff made earlier to him about Rachael: "It's too bad she won't live, but then again who does?" We hear the line repeated now as if Deckard is recalling it himself. He nods "yes," indicating he now understands what Gaff meant by it. The carefully placed origami is a surprising revelation—certainly for viewers, and maybe even for Deckard. As Scott explains, "If Gaff knew about that, it's Gaff's message to say, 'I've read your file, mate.'"[19]

Harrison Ford differed with Scott over his character's status, whether human or bioengineered, but the fact that Deckard is a replicant becomes a story premise in the sequel, *Blade Runner 2049* (2017).[20] In the follow-up, a young blade runner and replicant, Detective K (Ryan Gosling), is assigned to track down the legendary Deckard to solve a mystery. There's evidence that replicants are evolving, which could lead to a potential war with the replicant freedom movement, an underground resistance group. The film delves even deeper into the existential questions introduced in the original about human nature.

Could Machines Ever Think as Human Beings Do?

The Imitation Game is based on Andrew Hodges's fictionalized biography, *Alan Turing: The Enigma,* and it won the Oscar for Best Adapted Screenplay. Turing was a brilliant mathematician who pioneered developments in computing and artificial intelligence.

As we fade in from black, we hear music and the sound of Morse code being transmitted over opening graphics informing us that the film is "based on a true story" and begins in 1951, in Manchester, England. Alan Turing (Benedict Cumberbatch) sits at a table in a blue-hued interrogation room. Sound familiar? Detective Nock (Rory Kinnear) enters and throws a file down on the table. Cut to black, then the camera moves over a room littered with papers covered in drawings and mathematical symbols. Chemicals, test tubes and beakers, and electronic equipment are scattered about. "Are you paying attention?" Turing responds in a voice-over: "You think that because you're sitting where you are, and I am sitting where I am, that you are in control of what is about to happen. You're mistaken. I am in control, because I know things that you do not know."

We see a series of shots: a room of women operating a bank of radio transmitters, a radio operator at Secret Intelligence Service (MI6) Headquarters listening to a brief radio report about a break-in at Turing's house, and a woman delivering a message to the director of MI6. A close-up of the message reads: "Alan Turing has been robbed. Manchester police investigation pending." Turing's voice-over continues: "What I will need from you now is a commitment. You will listen closely, and you will not judge me until I am finished. . . . What happens from this moment forward is not my responsibility. It's yours. Pay attention." The directive addresses the detective as much as it does the movie audience.

Cut to Nock arriving at Professor Turing's home in a rainstorm to investigate the burglary. That Turing is insulting and dismissive makes the detective suspicious. Back outside, he tells a police sergeant, "I think Alan Turing's hiding something." Cut to a busy Euston train station in London, 1939. Britain has declared war on Germany. A younger Alan Turing, a brilliant mathematician with experience in code breaking, walks through a crowd of mostly children who are being evacuated from the city. He boards a train on his way to interview at Bletchley Radio Manufacturing, which is a cover for a top-secret government project.

We return from time to time to Nock's investigation of Alan's cryptic past, which leads the detective to suspect wrongly that Alan is a Soviet spy. The police discover that a male hustler robbed Alan. The police arrest Alan on indecency charges (homosexuality was illegal in Britain), which gives Nock the opportunity to interrogate him. These scenes leading to the interrogation serve as a framing device. The film's action shifts back and forth between this and two other periods in Turing's life.

The main action is set in England in 1939 at the onset of World War II. The newly created British intelligence agency MI6 acquired a Nazi encryption device called Enigma that was smuggled out of Berlin. To gain an advantage in the war, the British government recruits a team of brilliant cryptographers to collaborate on a top-secret project at a facility at Bletchley Park to crack what appears to be an unbreakable code. What makes the Enigma device extraordinary is that it is recoded daily and refreshed by the Germans at midnight. At 6:00 a.m. the cryptographers intercept a new day's messages, each day presenting them with an astronomical number of possibilities—one hundred and fifty-nine million million million, "if you'd rather be exact about it," Hugh Alexander (Matthew Goode), a master in chess, points out.

Alan is unbearably arrogant, cold, and off-putting, and lacks any sense of humor. He prefers working in isolation and interacts with the others only as necessary. While other team members hope to discover the secret of Enigma by deciphering daily codes, Alan sets his sights on building an electromechanical machine with computational capability that would eventually become the modern computer: "An electrical brain. A digital computer," Alan calls it, that will figure out Enigma's daily settings.

We begin to understand Alan through flashbacks to his days at Sherborne School for Boys that show him being bullied by his classmates for being "different" but bonding romantically with one, Christopher, who sparks Alan's interest in cryptography. Christopher tells him, "Sometimes it is the very people who no one imagines anything of who do the things that no one can imagine." This line of dialogue is repeated, creating a pattern that points to the story's overall meaning.

The addition of Joan Clarke (Kiera Knightley) to the exclusively male team introduces a gender theme. Joan's parents think it "indecorous" and forbid her to live and work in the male environs of the "radio factory." Alan pays them a visit, letting them overhear a feigned conversation with Joan to convince them she will be working with other "young ladies" who do clerical work. Afterward, when Joan asks why he helps her, Alan replies with Christopher's words precisely: "Sometimes it is the very people who no one imagines anything of who do the things that no one can imagine." Alan's relationship with Joan helps him understand the advantage of working with the others to accomplish their goal. "I'm a woman in a man's job and I don't have the luxury of being an ass," she explains to him. "If you really want to beat it—if you really want to solve your puzzle—you're going to need all the help you can get." It marks a turning point.

Now, at this juncture you should know that I watched *The Imitation Game* in a crowded theater on opening weekend. Sitting a few seats away, one row behind me, was a woman who expressed herself audibly throughout the film. This information will become relevant in a moment. Meanwhile, back to *The Imitation Game*.

The interrogation scenes bear an obvious resemblance in lighting and design to the one in the opening of *Blade Runner* (frame 4). Their inclusion in the film seems designed to function as a significant intertextual reference, signaling that, like *Blade Runner*, *The Imitation Game* is also centrally a metaphor for exploring the nature of humanity. The exchange between Alan and Detective Nock clearly recalls Mr. Holden questioning Leon

The Imitation Game © 2014 BBP Imitation, LLC

Frame 4. The interrogation scenes in *The Imitation Game* bear an obvious visual resemblance and draw a metaphorical comparison to the one in *Blade Runner*.

Kowalski to determine whether he is human or an android. Nock asks Alan, "Could machines ever think as human beings do?" Alan replies, "Most people say not." "You're not most people," Nock points out. "The problem is you're asking a stupid question," Alan says sharply. "Of course, machines can't think as people do. A machine is different from a person. Hence they think differently." Alan goes on, disclosing the film's subtext. "We allow for humans to have such divergences from one another. What does it mean to have different tastes—different preferences—other than to say that our brains work differently? That we think differently from one another?" Then he invites the detective to play "the imitation game," which is "a test of sorts for determining whether something is a machine or a human being."

The comparison to *Blade Runner* is unmistakable and metaphorically rich. As one writer points out, *Blade Runner* features "the interrogation of an intelligent machine that would barely exist in fiction (let alone its potential in reality) without Turing's foundational work in computing, World War II codebreaking, and artificial intelligence."[21] After telling Nock what he *really* did during the war, Alan confronts him directly: "Now detective, you get to judge. So, tell me: what am I? Am I a machine, am I a person, am I a war hero, am I a criminal?" Nock refuses to be the judge, leaving it to viewers to resolve the film's central dilemma, which escapes even Alan: "Well then you're no help to me at all." Right on cue, the woman behind me had an epiphany. She said softly, realizing, "He's an enigma." In that moment, *The Imitation Game* is suddenly much more than a chronicle of a top-secret project to break the Nazis' communication code. Alan Turing, and not the ostensibly unbreakable German code, is the real enigma.

In a final scene together, looking at Alan's computer, Joan tells him, "No one normal could have done that. . . . Now if you wish you could have been 'normal,' I can promise you, I do not. The world is an infinitely better place precisely because you weren't." Alan asks, "Do you really think that?" Joan completes the pattern: "I think that sometimes it is the people who no one imagines anything of who do the things that no one can imagine." With that the story lines come together to affirm the central theme established as a pattern throughout the film. The film draws a parallel between Turing's obsession with breaking the Enigma code and his own personal quest for self-understanding. At a deeper level, it tells a story about a gay man's deepest fears, desires, yearning for human love and acceptance, and finally, measuring a man's life and accomplishments. The narrator points to inherent human dignity, which is not dependent upon who we are or what we might accomplish and—if I might affix a Christian slant—comes in its fullest sense with being created in the image of God.

4

Creating an Illusion of Reality

Film Form and Content

This is the essence of visual storytelling: to convey meaning to the viewer in ways other than words—and to add levels of meaning *in addition to* the dialog and action.

—Blain Brown, cinematographer

Set in a Beverly Hills high school, *Clueless* (1995) is a witty coming-of-age film that has become "one of the quintessential texts of '90s nostalgia," writer Lindsay Zoladz observes. Loosely based on Jane Austen's *Emma*, writer-director Amy Heckerling's "razor-sharp script" fixed witticisms like "As if!" and "Whatever!" in the popular vernacular of the decade's teen culture. Heckerling said at a workshop I attended that she gathered ideas for the film's dialogue by listening to conversations among her teenage daughter and friends.

The movie's cleverness, as Zoladz points out, comes as "a cinematic sleight-of-hand: It's an excessively smart movie about 'dumb' people," or at least types of people who might "possess an intelligence the world doesn't give them credit for." One way that Heckerling achieves this is with snappy dialogue that fits with the movie's theme by creating a "glorious culture clash of the high-brow and low."[1] When Heather attributes to Hamlet the line, "To thine own self be true," Cher (Alicia Silverstone) corrects her: "Hamlet didn't say that." Heather insists, "I think I remember Hamlet accurately." Cher is just as sure but refers instead to the 1990 *Hamlet* movie: "Well, I remember Mel Gibson accurately, and he didn't say that. That Polonius guy did." When Tai asks Cher if she thinks Amber is pretty, Cher says, "No, she's a full-on Monet." Confused, Tai asks, "What's a Monet?" Cher explains: "It's like a painting, see? From far away, it's OK, but up close, it's a big old mess."

As a matter of fact, viewing distance is important in order to appreciate Impressionist art. Pierre-Auguste Renoir's celebrated *Dance at le Moulin de la Galette* (1876), housed at the Musée d'Orsay in Paris, depicts a scene at one of the city's open-air cafés. It's a painted snapshot of middle-class life, with people dancing, drinking, and dining on a sunny afternoon. If you get up real close (without setting off the museum alarm), you can see the texture of the brushstrokes, and standing so near does make the Renoir look like "a big old mess." At the right distance, however, you see that the brushstrokes create depth in the way the composition comes together. As the painting engages your imagination, you even get a sense of movement that comes from the contrasting colors, the poses of people in motion, and the sun appearing to flicker through the leaves on the trees.

In their respective media, Heckerling's use of dialogue and Renoir's application of paint demonstrate the basic relationship of form, style, and content in art. Wanting to break free from the way photography reproduced reality, Impressionist painters tried to convey *stylistically* the way an artist sees: a visual impression of a moment that captures and evokes feelings rather than a realistic reproduction of reality. The way the Impressionists experimented with formal styles as a means of expressing values and personal beliefs about life and human perception contributed significantly to their art being recognized as great and lasting.

Here and in the following chapter we consider the relation of form and content in the *cinematic* making of a fictional world rich in meaning. The aim is to start developing a critical framework that can enhance our understanding of a film and the way moviemakers create worlds of make-believe through form and stylistic design. This paves the way for discussion of a filmmaker's viewpoint, a film's potential meanings, and viewers' interpretive strategies based on a framework of expectations.

The Illusion of Reality

In a review of *Lincoln* (2012), film critic A. O. Scott comments on how the British-born Daniel Day-Lewis "eases into a role of epic difficulty as if it were a coat he had been wearing for years."[2] The acclaimed method actor is aware of his reputation for disappearing in his roles. "Without sounding unhinged,

I know I'm not Abraham Lincoln. I'm aware of that," he said. "But the truth is the entire game is about creating an illusion, and for whatever reason, and mad as it may sound, some part of me can allow myself to believe for a period of time without questioning, and that's the trick."[3]

The illusion of reality he refers to begins with the nature of the medium itself. The movement in a film is, of course, an optical illusion. A film consists of a series of frames, or photographs separated by frame lines (dark spaces) and projected at 24 frames per second. The optical technology used to record and project film exploits quirks in our visual perception; the frame lines go unperceived, leaving us to see a succession of pictures as continuous movement. In other words, the movement we perceive as taking place on the screen is actually happening in our minds.

In film, the camera creates our way of seeing; it is our window into the world of the film. The camera directs our attention and can alter our perceptions. Movies have a "dual capability," film scholar Stephen Prince explains.[4] By design, much of what we see and hear in a film *corresponds* with our real-life experience. However, things like camera movement, the editing together of shots from various positions, and the use of wide-angle or telephoto camera lenses can also *transform* our experience, giving us a view without counterpart in real life. In short, our entry into the world of the film happens with much greater complexity than our normal visual and social experience allows. And that's very much a part of the delight of movie watching.

The term *cinematography*, which is the art of moviemaking, combines three Greek words—*kinesis* (movement), *photo* (light), and *graphia* (writing)—to mean "writing with movement and light." In one sense, *cinematic* describes the intrinsic qualities of the medium: its unique storytelling capacity. A movie is an amalgam of movement, light, and sound that, together with editing and what is known as a *moving* or *mobile frame*, affords a distinct capability to manipulate space and time. The camera's freedom to move every which way in effect shifts "the spectator's position *within the shot*," explains film scholar Ed Sikov, who adds, "No other art form is able to accomplish this feat."[5] In other words, while watching a movie, we perceive both the movement of characters and objects within the movie frame—the height-and-width border that shapes and frames the movie's image—and the apparent movement of the frame itself.

These qualities differentiate film from performance arts like theater and dance and two-dimensional pictorial art—the animated portraits on the walls at Hogwarts School of Witchcraft and Wizardry aside. Actually, Maya Deren, an influential experimental filmmaker in the 1940s and '50s, likens film to an "animated painting." Deren locates the artistic potential of film in its "creative use" of reality. As she sees it, the photographing, or filming, of reality itself "is the building block for the creative use of the medium." This differs from traditional art forms, she explains, wherein "the creative process takes place as reality passes through the artist."[6] Now what might that mean? Well, it's not like Voldemort's spirit passing through Harry Potter, knocking him unconscious as the Dark Lord flies out the door (whoosh!) in *Harry Potter and the Sorcerer's Stone*. Try this:

Picture a young woman dancing.

An artist imaginatively paints an image of her on canvas, or sculpts her out of wood or metal; a writer describes her with words on a page. Using a camera, however, a filmmaker records the reality of the dancer's existence—that is, makes a photographic reproduction or "realistic" moving image of the young woman actually dancing. In traditional art forms, Deren argues, artists use various materials (oils, charcoal, ink, wood, stone, and so forth) to "create metaphors of reality." Filmmakers "paint" or "write," if you will, using photographed "reality" itself as a metaphor for ideas and concepts.[7] In that sense, among the arts, film arguably comes closest to representing reality.

"Seeing is believing," the proverb says. "It is seeing which establishes our place in the surrounding world; we explain that world with words, but words can never undo the fact that we are surrounded by it," novelist and art critic John Berger explains.[8] To the extent that movies create an appearance of reality that accords with the real world, it lends them a power that some find comparable with the authority of reality itself.

In a narrative film, "reality" is constructed by "taking artistic ideas and implementing them in the real world of the film set," says cinematographer Blain Brown. This reality is manipulated twice. First, during filming, with the camera capturing "realistically" whatever is placed in front of it. "We have taken the 'real reality' (the actors, the set, the props, the dialog) and broken it up into pieces: the shots that are 'in the can,'" Brown explains. Then during editing, "we can reassemble this reality in any way we choose. We can move things around in time and in physical relation to each other: changing the pace, the tone, the mood, even the events."[9] The film's final cut effectively creates a new artistically constructed or imagined reality.

Visualizing: Making It Believable

When we describe something as *cinematic*, we usually mean visually graphic or fast paced. *Variety*'s Todd McCarthy sums up nicely the cinematic quality of Dan Brown's novel *The Da Vinci Code*: "a strong story hook, very short chapters that seem like movie scenes, constant movement by the principal characters in a series of conveyances, periodic eruptions of violent action and a compressed 24-hour time frame."[10]

The wit and deductive reasoning that made Brown's book a runaway bestseller, however, came across as overblown exposition in the film version. "Sitting through all the verbose explanations and speculations about symbols, codes, secret cults, religious history and covert messages in art, it is impossible to believe that, had the novel never existed, such a script would ever have been considered by a Hollywood studio," McCarthy observes. "What one is left with is high-minded lurid material sucked dry by a desperately solemn approach."[11] Some stories then are more conducive to cinematic adaptation than others.

In Ted Chiang's short story on which the science-fiction film *Arrival* (2016) is based, aliens communicate with earth's linguists and scientists "via digital screens they've sent light years across the universe." The concept, as one journalist observes, is "highly scientific, not inherently cinematic." To make the film "Hollywood-ready," screenwriter Eric Heisserer made some drastic changes. He reworked the narrative, bringing the large, long-legged heptapods to earth so that Louise Banks (Amy Adams) could have face-to-face encounters with them, and he added "a pulse-pounding third act finale." The laborious translation process, not exactly "action-packed entertainment," was largely condensed into a montage sequence with a voice-over by Ian Donnelly (Jeremy Renner).[12]

Whether an adaptation or original concept, production of a narrative film begins with the written word—a screenplay—which serves as a blueprint for making the film. A screenplay *shows* rather than *tells* a story; it contains everything viewers will see and hear while watching the movie. Together the director, cinematographer, and production designer hone in on a shared vision for how to *visualize* the story, theme, characters, and setting. Visualization involves the faculty of imagining, the creative ability to form new mental images. In terms of the cinema, it has to do with interpreting dramatic elements in a screenplay by putting them into visible form, a process that has a symbolic character.

Film production requires intense coordination and technical expertise to create an overall design that includes everything from the actors' performance to camera placement and lighting, filming locations, wardrobe and set design, props, makeup and hairstyling, and special effects. All this aims to fashion an internally consistent fictional world that when screened exhibits *verisimilitude*—a convincing appearance of reality, or believability.

Let's look at *The Hunger Games* (2012), based on the first novel in the bestselling trilogy by Suzanne Collins. The story is set in the future in Panem (formerly North America), a dystopic, authoritarian nation divided into twelve districts and the Capitol. In retribution for a failed past rebellion and as a crushing reminder to squelch any future resistance, one boy and one girl from each district are chosen by a lottery drawing at an annual "Reaping." They serve their district as "tributes" who are forced to all fight each other to the death. As a further show of the Capitol's unyielding dominance and the districts' docility, the sadistic contest is televised live nationally—viewing is mandatory. When her young sister Prim's name is drawn, Katniss Everdeen (Jennifer Lawrence) volunteers to take her place alongside the male selection, Peeta Mellark (Josh Hutcherson).

A brisk, action-packed novel like *The Hunger Games* would seem ready-made for film adaptation, but Collins's page-turner was modified for effectiveness on the screen. Absent a voice-over narration, film viewers cannot "hear" what a character is thinking as you can when reading a novel. Instead, spectators come to know a character's internal thoughts, opinions, and even outlook by making inferences based on the character's actions, dialogue, and behavior. A screenplay, explains writing consultant Dara Marks, describes an "external line of action" that "expresses how a character internalizes and processes that action."[13] In other words, as the narrative moves forward, it reveals a character's motives by showing actions and their consequences. This consistent pattern traces the main character's arc, or change, over the course of the story. A script, then, depicts the film's subject (through character, dialogue, and action) and provides the basic plot (scene-by-scene) and dramatic structure (setup, conflict, escalating action, climax, resolution).

Fans of *The Hunger Games* novel were struck immediately at the change in narrative point of view. The novel relies on a first-person, present-tense narration. The reader's entrée into the dystopian world of Panem comes entirely through Katniss's immediate experience, which enhances a reader's emotional connection. The film version, however, employs an omniscient narrator, which makes viewers privy to events and conversations that Katniss either is unaware of (such as district uprisings) or might speculate about in the novel (the fireballs as part of the Gamemakers' behind-the-scenes manipulating of the action in the arena, for example).

To illustrate, readers learn about the deadly tracker jackers by way of Katniss's internal monologue. This occurs in the novel almost as an aside—as if in that moment she'd really be mentally recounting the history and genetic engineering of tracker jackers by the Capitol, but that's how readers suspend their disbelief (more on that later). In the film, instead of Katniss delivering the same exposition via dialogue, as the scene unfolds it cuts from Katniss in the arena to a segment of the Capitol's live television coverage. Hunger Games celebrity host Caesar Flickerman (Stanley Tucci) explains to Panem citizens watching the televised program (and us as film viewers) how tracker jackers are "genetically engineered wasps whose venom causes searing pain, powerful hallucinations, and in extreme cases, death." We hear the last part of Flickerman's dialogue over a shot of a nest buzzing with tracker jackers, taking us back to the arena, with Katniss then climbing a tree toward the threatening nest.

Adding Layers of Meaning

Film practitioners go to great lengths to ensure a film's verisimilitude. To create the "nonlinear orthography," the written language that the huge, long-legged heptapods used to communicate in *Arrival*, screenwriter Eric Heisserer and production designer Patrice Vermette found some inspiration from J. R. R. Tolkien's Elvish in *The Lord of the Rings* trilogy. The filmmakers "took a close look online at graphics of the One Ring etchings," according to one writer, and enlisted linguistic professor Jessica Coon, an expert in the Mayan language Ch'ol, to ensure "the film's depiction of linguists and translation is accurate."[14]

The aim of verisimilitude does not preclude incorporating elements for symbolic value or to express mood and emotion. In *The Hunger Games*, for example, the computer-generated flaming capes that Katniss and Peeta wear in the opening ceremony chariot parade are a dazzling symbol of their coal-mining district that is also intended to make them a favorite with sponsors who can aid their quest in the arena. Costume designer Judianna Makovsky found inspiration for the people of District 12, home of Katniss and Peeta, from photos of coal-mining districts in the first half of the twentieth century. "We wanted to make a very serious impact, and color was very important—to keep it mostly gray or blue . . . very cold because coal leaves a black dust everywhere," Makovsky said. In sharp contrast, the costuming of the Capitol's citizens is overstylized, with loud colors, pleats, flowers, ruffles, padded shoulders, and flamboyant hats. They are made to look ostentatious, like "over plumed, surgically enhanced peacocks," as writer Molly Creeden puts it (frame 5). To hint mockingly at their calloused viciousness, Makovsky insisted they be "powdered and eyebrowless," which gave characters like Effie Trinket (Elizabeth Banks) "a ghostly, haunting look."[15]

In another sense, *cinematic* refers specifically to the various methods and techniques that filmmakers use "to *add layers of meaning* to the content," as Blain Brown puts it.[16] These tools and conventions of the medium

The Hunger Games © 2012 Lions Gate Films, Inc.

Frame 5. The makeup and costuming of the Capitol's citizens in *The Hunger Games* is overstylized to look ostentatious. Being "powdered and eyebrowless," like Effie Trinket, gives them "a ghostly, haunting look."

comprise the generally accepted devices and artistic practices, and practitioners and spectators understand their function. They are the *means* by which a filmmaker organizes the film's design and communicates a creative vision—which directs our attention to the relationship between *form* and *content*.

In practice, form and content are essential and mutually dependent aspects of film—two sides of the same coin, so to speak. For the purpose of analysis, however, we can make a distinction. *Content* is what the filmmaker makes of the film's subject, or what the movie is about, which involves story, character, and theme. *Form* is how, or the means by which, the subject is conveyed and experienced. This experience of the form occurs through the interplay of the film's various elements that together give the film its overall effect, sense of unity, and measure of individuality. A film's form, then, is its general design or appearance, which viewers identify through a process of understanding how these various elements interact to create patterns of "the overall set of relationships among a film's parts," as film scholars put it.[17] The main categories consist of *narrative, cinematography, production design, sound, acting,* and *editing.* These cinematic tools allow moviemakers to harness the creative potential of the medium to express a creative vision.

Formal analysis has the important benefit of calling our attention to some method or technique related to its function in the film. Analysis of film form concerns itself not so much with *what* happens as *the way* it happens in a movie. It has to do with sorting out the ways different aspects of a film fit together to suggest meanings. Formal analysis aims to better understand how the cinematic imagination works and to look more closely at film *as film* to enhance our enjoyment, appreciation, and interpretive skills.

At one level, most narrative films are easy enough to understand—and that's by design. You only have to sit back and watch. We see an extreme long shot of the National Mall. Hey, we're in Washington, DC! There's the Lincoln Memorial, the Reflecting Pool, the Washington Monument! A shot of the Capitol Building fills the frame. Cut to a dimly lit interior corridor. We must be inside the Capitol! We hear suspenseful music as the camera follows the protagonist walking cautiously down the hallway. Cut to the frame filled with an office door ajar that moves ever so slightly. Sensing danger—gasp!—we fear for the hero's safety, while wondering, "Who's behind that door?" Do you understand what's happening? The filmmaker organizes shots, camera movement, editing, and music to elicit certain reactions so that viewers will respond right on cue precisely as intended.

If you saw *Harry Potter and the Half-Blood Prince* (2009), the sixth film in the franchise, you will remember the story has an unusual beginning in contemporary London. Muggles watch the sky darken as ominous grey clouds take the shape of Lord Voldemort's face. Death Eaters appear in the sky, swooping down with plumes of black smoke trailing behind. They fly with dizzying speed past London landmarks and through the narrow streets before targeting the Millennium Bridge, a pedestrian suspension bridge across the River Thames. The menacing creatures soar around the bridge in a corkscrew motion, the structure undulating, twisting, and rocking until the suspension cables snap and it collapses violently into the Thames. Wow! What a dramatic opening sequence! How did they do that?

The use of a dazzling digital tracking shot makes it seem like we're soaring right along behind the Death Eaters as they dive down and—whoosh!—zoom across London. After an establishing shot of the actual Millennium Bridge, the rest of what we see is an equally impressive display of CGI (computer-generated imagery) effects. Special effects (VFX) supervisor Tim Burke worked for several months with a team to create a CGI replicate that was in every way identical to the real bridge. Some creative license ("artistic interpreta-tion") had to be taken, however, when an actual "dynamics simulation" of the bridge collapsing proved "not as interesting as we wanted," Burke said. Based on footage of other bridges failing, Burke discovered that "a suspen-sion bridge would twist and roll like a sine wave created through a vibration," which had a more dramatic effect (frames 6a, 6b). "We took this idea and then developed it for the collapse, having the Death Eaters fly around the bridge in a spiral motion to create the twisting that brings the bridge down."[18] Now that's moviemaking magic!

Harry Potter and the Half-Blood Prince © 2009 Warner Bros. Entertainment, Inc.

Frames 6a, 6b. The special effects (VFX) team takes some artistic license in *Harry Potter and the Half-Blood Prince* when showing Death Eaters flying in a spiraling motion around the Millennium Bridge to bring it crashing into the Thames.

And here's more. You might recall being completely caught up in the story right from the opening series of images in Pixar's *Up* (2009). We see the quirky romance and the long and beautiful married life of childhood sweethearts Carl and Ellie Fredricksen. We watch as they grow old together, their hair turning grey; we witness their joys and disappointments, unexpected turns, sad revelations, and bittersweet moments. What makes the "Married Life" sequence so "remarkable a feat of motion picture bravery and technical virtuosity," as one writer describes it, is not only "the scope of the time covered" in just a few minutes of screen time, "but also the complex emotional issues it addresses."[19] How exactly does that happen?

Obviously, there is much more to film viewing than simply following the basic story; understanding some films is not always easy, let alone interpreting their deeper meaning. While leaving the theater after watching *Manchester by the Sea* (2016), I overheard a man complain to his wife, "I didn't get it." He said he couldn't keep track of what was going on during the movie. "That's because you never could understand a flashback," she answered matter-of-factly, which made them both laugh.

A flashback can be a single shot, a sequence, or a scene that viewers understand as something that occurred in the past now being defined by the present-day time frame set up within the film. The narrative design of *Manchester by the Sea* merges past and present for Lee Chandler (Casey Affleck)—both in the telling of the story and in the minds of viewers. Presenting events out of chronological order advances the present-day story and, concurrently, with the extensive use of unannounced flashbacks, discloses Chandler's backstory. In this way, we learn gradually about his current motivations and the reason for his enduring pain, grief, and inability to forgive himself. In this instance, to get at the film's explicit meanings depends on a viewer's ability to make associations between scenes in relation to their place and function in the narrative.

Call Sign Charlie

Let's look at how form and content reinforce each other to imply meaning in a short scene in *Top Gun* (1986). A bit of background: Navy pilot Lieutenant Pete "Maverick" Mitchell (Tom Cruise) and his Radar Intercept Officer Nick "Goose" Bradshaw (Anthony Edwards) are one of six F-14 crews selected to train at the Navy's elite Fighter Weapons School at the Miramar Naval Base in San Diego. As his call sign implies, Maverick is egocentric, evidenced in his

Top Gun © 1986 Paramount Pictures Corporation

Frame 7. An establishing shot in *Top Gun* gives viewers a sense of where the action is taking place and where characters are in relation to one another.

unorthodox flying style as well as his professional and personal relationships. His *character arc*—a term writers use to describe the way a character changes over the course of the story—moves from self-centeredness to an awareness of the necessity of cooperating with others professionally (the main plot) and considering the needs of others personally (related subplot).

His first night there, Maverick "crashed and burned" in a corny attempt to pick up an attractive woman at a local bar, coolly referred to as a "target-rich environment." The imagery associates a sexual encounter with an aerial conquest. The next morning, an *establishing shot*, here an extreme long shot, shows a small group of pilots sitting classroom style in a huge outdoor aircraft hangar; an American flag hangs overhead, and F-14 Tomcats are parked nearby on the tarmac (frame 7). Commander "Jester" Heatherly informs the pilots that they will be "trained and evaluated by a few civilian specialists" who are "our very best source of information on enemy aircraft." He introduces one such civilian specialist, call sign "Charlie."

Top Gun © 1986 Paramount Pictures Corporation

Frames 8a, 8b, 8c. In *Top Gun*, camera placement and editing together introduce viewers to the astrophysicist, call sign "Charlie," in a highly sexualized way.

Heatherly's dialogue—"She has a PhD in astrophysics and she's also a civilian contractor, so you do not salute her"—is incongruous with the highly sexualized way the camera shows Charlie (Kelly McGillis): A medium close-up tracking shot from behind focuses the viewer's attention on her shapely legs in sheer stockings with a black seam as she walks down a center aisle. The editor cuts to a close-up (for emphasis) of Maverick looking down over his shoulder at her legs, and then up as she walks by him, just as Heatherly says, "But you'd better listen to her because the Pentagon listens to her about your proficiency." He hands the session over to Charlie. When she turns around, the audience—including a discomforted Maverick—recognizes her as the target of his tactless sexual advance the night before (frames 8a, 8b, 8c).

Charlie starts talking immediately about the F-5's "thrust-to-weight ratio" and how the MiG-28 has a "problem with its inverted flight tanks. It won't do a negative G pushover." The lines of dialogue are laced with not-so-subtle sexual innuendo. She's interrupted and corrected by Maverick (and Goose). They "happened to see a MiG-28 do a 4G negative dive" in the film's opening sequence. "So you're the one," Charlie says to Maverick, who has clearly regained the upper hand. He smiles at her and replies smartly, "Yes, ma'am."

Since there were no women officers at the Miramar Naval Base, at the bidding of Navy consultants, the screenwriters changed Charlie's original occupation easily enough from aerobics instructor to civilian astrophysicist. Her profession has no real bearing on the story; the character's sole purpose is to serve as Maverick's love interest, which is implied in the way the editing of sound and image work to represent her in this scene. Can you see how cinematic techniques are the means to convey meaning here, with a certain attitude about men and women, sex and romance?

Finally

A word of caution before moving on: Filmmakers employ filmic techniques in ways familiar to audiences in order to ensure they "get" the intended meaning of the moment. A high-angle shot signals power or authority, for example, or a close-up of a face half in shadow often means the person is duplicitous. We have to be careful, however, when talking about the meaning of design elements, not to slip into overly simplistic interpretations. Use of cinematic elements can be more nuanced, open to suggesting various meanings in different contexts. Emmanuel Lubezki, who won the Oscar for Cinematography three years in a row for *Gravity* (2013), *Birdman* (2014), and *The Revenant* (2015), said, "The language of film is further and further away from the language of theater and is closer to music. It's abstract but still narrative."[20]

A filmmaker can make use of the same technique for different purposes. The critical question has to do with both effectiveness and fittingness—that is, how well a technique stylistically expresses a specific moment in the film or its overall meaning. We understand a movie and interpret its meaning based on the film's *disclosure*—the way it reveals new or previously hidden information. The film does this by the way it handles events and portrays characters, as well as prominent features of the story's setting, visual imagery, sound, acting, cinematography, production design, and so forth. By means of filmic elements, movies engage our cognitive processes—perception, memory, use of language, and problem solving—as well as our emotions and imagination. All this makes up the unique and creative capacity of film to tell stories *cinematically*.

MOVIE MUSING

The "Married Life" Sequence in *Up* (2009)

> Cinema is a language and within it are the specific vocabularies and sub-languages of the lens, composition, visual design, lighting, image control, continuity, movement, and point-of-view.
>
> —Blain Brown, cinematographer

Pixar's *Up* won an Oscar and Golden Globe for Best Animated Feature Film and earned $735 million dollars worldwide. Critics raved especially about the opening sequence, calling it "a masterclass in narrative exposition" and "one of the most extraordinary openings to a film, far less an animated film, ever to have been crafted."[21] Aren't you at least a bit curious about what makes that opening sequence so compelling and emotionally captivating?

The film starts with a timid nine-year-old Carl watching a newsreel in a theater about the discrediting of his idol, explorer Charles Muntz. On the way home, he meets the energetic and talkative Ellie, who shares his dream of restoring Muntz's reputation by finding "Paradise Falls, a land lost in time" and a giant exotic bird that lives there. "I just don't know how I'm going to get to Paradise Falls," Ellie says, making Carl promise that he'll take them there in a blimp. "Swear you'll take us, cross your heart."

The filmmakers convey the tender and heartbreaking love story of Carl and Ellie Fredricksen by means of a very effective *montage*, a sequence that achieves its emotional energy by condensing a passage of time or events into thematically related shots or images. The sounds and images in the "Married Life" sequence are organized to create an emerging pattern. We *see* a series of brief shots edited together; we *hear* no dialogue, only a musical sound bridge (a song composed by Michael Giacchino).

In the original idea, the story begins with a series of short scenes containing dialogue. The decision not to include dialogue or sound effects was made later based on the screenwriters' shared experience of growing up in "homes where our folks were taking Super-8 films of our family," writer and director Pete Docter explains. "And when you go back and look at those, they're also silent, but there's something powerful about having no sound." They wanted the effect of audiences being "actively engaged by creating this missing element, so it comes to life in your own head."[22]

The montage is a complete story in itself that functions as a prologue to the main narrative. The sequence creates strong feelings of empathy for Carl and a desire that he fulfill the dream of adventure he longed to share with Ellie. As a reviewer notes, although other characters see Carl as "a cantankerous old git," with the knowledge we have of the montage sequence, "we can understand exactly why he sees the world in shades of grey, and admire him for still having a sense of adventure in his heart despite all the sadness that encases it."[23]

Let's look at the sequence more closely: It begins with a camera flash at Carl and Ellie's church wedding and establishes a pattern using a repetition of shots and images (especially balloons) to mark both the passage of time and changes in the conditions of their lives (frame 9a). At one point Ellie and Carl lie on a picnic blanket looking up at the sky, as clouds turn into the shape of babies. Cut to them decorating a brightly colored nursery filled with daylight. In the first of several poignant moments, the camera pans right, passing through the wall into a darkened hallway and remains there. We see Carl and Ellie through an open doorway with a doctor in a neon-lit examination room, Ellie's head in her hands. Carl stands behind her with his hands on her shoulders comforting her. A poster of a pregnant woman is on the wall behind them (frame 9b).

Up © 2009 Disney Enterprises, Inc. / Pixar

Frame 9a. The "Married Life" sequence in *Up* is a complete story in itself that condenses the passage of time and conveys the heartbreaking love story of Carl and Ellie.

Up © 2009 Disney Enterprises, Inc. / Pixar

Frame 9b. A simple camera panning shot conveys a significant event.

Cut to shots of Carl at home looking out an upstairs window at Ellie sitting alone in a chair in the middle of the yard. Cut again to a shot of Ellie, sitting upright, her eyes closed as she takes a deep breath. Carl joins her, and they share a sad smile. Ellie's "My Adventure Book," one of several recurring motifs, restores their childhood dream. A series of shots showing them saving for the trip by putting coins in a "Paradise Falls" jar is juxtaposed with others implying costly medical needs, car and house repairs. A collage of close-ups shows Ellie's disembodied hands fixing Carl's ties. It ends with her straightening Carl's black bow tie and the camera turning to show the two of them looking in a mirror—grey-haired now, but still deeply in love. The series of shots that follow show them in old age, still doing everything together, and then Carl caring for Ellie, who is sick in bed (frame 9c). The sequence ends with Carl returning home after Ellie's funeral and a fade to black.

A repetition of earlier shots conveys new meaning now: Carl wakes up in bed, the blankets on the other side undisturbed. He eats breakfast, washes a window, and dusts the fireplace mantel where a picture of a young Ellie and her binoculars remain. All by

Up © 2009 Disney Enterprises, Inc. / Pixar

Frame 9c. Repeating images (like window washing) mark the passage of time and changes in the lives of Carl and Ellie.

Frame 9d. Recurring images suggest Carl's enduring love for Ellie.

himself. Their dreams deferred, Carl is widowed, sad, stoic, and alone in reconciling the loss of his one and only love. We see Carl sitting on the front porch; an extreme long shot shows his house and yard framed by a white picket fence looking like a square island surrounded by construction crews at work on huge buildings. He finds a brochure for a retirement village in the mailbox that still bears Ellie's now faded paint markings (frame 9d). These images drive the narrative forward, adding another layer to the montage's central tragic theme about our "helplessness against the often-cruel, vindictive power of fate," as one writer observes.[24] In less than five minutes the sequence covers a lifetime lasting nearly sixty years.

For one woman in her seventies, the movie was a special gift. She wrote to the film's creators telling them that her husband had died just before the release of *Up*. Seeing the movie "turned out to be a very restorative thing for her," Docter learned. Somehow, while watching the movie, "she felt like she was getting to spend a little more time with her husband," he said, adding, "It was very meaningful to me that that film could do that for someone."[25]

MOVIE MUSING

Creating the Illusion (and History) in *Lincoln* (2012)

> But if Spielberg's narrative is a little off, his principal argument isn't.
>
> —Joshua Zeitz, *Atlantic*

Daniel Day-Lewis won an Oscar for his performance as Abraham Lincoln, drawing praise for the way he portrayed the US president as "tender and soulful, convincingly weary and

Up © 2009 Disney Enterprises, Inc. / Pixar

stoop-shouldered," writer Charles McGrath observes.[26] Day-Lewis makes him appear—emotionally and physically—as if the weight of the world is on his shoulders (frame 10). It was the British-Irish actor's rendition of Lincoln's voice, however, that fascinated critics the most. They wondered if a Londoner who speaks with a British accent could "really fill out the 16th president's stovepipe hat."[27]

There are no audio recordings of Lincoln speaking. But there is historical evidence that, contrary to the popular imagination, Lincoln had a reedy, nasal-sounding voice and spoke with a folksy twang he acquired while living in Kentucky, Indiana, and Illinois. Day-Lewis decided that Lincoln's high-pitched voice carried better with a large crowd and made him more effective as a public speaker. Gradually, he said, "I began to hear a voice that, as I grew closer to the man, that seemed to give me the full expression of his character."[28] In the same vein, *Lincoln* production designer Rick Carter relied on extensive photographs to make sure the period Victorian furniture, the maps and documents, even the wallpaper pattern was copied meticulously to make the White House interiors serve as "a visual metaphor for his [Lincoln's] mindscape."[29]

The award-winning *Lincoln* also reveals crucial dynamics in re-creating historical events in a commercial Hollywood film. *Lincoln* covers an intense period of four months, showing the president's political strategizing and maneuvering to secure passage of a Constitutional amendment to abolish slavery as the Civil War is nearing its end. The plot moves forward toward its climax: a gripping reenactment of the historic vote.

While watching the film, Connecticut Congressman Joe Courtney was caught up in the suspense as the roll call vote began, only to be stunned to hear two of Connecticut's three House members vote against the amendment. As it is, the Congressional Record shows that the entire delegation from Connecticut voted in favor of abolishing slavery—an

Lincoln © 2012 DreamWorks II Distribution Co., LLC / Twentieth Century Fox Film Corporation

Frame 10. Actor Daniel Day-Lewis makes Lincoln appear emotionally and physically as if the weight of the world is on his shoulders in the historically based drama *Lincoln*.

easily verifiable fact. Courtney wanted a public apology from director Steven Spielberg and wanted the vote count corrected in the DVD release.

Screenwriter Tony Kushner had no qualms admitting the disparity in the Connecticut delegation's vote. The liberties he took in organizing the scene were designed to make it more compelling and focus its emotional impact. Two of the Connecticut delegation's votes, along with the names of the men casting them, were changed to emphasize the narrow margin of victory. As the voting begins, the loud "Nay's" heighten suspense by making the outcome seem anything but sure. The Missouri vote is split, followed by two of three New Jersey's "indisposed" House members abstaining. Illinois casts two votes against the amendment. Cut to a close-up of a pensive Lincoln waiting in the White House.

"The closeness of that vote and the means by which it came about was the story we wanted to tell," Kushner explains in response to the criticism. "In making changes to the voting sequence, we adhered to time-honored and completely legitimate standards for the creation of historical drama, which is what *Lincoln* is. I hope nobody is shocked to learn that I also made up dialogue and imagined encounters and invented characters."[30] For one, in the film's opening sequence, two black Union soldiers, one reticent and the other rather bold, confront Lincoln with the prospect that equal pay, and eventually black commissioned officers, might bring, "in a hundred years, the vote" (a foreshadowing of the Voting Rights Act of 1965). Two white soldiers, who heard Lincoln speak at Gettysburg, join the conversation and recite the opening of Lincoln's now immortalized address, "Four score and seven years ago . . ." As they leave to join their company, the reserved black soldier remains behind and proudly delivers the closing line: "that we here highly resolve that these dead shall not have died in vain."

It's an absorbing way to begin the story. But historian Harold Holzer points out that "it is almost inconceivable that any uniformed soldier of the day (or civilians, for that matter) would have memorized a speech that, however ingrained in modern memory, did not achieve any semblance of a national reputation until the 20th century."[31] Nevertheless, the recitation of the now celebrated speech and image of Lincoln visiting the war front and discussing racial equality with black Union soldiers highlights the issue dividing the nation and serves as a kind of thesis for the story that follows.

A dramatic payoff comes after the vote is tallied. Thaddeus Stevens (Tommy Lee Jones) is the Republican chair of the Ways and Means Committee and the film's antihero. He works cautiously with Lincoln to abolish slavery, and after the legislative victory he shows the bill to Lydia Hamilton Smith, his partner of twenty years under the guise of being "his black housekeeper," which was, as one writer notes, "the worst-kept secret in Washington."[32] One of the film's closing scenes shows them lying in bed together with Lydia reading the words of the Thirteenth Amendment. The effect is to bookend the story by recalling, with some closure now, the earlier scene of the black soldiers reciting Lincoln's Gettysburg Address.

In Congressman Courtney's view, artistic license, in this instance at least, does not justify amending history. That historic vote represents the sacrifice of over four thousand Connecticans who died in the Civil War, and they, insisted Courtney, "deserved a better legacy than the screen play portrayed."[33]

Without taking sides, Civil War expert Matthew Warshauer provides some historical nuance. Even if the Connecticut delegation supported abolition, their constituents were deeply divided over slavery. After passage of the Thirteenth Amendment, on two different occasions, Connecticut citizens voted against removing the word "white" from the state constitution's statement on voter entitlement. *Lincoln* clearly misrepresents the Connecticut delegation's vote, a *Wall Street Journal* reporter observes. "But in tinkering with history, Steven Spielberg may accidentally have more accurately depicted 1865 Connecticans' complex and conflicted feelings about slavery itself."[34]

When it comes down to it, dramatic import will most likely be a filmmaker's top priority. And understandably so. That puts the onus on the audience to sort out fact from fiction and decide what matters in thinking critically about the meaning a movie conveys. As Day-Lewis said, "But the truth is the entire game is about creating an illusion."[35]

5

Connecting the Dots

Style and Meaning

I will persist in recognizing the morality in art by exploring the
art in art.

—Richard Alleva, *Commonweal*

Reports of an increase in crime in the 1990s fueled public anxiety about
violent movies and their potentially negative social effects. Oliver Stone's
road film *Natural Born Killers* (1994) and Quentin Tarantino's highly stylized
Pulp Fiction (1994) ranked high on the list.

Natural Born Killers indulges in a bloody cross-country murder spree per-
petrated by two young lovers that the media unabashedly make into celebrities.
Rolling Stone's Peter Travers called it "a surreal splatterfest [that] soars on its visual audacity."[1] Stone's purported aim was satire and to indict real-world media
exploitation of violence. *Pulp Fiction*, which won the Palme d'Or at the Cannes
Film Festival, drew rave reviews and turned independent art house producers
into a force in American filmmaking. The film's nonlinear plot, colorful cast of
underworld types, and inventive dialogue left audiences "with a stunning vision
of destiny, choice and spiritual possibility," *New York Times* critic Janet Maslin
wrote.[2] Both films are sexually frank, contain dialogue filled with obscenities,
and show scenes featuring drug use and orchestrated, graphic violence.

An instructive exchange took place between Richard Alleva, who writes for
Commonweal, an independent Catholic journal of opinion, and reader John D.

Hagen Jr., who faulted Alleva for appraising the films "exclusively from an aesthetic standpoint" and for being "all about style, without the least tincture of moral critique." He expected more from a Catholic reviewer and charged that *Commonweal*'s reviews generally "treat the arts as a sort of intellectual parlor game, without any social or moral ramifications or points of reference in the gospel."[3]

Alleva responded with a question: "How can you get at the moral sickness or health of a movie without examining its art or lack of art?" He continued:

> Sooner or later, a movie's or novel's moral delinquency betrays itself through aesthetic delinquency. Plot illogic may signal unconcern with human motive. Mindlessly obscene dialogue betrays indifference to the substance of human speech, a moral as well as an aesthetic failing. Mindless editing choices or camera set-ups may reveal a basic lack of interest in the humanity of the situation posited by the script. . . . Planning the sequence of events in a story can also show moral choice.

Alleva stood firm. "*Pulp Fiction* is an adolescent, ultraviolent, foulmouthed romanticization of the gangster milieu," he maintained. "But it is also exhilarating, mind-teasing, breathtakingly well-made—and fundamentally moral." Hagen "can see the isolated incidents of immorality that dot the landscape of *Pulp Fiction*, but he can't connect the dots to see the pattern. But without the pattern—no morality!" The *Commonweal* critic pledged, "I will persist in recognizing the morality in art by exploring the art in art."[4]

Form + Content + Style =

As the *Commonweal* exchange shows, the harmonizing of form, content, and style can affect interpretations of a film. Why? Because form expresses content with a certain slant or viewpoint. A film is designed to allow us to "see that content *in a particular way*," as film scholars observe. "Form enables the artist to shape our particular experience *and interpretation* of that content."[5] Consider, for example, how movies can offer different viewpoints about war. *Sands of Iwo Jima* (1949) glorifies the camaraderie and fighting spirit of Marines during World War II. *Platoon* (1986) shows a platoon and, metaphorically, America at war with itself in Vietnam. *Saving Private Ryan* (1998) recalls the fear and dedication of infantrymen during the momentous D-Day landing on Omaha Beach. *The Hurt Locker* (2008) treats war as a drug and one soldier's addiction. *American Sniper* (2014) probes the psychological effects of warfare on individuals who pledge to fight for God and country. These films all deal with the same subject matter but represent different attitudes.

Here style comes into play. *Style* has to do with the distinctive ways that filmmakers use available methods and techniques to create patterns of meaning. A few brief illustrations here make the point.

Ang Lee's movies (*Crouching Tiger, Hidden Dragon*; *Brokeback Mountain*; *Life of Pi*) are typically slow-paced and deliberate, with sweeping, elegant cinematography. Lee prefers intentional character explorations that focus on themes like family, duty, hidden desires, and societal expectations. We feel constant movement in Kathryn Bigelow's films (*The Hurt Locker, Zero Dark Thirty*), which are known for tight action sequences and a journalistic storytelling style (in collaboration with screenwriter Mark Boal). Depictions of heroines, like Maya in *Zero Dark Thirty*, show "the struggles and triumph of a strong woman making her way in a world dominated by men."[6]

Steven Spielberg (*E. T. the Extra-Terrestrial, Jurassic Park, Minority Report, Bridge of Spies, The Post*) relies on the large orchestral scores of composer John Williams, which fit with the director's sentimental flair. An influential signature of Spielberg's style is a camera moving in for a facial close-up to show a character's reaction to what is happening offscreen—known as the "Spielberg Face." The convention cues viewers in to the emotional significance of an epic turning point. "Eyes open, staring in wordless wonder in a moment where time stands still," one commentator explains, the shot conveys "sudden shock or creeping dread, the trauma of remembering the past or of confronting the future, discovering humanity in another person, or discovering humanity in oneself."[7]

Style also involves a fittingness in the way form and content together reveal the film's slant on the subject—the filmmaker's way of imaginatively owning it. Form, content, and style then are interactive; their use aims for consistency in expressing the film artist's perspective.

While most Hollywood films center on a main protagonist and tight resolution, Spike Lee (*He Got Game, Crooklyn, Jungle Fever, BlacKkKlansman*) uses an ensemble cast, striking camera angles, bold primary colors, and ambiguous endings to explore race in America. Quentin Tarantino's movies (*Pulp Fiction, Inglourious Basterds, Django Unchained*) display a fascination with evil. Highly stylized, they feature graphic, sometimes exaggerated violence that can be unsettling in how it elicits contrary reactions in viewers, ranging from shock to laughter.

The protagonists in Martin Scorsese's films (*Raging Bull, Goodfellas, Hugo, The Wolf of Wall Street*) are often outsiders or unconventional heroes. Scorsese likes to use a moving camera, however subtle, to keep the narrative always advancing and because, as Roger Ebert explains, "movement suggests voyeurism and a static camera indicates a gaze."[8] It's a more involved and personal way of viewing. In contrast, David Fincher (*Se7en*, *Fight Club*, *The Social Network*) rarely moves the camera, favoring a stationary setup on a tripod over handheld shots; the idea is to make the camera seem omniscient, simply showing what's happening. Unlike Spielberg, he uses close-ups sparingly, believing they too clearly signal the audience that something is important.[9]

Is the Top Still Spinning? The Search for Pattern

As I mentioned earlier, meaning is not inherent in a film. Rather, as we have seen, meaning takes shape through the interaction of the spectator's framework of expectations with the film's form: the means by which the filmmaker organizes the film's design and expresses a creative vision. A film's meaning is finally the result of a process by which viewers come to make sense of the film by gathering and sorting information into a coherent story. That process begins with a search for pattern—that is, by connecting the dots.

Pattern refers to the film's underlying structure that organizes aspects of the film in working together. We watch a movie expecting that a pattern exists, and cues within the film guide us. These come via repeated elements and notable methods and techniques used throughout. Uncovering patterns helps us identify key motifs, which in turn leads to an understanding of the film's meaning, the central idea or perspective expressed by the film's form.

Throughout the perplexing plot of *Inception* (2010), a "subconscious heist movie," team leader Dom Cobb (Leonardo DiCaprio) uses a totem, a spinning tractricoid top, to keep track of reality as he travels through a tangled maze of dreamworlds.[10] Spinning the top is his "reality" test. If the top falls over, he is awake (in his own reality), and if it continues spinning, he knows he's in a dream state. The repeated image of the spinning top filling the screen establishes a pattern that sets up the film's much-talked-about ambiguous ending. Cobb spins the top and is distracted when he sees his children. The camera moves over to the top, which appears to be wobbling, and then the film cuts to black, leaving the audience wondering whether Cobb has really (in reality) returned to his children (frame 11). The film's open ending expresses a crucial issue. "The question of whether that's a dream or whether it's real is the question I've been asked most about any of the films I've made," writer-director Christopher Nolan said. "It matters to people because that's the point about reality. Reality matters."[11]

The biographical sports film *42* (2013) tells the story of Jackie Robinson breaking the racial barrier in professional baseball. For both moral and

Inception © 2010 Warner Bros. Entertainment, Inc. / Legendary Pictures

Frame 11. The repeated image of a totem, a spinning tractricoid top, establishes a pattern that sets up the ambiguous ending in *Inception*.

moneymaking reasons (increased ticket sales to African Americans), Brooklyn Dodgers general manager Branch Rickey (Harrison Ford) wants to desegregate the national pastime. He identifies Robinson, a star in the old Negro baseball leagues, who signs a contract to become the first African American player in the all-white major leagues. This story about integrating Major League Baseball takes place in the mid-1940s. That's less than a decade before the 1954 Supreme Court landmark ruling (*Brown v. Board of Education of Topeka*) declaring that racial segregation in public schools was unconstitutional. Robinson endures relentless verbal abuse from fans and players. The manager of the Pittsburgh Pirates is especially vicious in a scene with Robinson at bat that re-creates one of the darker moments that actually occurred during a 1947 Pirates-Dodgers game.

We have no actual footage showing what Robinson did between being on deck and being at the plate. Aware that "baseball players have certain rituals or habits that they develop," actor Chadwick Boseman said, he went with instinct while filming one of his first at-bats. Whenever Robinson steps up to the plate, he grabs a handful of dirt and rubs his hands in it. "In some sense, it was a prayer and in another sense, it was getting his hands ready to hold a bat."[12]

At his first bat in the film, while Robinson rubs dirt on his hands, spectators boo, one yelling, "Hey, n—— boy! Whatcha doin' playin' baseball?" A young black boy sitting in the stands with his mother closes his eyes, folds his hands, and prays: "Please God, please let Jackie show them what we can do." Later in the film, Robinson receives death threats before a game in Cincinnati. This time we see a young white boy in the stands. At first, he looks scared and confused by angry fans hurling racial insults when Robinson takes the field. But then, imitating his father, he shouts at Robinson: "N——! We don't want you here!"

As the game is about to begin, shortstop Pee Wee Reese (Lucas Black) jogs over to Robinson at first base. He puts his arm over Robinson's shoulders as they talk, drawing boos from the crowd. Reese is intentionally making a scene to show his family and friends that he embraces his black teammate. Now the film inserts a close-up of the white boy looking contrite. "Maybe tomorrow we'll all wear 42," Reese tells Jackie. "That way they won't tell us apart." This line of dialogue no doubt intends to foretell Major League Baseball's annual honoring of Robinson. On April 15 every year, all players, coaches, managers, and umpires on every team wear the number 42, which was retired across the league in a unique tribute to the trailblazing Hall of Famer.

Again, after a game in St. Louis, in a crucial scene, Branch Rickey tells Robinson that while driving by a sandlot baseball field that morning he saw

Frames 12a, 12b, 12c. A pattern in 42 suggests that Jackie Robinson's courage and determination is having a positive influence on the next generation; racial progress is being made.

a young white boy imitating Robinson's batting ritual. "He was pretendin' he was you. Rubbin' dirt on his hands, swingin' with his arms outstretched like you do. A little white boy pretending he's a black man." The pattern—the repeated batting ritual, racist spectator rants, and the boys—suggests that despite the hate, insults, threats, and abuse that Robinson has had to endure, progress toward racial equality is being made (frames 12a, 12b, 12c). His courage and determination to be an outstanding baseball player is having an indelible influence on the next generation.

What's the Movie About? What's It *Really* About?

Film analysis works through a film's straightforward message to understand its more complex meanings that enrich our understanding and experience with the film. There are different ways to understand how a film is invested with meaning. Let's consider three related layers of meaning: *explicit*, *implicit*, and *interpretive*.

Explicit meaning refers to what a movie communicates directly to viewers— all that is presented, what we hear and see in the film's audiovisual world. When asked what a movie is about, most people describe the basic details of the story: setting, characters, conflict, and resolution. For example, *Arrival* is about a team of experts trying to communicate with alien visitors in order to avert an impending global nuclear strike on them by terror-struck national leaders. The *Harry Potter* series is about an orphaned boy's quest to learn magic at Hogwarts School of Witchcraft and Wizardry and defeat an evil wizard determined to kill him. *Rocky* (1976), a classic American underdog story, is about a lonely, down-and-out boxer who gets an unexpected opportunity to fight for the heavyweight championship of the world. *Do the Right Thing* (1989) is about a day in the life of a racially diverse community in the Bedford-Stuyvesant neighborhood of Brooklyn, New York. Explicit meaning comes from what occurs right on the surface of the film; it is readily apparent, and its telling suggests underlying meanings.

Implicit meaning lies just beneath the film's surface presentation; its power relies on nuance instead of direct expression. This kind of meaning arises by association or an implied connection among characters and story events. At a deeper level, *Arrival* is about the nature of humanity, communication, time, and history. In the *Harry Potter* films, a coming-of-age theme, bravery confronting death, and the eternal struggle between good and evil are intertwined. The implicit meaning in *Rocky* deals with determined hard work in pursuit of your heart's desires, realizing your own potential as the path to personal redemption, and affirmation of the American rags-to-riches myth.

Do the Right Thing implies a different version of the American dream, one that centers on tensions between love and hate, violence and nonviolence, in resolving community conflict.

Implicit meaning largely concerns theme. Theme is a story's heart, the main point or what the story is essentially about. It is a central unifying idea at the core of the story that finds expression in the narrative and the film's audio-visual world. We discover it, in other words, through attention to characters' actions, dialogue, sound, imagery, and consequential events in the narrative.

Themes tend to be broad ideas, nearly universal, even as the story and characters belong to a specific time or culture. "Love conquers all," whether in the slums of Mumbai (*Slumdog Millionaire*, 2008), in a trendy district in West London (*Notting Hill*, 1999), or amid the dazzling cityscape of Singapore (*Crazy Rich Asians*, 2018)—and even in an enchanted swamp (*Shrek*, 2001). "Good triumphs over evil" in countless movies, from John Wayne to James Bond, the adventures of Harry Potter and comic-book superheroes. But not in *Chinatown*, *Memento*, *Se7en*, or *Fight Club*. Theme is sometimes thought of as the "moral of the story": crime doesn't pay, good guys finish first (or last), honesty is the best policy, or love means sacrifice. However, when theme turns into a "moral" or "message" that becomes heavy handed, it can overpower the story as the film becomes pedantic or preachy.

Other kinds of implicit meaning enrich theme. For instance, a film might include references to things, persons, places, or events in the real world with importance familiar to audiences. These demonstrate how *referential meaning* can invest a story with deeper significance.

That *Rocky* (1976) is set and shot on location in Philadelphia, the nation's birthplace, during the year of the Bicentennial celebration, enriches the film's qualities as an affirmation of the American myth. Noticeable mentions of America as the "land of opportunity" and of Rocky's shot at the heavyweight championship as a "Cinderella story" also appear. Other references locate the story in the boxing world: On the wall in Rocky's apartment we see a poster of his namesake and hero, middleweight champion Rocky Graziano. Heavyweight champion Smokin' Joe Frazier, who had just retired in 1975, makes a cameo appearance in the ring before Rocky's match with Apollo Creed begins.

Allusions in Spike Lee's *Do the Right Thing* (1989) put the film in the context of 1980s racial politics in New York City. We see graffiti on a brick wall that reads "Tawana Told The Truth!"—referring to the Tawana Brawley allegations of rape and abuse in 1987. A Korean shop owner makes a derisive, self-reflexive remark, "How I'm doing," in reference to the oft-used catchphrase of New York City Mayor Koch, who was up for reelection in 1989 (and lost). The film ends with a scrolling onscreen graphic—quotations by Martin Luther King Jr. and Malcolm X with their differing agendas—that lend the film and its theme historical context and ongoing significance.

Filmmakers use *intertextuality* to suggest a relationship between two different "texts." For example, an intertextual reference within a film to another film, a novel, or a poem hints at a connection in terms of theme, setting, or genre, or it nods to the influence of another film or filmmaker. Audiences familiar with the other text take pleasure in making the discovery, and evoking the other artwork shapes the film's meaning. For example, we can find many allusions in director Nora Ephron's *Sleepless in Seattle* (1993) to the classic romance *An Affair to Remember* (1957). Annie (Meg Ryan) and her editor (Rosie O'Donnell) cry while watching the 1957 tearjerker on TV; meanwhile, across the country, Sam (Tom Hanks) mocks it as "a chick's movie," a nickname for *Sleepless*'s own genre. Taking a page directly from *Affair*, Sam and Annie meet on top of the Empire State Building in the final scene.

George Lucas's celebrated *Star Wars* (1977) contains so many references to other films that one writer describes it as "a world 'mediated' through other movies" that could have been titled "Genre Wars."[13] At once nostalgic and inventive, *Star Wars* is a hodgepodge of popular culture that makes various references to American westerns, space adventure serials, World War II dogfighting films, Japanese samurai movies, science fiction, *Casablanca*, and the Nazi propaganda film *Triumph of the Will*. This filmic pastiche is held together by the mythic storytelling pattern outlined in Joseph Campbell's *The Hero with a Thousand Faces*.

A key scene in John Ford's influential western *The Searchers* (1956) factors prominently in *Star Wars* (1977): The cowboy hero, Ethan Edwards (John Wayne), is lured away by a renegade band of Comanche Indians and returns to find his brother's homestead ablaze and family killed. In an obsessive quest for revenge, Ethan sets out to find his surviving niece. Likewise, Lucas recreates the scene in *Star Wars* as a catalyst for the hero's adventure. While Luke Skywalker (Mark Hamill) is off in pursuit of runaway droid R2D2, Imperial storm troopers kill his uncle and aunt and destroy their abode. Luke begins his journey now to become a Jedi Knight. Along with other elements, this pivotal moment identifies *Star Wars* with the mythology of the traditional American western.

Interpretive Meaning

A third layer of meaning, *interpretive meaning*, deals with understanding and explaining the deeper, overarching significance of a film. Again, as much as movies are designed to guide viewers toward intended meanings, viewers play an active role in creating meaning.

"That's a cool shot."

"I don't like that the camera's moving all the time."

"It feels like I've seen this movie before—a hundred times."

"I wouldn't have the courage to do what she's doing (or did)."

"I really liked the music."

"How did they shoot that?"

"I forgot it was Meryl Streep on the screen."

"I love Steven Spielberg's films."

"I enjoyed it—a lot—but what does it all mean?"

I've heard people whisper things like this during a film or make remarks to this effect in the theater lobby after. These comments about the making of the movie, about its effects, meaning, and artistic merits, are the start of film analysis.

Film analysis or interpretation takes shape as a conversation that shares and explores ideas based on a common experience or encounter. Moviegoers will often talk about the film itself and their experience with it, comparing it with others, consulting critics and even, sometimes, academics. We exchange ideas and get reactions to reach a deeper understanding of the movie and its possible meanings, as well as judge its merits and import. That is the central aim of criticism. Because a person's ideals and standards inform these discussions and judgments, opinions differ and require mutual respect and healthy discernment.

Viewers might consider any number of factors in thinking critically about a film, including aesthetic standards and moral, cultural, ideological, and religious priorities. We have already seen that together these make up a framework of expectations that we apply in various ways, depending on the film, and, I should add, with more or less skill and sophistication. That's not meant to be snooty. I've heard elementary schoolers make informed comparisons of *Frozen* to other Disney princess films. And I've listened to college students wax eloquent about themes, about the ins and outs of the story lines, and about differences between the novels and movies in the *Harry Potter* series. In different ways, they are gauging how well a film fits with their expectations.

While in a theater watching *Noah* (2014), an epic film based on the Bible's account of the Genesis flood, a man behind me quietly scoffed at every single flourish the story took with the biblical narrative. The snakeskin talisman handed down from Adam ("Humph!"). The gigantic earth-encrusted angels that help build the ark ("You're kidding!"). The antagonist, Tubal-Cain, becoming a stowaway on Noah's ark ("This is a joke."). His wife shushed him. Later, toward the end, a dove returns to Noah with an olive leaf in its mouth; it is a sign, laced with religious symbolism, that the floodwaters have receded and it is safe to leave the ark. He remarked, a bit sarcastically, "Well, at least they got *that* right."

Spectators most likely have a different reaction (of sorts) to the *Star Wars* movies, which we have no doubt are pure sci-fi fantasy. In *The Force Awakens* (2015), Han Solo (Harrison Ford) realizes that Finn (John Boyega) has no plan to disable the Starkiller Base's shields. Solo stresses the gravity of the situation: "People are counting on us. The galaxy is counting on us." Finn replies offhandedly, "Solo, we'll figure it out. We'll use the Force." What!? "That's not how the Force works," Han insists. It's one of the funniest lines in the movie. And we laugh—as if we too know how the Force works!

The humor also comes from our familiarity with Solo's character arc—from skeptic to believer—that in some sense we share. During a quiet scene earlier in the film, Han admits to Rey (Daisy Ridley): "Thought it was a bunch of mumbo-jumbo. A magical power holding together good and evil, the dark side and the light. Crazy thing is, it's true. The Force. The Jedi. All of it. It's all true." We likewise became convinced, having previously witnessed the power of the Force in the *Star Wars* fictional universe. We enter the theater already believing that what Obi-Wan Kenobi describes as an "aura that at once controls and obeys" is real and exists, if only "a long time ago in a galaxy far, far away."[14]

These two illustrations show how moviegoers will often think about movies differently to the extent that they perceive them to be fiction or nonfiction, what Stephen Prince calls the *fictive stance*.[15] If the story is fiction, audiences don't hold filmmakers to the same standards of truth and honesty as they do for nonfiction films. This helps us understand some of the hoopla surrounding *Noah*. As it was, Paramount's Bible-based spectacle reportedly "landed poorly with more literal interpreters of Scripture."[16] As much as the viewer behind me expected *Noah* to adhere to the book of Genesis, devotees of the *Star Wars* films are just as adamant that the story, production design, and character actions go "by the book" of the *Star Wars* fictional universe. Fans who spent time theorizing about the identity of Supreme Leader Snoke and Rey's parentage were unhappy with the uncomplicated way *The Last Jedi* resolved the intrigue, while others were upset with the more inclusive cast of characters (presumably because the franchise heretofore did not include many women or people of color).[17]

From start to finish, movies blend art and outlook. Artists and spectators make creative and critical judgments that are in some measure based on beliefs about the nature of both art and life. A filmmaker's perspective might permeate his or her work in many ways that find expression in the film itself. These might include personal convictions, accepted cultural values, business imperatives, and other factors accounting for the creation and character of the film. For example, evangelicals produced *Son of God* (2014) to reach millions of people with the story of Jesus. Ava DuVernay's directorial choices in *Selma* (2015) came from her point of view as a black female filmmaker. Darren Aronofsky's *Noah* (2014) was designed in part to be a blockbuster film that would appeal to a worldwide audience. In their own way, each of these ambitions shaped the film's final cut.

Likewise, our vantage points influence how we interpret a film and assess its worth. One critic found *Schindler's List* (1993), Steven Spielberg's award-winning film on the Holocaust, "very offensive from a Christian perspective." The reason? There is "extensive nudity in concentration camp scenes . . . graphic sex scenes between unmarried individuals . . . [and] 19 obscenities, 8 profanities and several vulgarities." In response to this critic, British scholar John Coffey thought that letting decency outweigh cultural import greatly diminished the significance of the historically based story: "Faced with one of the great moral evils of our century, these reviewers could do little more than tot up the number of swear words."[18]

Roger Ebert raved about *Schindler's List* for showing "the Holocaust in a vivid and terrible way." He pointed out the extent to which everything in the film serves the meaning Spielberg attached to these events. "The movie is brilliantly acted, written, directed and seen," Ebert wrote. "Individual scenes are masterpieces of art direction, cinematography, special effects, crowd control."[19] Even if the film is a cinematic masterwork, that is not enough, however, to satisfy someone with a personal connection. After learning about his father's experience of starvation and brutality in a Nazi concentration camp, a film critic who identifies himself as the son of a "Schindler Jew" writes that Spielberg's movie does not so much contribute to "an understanding of the Holocaust as cloak its horrors." He believes "the Holocaust deserves to be rendered truthfully in all its detail because it challenges and contradicts any advances made by human beings."[20] So here we have four different slants on the epic historical drama based on different vantage points and expectations for the film as art, morality, culture, and history.

Critical engagement draws attention to the way different interpretive possibilities might take shape based on a viewer's perspective. Scholars recognize three broad strategies. Like-minded viewers might be inclined to uncritically accept mainstream values expressed in a film (often called the *dominant* reading). Two other strategies, often talked about as "reading against the grain," involve scrutinizing ideas and attitudes to become aware of weaknesses, silences, and contradictions that might exist in the film's outlook. Based on their own viewpoints, viewers might stake an oppositional position by challenging or rejecting the prevailing outlook (a *resistant* reading). Or, somewhere between these two readings, spectators might adopt a critical posture without merely accepting or outright rejecting the film's outlook (a *negotiated* reading).[21] These different interpretive strategies show how perspectives play a central recognizable role in film interpretation and, along with other factors, make an important and even necessary contribution to the film experience.

While it is possible for viewers to discover meanings unintended by a filmmaker, interpretation is not boundless. It should be anchored in the film's form to avoid becoming impressionistic or mere conjecture. Interpretation starts with and ought to be based on what the film discloses through formal elements: methods, techniques, and patterns. Just as important to keep in mind is that filmmakers, critics, and spectators are more or less aware of their viewpoints, their framework of expectations, when talking about film. This rests on a key premise of this book: perspectives matter in both designing and interpreting movies.

To Entertain or Enlighten: That Is the Question

A Christian film promoter works with this premise: "What religious people want most when they go to the movies, like people who aren't religious, is to be entertained."[22] So let's start there. What if we think of being entertained as essential—not the end but the beginning of a worthwhile and satisfying experience with a film? This experience then starts us thinking more deeply about the movie itself and our encounter with it.

We might begin talking about a film, its meaning, and artistic merits by asking, "Do I find this movie entertaining and in some way enlightening?" Because in as much as it is *entertaining*, a well-made film, one with a compelling story and realistic characters, can also be *enlightening* or persuasive in its view of life. Think about it. We're lost for two hours in a fictional story that impresses us as being "real," engages us in the lives of characters, while expressing an outlook on what occurs throughout the film. Asking *why* and *how* this happens involves us in discussion of the craft of filmmaking and the nature of audience reception and interpretation.

If we find a movie entertaining and enlightening (or not), we might ask, for example, *how* formal elements work together to create representations of life that make them so believable (or not). How do movies play with our emotions and thoughts, and perhaps even get us to transfer interpretations to the real world? These kinds of questions draw attention to the ideals and values expressed in a film, which leads us back to the film's perspective and how it is conveyed. In short, movies invite viewers to look, to question, to engage the story, characters, and filmmaker's vision, to interact, and to discover new ways of thinking about life and the world.

As it is, we expect some movies to do no more than entertain us, while others we expect to offer thoughtful and heartfelt stories about things that matter to us. We might watch movies for the sheer delight of being thrilled, frightened, or otherwise emotionally captivated, or for insight into the human condition, or as a way of reflecting on ourselves, others, or society. We assess them, accordingly, for their entertainment value, truthfulness to actuality, or artistic proficiency. All the same, we should not lose focus on the essentially artistic character of film. The stylistic use of filmic techniques is the *means* of the film's disclosure, the way the film "tells" its story, reveals character, and ultimately fulfills roles and purposes in our lives and culture.

MOVIE MUSING

Pattern and Meaning in *The King's Speech* (2010)

> Watching [Colin] Firth agonisingly stammer his way through the closing
> speech at the Empire Exhibition at Wembley Stadium in 1925 is a master-
> class in acting.
>
> —Alan Frank, *Daily Star*

The opening sequence in *The King's Speech* (2010) sets up the main problem and establishes a pattern that points toward the film's resolution and the story's larger meaning. It is carefully crafted to make viewers feel the fear, anxiety, and embarrassment that Bertie (Colin Firth) feels. This occurs through a combination of techniques that build toward the scene's climax: the moment Bertie begins to speak.

An opening graphic informs us: "1925. King George V reigns over a quarter of the world's population. He asks his second son, the Duke of York, to give the closing speech at the Empire Exhibition in Wembley, London." The film cuts to a BBC microphone shot in close-up to make it look formidable, followed by numerous shots of the microphone. Nondiegetic piano music (coming from outside the story world) plays on the soundtrack over these shots and the opening credits. A news reader, preparing to go on the air, gargles—the first diegetic sound we hear (that is, the first sound within the film's world).

Though we're not sure why, Bertie looks apprehensive; remarks by other characters seem to only make him more nervous. "Let the microphone do the work, sir," the chief BBC engineer tells him. "I am sure you'll be splendid. Just take your time," the archbishop of Canterbury advises. Bertie's wife, Elizabeth (Helena Bonham Carter), appears loving in her concern, giving him a kiss on the cheek and then quickly rubbing off a spot of lipstick.

The BBC news reader sits with a straight back at a desk in front of the microphone. A red transmission light flashes once, twice, three times. "Good afternoon. This is the BBC National Programme and Empire Services," he begins, speaking impeccably, telling listeners (and us) about the speech they are about to hear at the closing of "the largest exhibition staged anywhere in the world." As he continues, we see Bertie climb a staircase, and at the top a gentleman reminds him: "Remember, sir. Three flashes, then steady means you're live." The camera tracks in for a close-up of Bertie, who looks simply terrified. We see a shot of a long wall of broadcast transmission equipment as the news reader announces, "And today His Royal Highness the Duke of York will give his inaugural broadcast to the Nation and the World." Cut back to Bertie, who looks like a dead man walking.

The Duke of York enters the stadium; everyone rises, then takes their seat. We see from Bertie's point of view: the red transmission light blinks once, twice, three times, and then glows solid. The redundancy related to the red transmission light—it's been referred to three times—is to ensure that viewers don't miss its practical function to signal that the speaker is on the air. It also creates unease and builds suspense toward the scene's climax: the unnerving moment when Bertie has to deliver a speech on behalf of his father, the king, before a packed Wembley Stadium and worldwide broadcast audience

The King's Speech © 2010 Speaking Films Productions Ltd

Frames 13a, 13b. Shots including a BBC microphone and red transmission light are designed to look intimidating as a way of representing Bertie's anxiety and embarrassment in *The King's Speech*.

(frames 13a, 13b). It establishes a pattern regarding preparation and performance—with a payoff to come later in the story.

Bertie stands in front of the intimidating microphone in tense silence. As he starts speaking and we hear his voice for the first time, he struggles, his painful stuttering amplified, echoing in the stadium. Shots of people in the crowd show growing discomfort. We feel Bertie's fear, anxiety, and humiliation. Close-ups show characters with looks of disappointment, embarrassment, and then there's his wife's look of loving concern. Now we understand the reason for all the prior apprehension.

The scene reveals Bertie's deep internal conflict; the Duke of York and (though yet to be revealed) future King of England cannot speak with the eloquence expected of royalty. The problem for Bertie to overcome is clear. Viewers cannot help but feel empathy for him.

Much later in the story, with fears of a second world war rising, Archbishop Cosmo Lang makes a remark that emphasizes the high stakes of Bertie's speech treatment: "In Nuremberg stadium, Herr Hitler mesmerizes millions, whilst the Duke of York cannot successfully order fish and chips." Another scene makes the comparison even more pointed. Bertie watches a newsreel of Adolph Hitler delivering an impassioned speech in German before a massive troop rally. "Papa, what's he saying?" his young daughter asks. "I don't know, but he seems to be saying it rather well," Bertie replies with a look of consternation. The scene was designed to strike a contrast between the two national leaders. "That's an incredibly powerful line, because Hitler is sort of the antithesis to Bertie's character, who can't say things very well," cinematographer Danny Cohen said. "And there was fluency to whatever [evil things] Hitler might have said. The delivery was always better than how Bertie could deliver his speeches, so that was a quite interesting, complex contradiction."[23]

In the film's climax, Bertie delivers a broadcast speech of far greater significance than the one at the closing ceremony of the Wembley Exhibition. In contrast to the huge stadium setting, Bertie speaks from a small room, made even smaller with colorful sheets stretched loosely across the ceiling and draped on the walls. He stands at a wooden podium. In a series of intimate close-ups of Bertie and speech therapist Lionel Logue (Geoffrey Rush) conversing, the dreaded microphone looms large between them. Some shots make use of wide-angle lenses that distort Bertie's face, making him look even more uncomfortable. "However this turns out, I don't know how to thank you for what you've done," Bertie says. "Knighthood?" Lionel replies lightheartedly.

We see the red transmission light flashing on Bertie's face in close-up (reminding us of his disastrous Wembley speech). "In this grave hour, perhaps the most fateful in our history," Bertie begins his address to the nation and the world. Now, in contrast, his throat relaxed, his hands steady, Bertie rises to the occasion. He speaks slowly, the pace measured, but without stopping; his voice comes across calm and confident. Bertie's transformational character arc is complete. With the help of his speech therapist and now friend, Bertie is prepared to serve as king and assume national leadership at the start of the Second World War.

MOVIE MUSING

Dramatizing Drone Warfare in *Eye in the Sky* (2015)

In war, truth is the first casualty.

—Aeschylus

Like an epigraph, an opening graphic with the Aeschylus quotation appears. It is animated to make the word "truth" disappear, suggesting something about theme, and another graphic follows, establishing the opening scene's specific location and time: "Eastleigh, Nairobi, Kenya, 07:00 AM East Africa Time." The action starts with a fade in from black as the door of a brick oven opens. With a moving shot that starts inside the oven (think about that), the camera follows a loaf of bread as Alia Mo'Allim's mother, Fatima, takes it out of the wood-fire oven. That we cross this cinematic threshold from one world into another via the oven is highly metaphorical.

Fatima (Faisa Hassan) runs a small bakery business out of their home, which opens to a dirt courtyard inside the walls of their compound in a densely populated Nairobi suburb. Outside, Fatima's husband, Musa (Armaan Haggio), finishes repairing a hula hoop made of spare bicycle parts strewn around the courtyard. Daughter Alia (Aisha Takow), a charming, playful little girl, expresses sheer delight and skill twirling the brightly colored hula hoop. We cut to an extreme long shot of Alia playing in the courtyard. As the camera moves back and upward, we get a bird's eye view of the surrounding neighborhood, the dirt streets filled with people. An armed military vehicle patrolling the area especially draws our attention.

An extended montage sequence establishes the story's global setting and introduces us to a cast of characters in at least eight locations around the world, including Nairobi, London, Las Vegas, Pearl Harbor, Beijing, and Singapore. That same morning on his way to work, Lt. Gen. Frank Benson (Alan Rickman) looks perplexed standing in a store in front of a wall of shelves filled with different kinds of Baby Annabell dolls. He's supposed to buy one as a present for his granddaughter. Unable to recall which one she wants, he decides to get the "Time to Sleep" doll and leaves a voice message asking his daughter to confirm his choice. Cut to Alia, who is reading when her mother calls her. As she does several times a day, Alia takes a basket with loaves of bread fresh out of the oven and sets them out on a wooden table around the corner to sell in the square. When Benson arrives at the British cabinet offices in Whitehall, London, he gets a return call and asks a staffer to exchange the doll he bought for a "Baby Moves" one, remarking, "Apparently there's an important difference." A pattern starts to emerge in the parallel between the two girls, who will go about their days oblivious to the geopolitical events unfolding with different proximity. The deliberate inclusion of the toys—a hula hoop and a doll, symbolizing their youth and innocence—humanizes the girls, making the thought of their being potential victims of a terrorist attack all the more atrocious. It adds another layer to the film's theme of the cost of war.

Meanwhile, at the Permanent Joint Headquarters in Northwood, London, the no-nonsense Lt. Col. Katherine Powell (Helen Mirren) has received confirmation that high-level terrorist operatives she's been tracking for six years are in a safe house, which it turns out is right next door to the Mo'Allim residence. A super high-tech surveillance mini-drone (a winged cyborg beetle) inside the safe house shows two suicide bombers being armed for a mission estimated to kill up to eighty civilians. Powell's directive is to capture the terrorists, and Kenyan Special Forces are ready to make the arrest. But with knowledge of the impending bombing, Powell's mission is changed from capture to kill. British and US military personnel go about coordinating a Hellfire missile attack from a US aerial drone. Securing official approval, however, for a joint British-US military initiative via the chain of command proves trying and complicated and propels the narrative forward with what one critic calls "endlessly argumentative action."[24]

The pilots at Creech Air Force Base in Nevada are cleared for engagement and begin the launch protocol when Alia returns with another basket of bread to sell, delaying the drone strike. Her stand is within the kill zone, sparking an international dispute over the rules of engagement, the risk of collateral damage, and the legality of the operation (due process and the right to kill British and American citizens). United States and British military personnel wrangle with policymakers and consultants over authority and legal interpretations. Benson's job is to facilitate these deliberations via phone, messaging, and video monitor conferencing. The narrative twists and turns on balancing and prioritizing public safety, fighting terrorism, military and political accountability, and public relations. The moral dilemma, potentially killing an innocent little girl in order to prevent an impending terrorist attack, surfaces in actions taken to get Alia out of the kill zone.

A crosscutting sequence deepens the pattern by juxtaposing actions signifying life and death. We see shots of the militants strapping suicide vests on two adolescent boys and loading explosives into vest pockets—one by one. Just outside the safe house compound, Alia sits at her table waiting patiently for the next customer. The story seems to be unfolding in real time, which enhances suspense. The pilots prepare to launch the Hellfire missile. With US and British officials monitoring these events, we tensely count down the remaining loaves to be sold so that Alia will vacate the area and be out of harm's way (frame 14).

The moral ambiguity in the tortuous decision-making process hangs over the closing scenes, leaving no one unscathed—not least the US drone pilot, Steve Watts (Aaron Paul), whose job is to pull the trigger and who, as film critic Ann Hornaday points out, provides the "most plaintive moral voice."[25] Last to leave the situation room are Lt. Gen. Benson and British political adviser Angela Northman (Monica Dolan), who has clearly

Eye in the Sky © 2015 eOne Films

Frame 14. A sequence with shots of militants juxtaposed with Alia waiting for the next customer signify life and death and increase suspense in *Eye in the Sky*.

been most at odds with him. Their final scene together brings the movie's theme into focus. "What happened today was disgraceful," she says in a reprimand. Benson tells her that he saw the aftermath of five suicide bombings. "What you witnessed today, with your coffee and biscuits, is terrible. What these men would have done would have been even more terrible. That is how it is," he replies tersely and with utter seriousness. "Never tell a soldier that he doesn't know the cost of war."

Afterward, a weary Benson has all but forgotten about his personal dilemma that morning until the staffer gives him a shopping bag with the "Baby Moves" doll. What seems so mundane compared to the day's happenings is likely to bring the same delight to his granddaughter as the repaired hula hoop did for Alia in the film's opening. When we cut to Alia's parents bringing her to a hospital in Nairobi, the two scenes bookend the day's events and complete the pattern set up at the beginning.

Reviews of *Eye in the Sky* (2015) were very favorable (97 percent among top critics on Rotten Tomatoes). The consensus was summed up, "As taut as it is timely, *Eye in the Sky* offers a powerfully acted—and unusually cerebral—spin on the modern wartime political thriller."[26]

Critics appreciated the movie's hard look at drone warfare and its various viewpoints on the subject. James Berardinelli finds the film "compelling, offering the best elements of a drama and a thriller." Without forcing "an audience into picking a side, it illustrates facets of a complex issue without bias." At the thematic core of this edge-of-your-seat thriller is an unresolved debate on the ethics of drone strikes. "There's no 'right' or 'wrong'—only points and counterpoints," Berardinelli notes.[27]

In one sense, the film does not provide too "overtly critical a view of drone warfare," *New York Times* critic Stephen Holden concludes, but instead "allows the story's absurdist elements to speak for themselves."[28] In the darkly humorous comparing of trivial annoyances to the life-or-death magnitude of the missile attack, we detect hints of the black political satire of *Dr. Strangelove or: How I Learned to Stop Worrying and Love the Bomb* (1964). The British foreign secretary is suffering from food poisoning in Singapore; with aides present, he comes out of the hotel bathroom in a white robe to take a pressing Skype call. The US secretary of state is irked at having to take an urgent phone call that interrupts his game of ping-pong in Beijing: "Why the hell are you wasting my time referring this to me?" he snaps. "Yes, all three are on the president's kill list. Tell them to take them out now!" These corresponding scenes also highlight a "tendency to caricature U.S. administration officials as far less thoughtful and painstaking" than their British counterparts, as Ann Hornaday and other critics note.[29]

Hornaday joins those praising the film as "the rare military drama that conveys both the graphic physical effects of war and its lingering psychic cost." She offers a different take, however, on the frustrating bureaucratic bickering. In her view, the movie "makes a propagandistic case for drone warfare, if only in depicting the decision-making process as so thoughtful, agonizing and comprehensive."[30] In this sense, showing all the different viewpoints highlights the moral complexity, and serves only to legitimize the use of drone technology as highly strategic and unavoidable given geopolitical circumstances.

A *Commonweal* critic follows much the same line, citing a 2015 report that civilian casualties accounted for well over ten percent of the nearly four thousand people killed in US drone strikes. He remarks, "You'd never know this from watching *Eye in the Sky*." The problem lies in using Hollywood conventions, "the focus on individual characters and fates, the impulse for sympathetic roles and portrayals," to dramatize a subject so ethically controversial and politically charged. "The atmosphere of moral agony and tragedy that suffuses *Eye in the Sky* reflects standard-issue Hollywood sentimentality; but in a political sense, it offers Americans reassurance that our drone warfare is morally justified," he explains. "Ostensibly, *Eye in the Sky* sets out to present divergent points of view in a neutral fashion; but in the end, there's little doubt about the bottom line."[31]

A reviewer at *RogerEbert.com* raises a different but related issue. *Eye in the Sky* is "a polished, often riveting thriller about an important topical issue," but is the topic more appropriate for a documentary than a fictional film? "Because the subject is a very potent and contentious one, we don't just want excitement in its treatment; we want clarification and illumination," he remarks. "But how much of what we see here is accurate and factually based, and how much is dramatic license?"[32] This highlights the importance of the fictive stance in the way spectators approach the film.

The filmmakers utilize cutting-edge technology: a hummingbird drone (based on existing hardware) that does surveillance outside the safe house, and a smaller beetle-like drone that is under development, but not in operation. For accuracy, director Gavin Hood discussed the beetle drone's capabilities with its developers and turned one of its problems into a dramatic situation: "It's not the size of the cameras, or transmitting images, or even making something mechanical fly like an insect," Gavin explains. "The problem is battery life. So we put that in the movie, because flight and transmitting high definition imagery sucks too much juice."[33]

The beetle drone penetrates the safe house and serves an important dramatic purpose. It provides the team in the situation room—and the movie audience—with visual up-to-the-minute intelligence on what the terrorists are plotting. It's also incredibly entertaining, the filming and editing "amping the tension," as one critic observes, "effectively contrasting the chilly confines of the interiors and the menace in broad daylight of the exteriors."[34] The beetle drone visuals let us count both the loaves of bread and the explosives inserted in the suicide vests. Suppose the military and government overseers—and film viewers—were not privy to the goings-on inside the safe house? How would not knowing about the imminent suicide mission affect their decision-making and subsequent actions, as well as our judgment of them? Form matters in both storytelling and interpretation.

MOVIE MUSING

Art and Ethics in *Rear Window* (1954)

Hitchcock combines technical and artistic skills in a manner that makes this
an unusually good piece of murder mystery entertainment.

—William Brogdon, *Variety*

Alfred Hitchcock, the "Master of Suspense," is one of the most celebrated and accomplished filmmakers of all time. His compulsive control over every aspect of his productions stamped them with his signature style. Throughout his career, as writer David Sterritt notes, Hitchcock "remained an artistically ambitious filmmaker who wanted to explore serious issues—social, philosophical, and cinematic—in serious ways for serious moviegoers."[35] To put it another way, Hitchcock created provocative and artistically inventive movies, "rattling-good thrillers," that were also hugely popular and critically acclaimed. The adjusted box-office grosses show Hitchcock's classic *Rear Window* (1954) edging out *Psycho* (1960)—with its famous and shocking shower murder scene—as his biggest commercial hit. Both are highly praised films lodged on the American Film Institute's 100 Greatest American Movies list, along with Hitchcock's *Vertigo* (1958) and *North by Northwest* (1959).

The *Rear Window* screenplay by John Michael Hayes is based on "It Had to Be Murder," a short story by Cornell Woolrich; two gruesome real-life murder cases also reportedly inspired Hayes's script. L. B. "Jeff" Jefferies (James Stewart), the main protagonist, is an adventurous, globe-trotting news photographer. He's trapped in his third-story lower

Fifth Avenue apartment during the height of summer recuperating from a broken leg. Restless and bored, Jefferies passes the time observing the activities of the apartment building's occupants whose rear windows all face a common interior courtyard. Soon enough, he starts tuning in to his neighbors' private lives like a daytime soap opera.

The setup is masterful, establishing the apartment/courtyard setting so precisely from the vantage of Jefferies's apartment that throughout the film, simply by the direction Jefferies looks, viewers know exactly whose apartment window he's watching. Hitchcock also makes brilliant use of point-of-view shots and association editing; shots of incidents that occur are intercut with others of Jefferies reacting to what he is seeing. Their meaning comes from the association between the shots.

The film opens with orchestral (nondiegetic) music accompanying the credits; afterward, we hear only diegetic sounds—that is, sounds from within the film's world. A series of shots by a moving camera introduce the setting—an apartment complex and interior courtyard—and the residents starting their day. A close-up of a wall thermometer, the red mercury indicating a temperature above 90, matches another of a man asleep and sweating. The camera moves down his body and pulls back revealing that he's in a wheelchair wearing a heavy cast from foot to hip bearing an inscription: "Here lie the broken bones of L. B. Jefferies." As if to answer the question of what happened, the camera pans quickly across the room, lingering on a smashed camera, photos of a race-car crash and explosions, more photographic equipment, a framed negative photographic image of a beautiful woman, and then the positive image of her on the cover of *Parisian Fashions* magazine.

A fade out and in with black appears here and throughout the film. The effect is to slow the pace of the narrative, giving a sense of Jefferies's boredom, and to suggest that a good amount of time passes between scenes. Jefferies talks with his editor on the phone about his broken leg while watching the morning rituals of his neighbors. Two young women sunbathe on a rooftop, attracting the attention of a helicopter pilot—a voyeuristic image hinting at one of the film's key themes. Among the apartment dwellers we see a neighborhood busybody; a struggling composer-pianist; a shapely ballerina he nicknames "Miss Torso," who spins and stretches in scanty attire and has to fight off her male guests; and on the first floor an aging spinster he calls "Miss Lonelyhearts," who has imaginary dinner dates. Freshly arrived newlyweds keep their blinds pulled down; an elderly couple sleep on a mattress on the fire escape to find some relief from the summer heat. Jefferies notices a sullen traveling salesman in a second-story apartment who argues constantly with his bedridden, shrewish wife who seems to take pleasure in making his life miserable. The camera has us peering into the lives of the apartment dwellers, who do not interact whatsoever with Jefferies and are unknowingly entertaining him—and us—as if part of a daytime drama. It is enough to spark our curiosity about their personal lives.

Jefferies maintains an emotional distance from his elegant and drop-dead gorgeous girlfriend, Lisa Fremont (Grace Kelly), whose picture we saw earlier on the *Parisian*

Fashions magazine. We first see Lisa in a tight close-up, leaning toward the camera (us) and gently kissing Jefferies. Lisa's patience with Jefferies is wearing thin; the Park Avenue model and high-fashion consultant is pressuring him to marry her and settle down by opening a Manhattan studio. Their gendered lifestyles (male/active, female/passive) contrast markedly. Lisa, glamorous and refined, urges Jefferies to give up his thrill-seeking ventures and become a studio fashion photographer. "I'm gonna get married and then I'll never be able to go anywhere," he says with disdain to his editor. He rationalizes that Lisa is "too perfect, too talented, too beautiful, and too sophisticated," claiming she's pampered and incapable of enduring the arduous travel and tough conditions of exotic places. Like many of Hitchcock's protagonists, Jefferies's life is at a point of paralysis, his inability to act symbolized by the heavy cast from foot to hip that confines him to a wheelchair.

The plot turns one night when Jefferies hears a woman's scream and glass breaking under cover of darkness. As he drifts in and out of sleep, he sees the traveling salesman coming and going from his apartment across the courtyard toting his sample case during a rainstorm. Early the next morning, while Jefferies sleeps soundly in his wheelchair, we see the salesman leaving his apartment with a woman. We'll return to this crucial scene that presents us with a shift in narrational point of view in a moment. Meanwhile, the salesman's behavior makes Jefferies increasingly suspicious. After piecing together clues, he calls his police detective friend Thomas J. Doyle (Wendell Corey); they flew reconnaissance planes together during World War II. Doyle's checking reveals that witnesses saw the salesman, Lars Thorwald (Raymond Burr), and his wife leaving together the previous morning.

Though it appears Jefferies has overreacted, he remains nonetheless doubtful. When he tells Lisa that he saw Thorwald taking his wife's jewelry out of her purse, Lisa is sure of foul play—no woman would leave without her jewelry. The practical "feminine" matter is enough for Lisa to accept Jefferies's suspicions and marks a key moment. It affirms a central thematic tension in Hitchcock's films "between love and faith on the hero's side, doubt and suspicion on the other side, which include yet-to-be-enlightened heroines, the police, and others representing obstacles to the hero's progress," Sterritt explains.[36] Jefferies, Lisa, and the nurse, Stella (Thelma Ritter), team up now in search of evidence that will prove Thorwald murdered his wife and disposed of her body. In a gender-role reversal, the women become the adventurers with the incapacitated Jefferies able only to observe from the confines of his wheelchair and apartment. Jefferies's diversion turns ethically serious, and then dangerous, putting his and Lisa's lives at risk.

A determined Lisa scales the fire escape and climbs through an open window into Thorwald's apartment looking for his wife's wedding ring. Jefferies and Stella are momentarily distracted by Miss Lonelyhearts and don't see Thorwald returning until it's too late to warn Lisa. Jefferies calls the police and can only wait. The effect is to make viewers feel Jefferies's paralysis; with him, all we can do is watch when Thorwald assaults Lisa and she cries out for help.

The police arrive, and as they are getting her statement, aware that Jefferies and Stella are watching, Lisa puts her hands behind her back and points out Mrs. Thorwald's wedding ring on her finger—signaling the success of her mission. Thorwald sees the gesture and realizes it's to someone across the courtyard; he looks directly at Jefferies and Stella, who jump back and turn off the lights. It's as if Thorwald is looking back through the movie screen at them—and us. Afterward, Lisa is taken to the police station, Stella goes off with bail money, and in a highly suspenseful scene, Thorwald comes after Jefferies, resulting in physical confrontation. Thorwald wrestles with Jefferies and pushes him out the window. Doyle and police officers arrive in the nick of time to break his fall and apprehend Thorwald, who confesses on the spot to the murder and discloses all the gory details. When Lisa holds Jefferies in her arms at the end of the climax (a gender-reversed image), the look on his face is priceless—a mix of sensual desire and mutual respect now.

Criteria for Assessing Art

Film scholars apply four widely accepted criteria for assessing art to make judgments about the relative quality of movies: coherence, intensity of effect, complexity, and originality.[37]

The first, *coherence*, has to do with how well the elements in the film are organized and work together to create meaning. Film elements can be understood and evaluated according to their function and fit within the film's overall pattern. The apartment dwellers in *Rear Window* are in various stages of life and relationships: single, newlywed, married (happily or unhappily). The narrative weaves them together as a kind of Greek chorus for reflection (both ours and Jefferies's) on both the personal tension between Jefferies and Lisa and the suspected murder. Conversation about the ups and downs of relationships between men, women, feminine intuition, love, romance, and marriage fills the dialogue. In addition, Hitchcock's calculated reliance on point-of-view shots and association editing aptly produce their intended effect and cohere with the movie's main motifs. "*Rear Window* is Hitchcock's most uncompromising attempt to imprison us, not only within a limited space, but within a single consciousness," as film scholar Robin Wood puts it. "From the beginning of the film to the end, we are enclosed in the protagonist's apartment, leaving it only when he leaves it (precipitately, through the window!)."[38]

The second criteria is *intensity of effect*. In what measure is the film crafted to engage viewers emotionally and intelligently with a riveting and believable story? As the suspense and drama build in the pivotal scene described earlier, Lisa climbs a fire escape and enters Thorwald's apartment through a window in search of evidence. Thorwald returns unexpectedly; Jefferies and Stella can only watch, powerless to help Lisa as she struggles

Rear Window © 1954 Alfred J. Hitchcock Productions

Frame 15. The inventive *Rear Window* weaves a gender-role reversal and sub-plots together with a murder mystery to enhance the main story line and enrich the film's theme.

with the expected murderer and cries out for help. The scene merges the main plot (the murder mystery) with the main subplot (Lisa and Jefferies's strained relationship) both narratively and thematically, while also playing on a voyeurism motif.

Rear Window exhibits a third criteria, *complexity*, by working on multiple levels and weaving several patterns together that deepen and enrich the film's overall meaning (frame 15). The motive for murder connects in one way or another to the lives of all the neighbors, who share not only the common courtyard but a mix of delights, desires, doubts, or disappointments over love, romance, and companionship. Jefferies and Lisa end up in a gender-role reversal that leads to solving the crime and their relationship differences—well, maybe. What's more, the story's disclosure occurs as a result of Jefferies's morally dubious snooping on his neighbors, an underlying theme. When Jefferies asks Lisa about the morality of spying "on a man even if you prove he didn't commit a crime," she replies, "I'm not much on rear window ethics."

Finally, a film benefits from *originality*, which has to do with subject selection, unique storytelling, and creative presentation. That is not to say a film has to be entirely new or different; it can be enough to put a fresh or clever twist on a familiar formula or convention.

Rear Window follows the usual crime story format. In this case, an ordinary community of apartment dwellers is disrupted by a murder, and once the crime is solved, normalcy returns, with suggestions now of a heightened awareness. The story also adheres to the basic features of a classical Hollywood film, something we'll consider more in chapter 7. The goal and motivations of the main protagonist (Jefferies) are clear. The story moves forward in a linear fashion with one event leading to the next until it reaches a complete resolution—if also a hasty one. The main line of action—solving the crime—interacts with related subplots involving the main characters and other apartment dwellers. Hitchcock's suspense thriller, however, is quite innovative for a conventional murder mystery.

Hitchcock enjoyed experimenting stylistically with his films, stretching classical Hollywood conventions. *Rear Window* was shot entirely on one set, the apartment courtyard, and it creates suspense with relatively little action taking place. Until very near the end, during the climax, which includes shots from the courtyard, we see everything the way Jefferies does, looking out from his apartment window. Moreover, we experience almost the entire story from Jefferies's limited (first-person) point of view, as if we're trapped with him.

Jefferies watches Thorwald coming and going out of his apartment wearing a black raincoat and carrying a large suitcase several times during a rainy night. At one point, Jefferies looks at his watch. We see a close-up of the watch, fade to black, then fade in to another of the watch showing that more than an hour and a half has passed. Thorwald returns, then leaves again. Fade to black, signifying hours passing again. Fade in with morning light; the rain has stopped. The camera shows Jefferies asleep in his wheelchair, and then pans right, across the courtyard, to show Thorwald and a woman leaving his apartment, and then pans back left to Jefferies, who remains asleep. We witness an event that Jefferies is unaware happened. Can you see how the camera itself *is* the narrator, the storyteller?

For just a brief moment, the narration shifts to an omniscient point of view with the camera revealing to the audience an important narrative clue. It turns out to be a red herring that, by sowing doubts, influences the way we perceive events as the story progresses. As Robin Wood describes it, the inclusion of this shot "brings home to us the fact that Jefferies *could* be wrong: by making the identification of the spectator with Jefferies's consciousness not *quite* complete, Hitchcock enables us to feel just that small amount of uneasiness necessary for us to question the morality of what he is doing—our own morality since we are spying with him, sharing his fascinated, compulsive 'Peeping-Tom-ism.'"[39] The momentary shift in narrative perspective also suggests to viewers the existence of an unseen presence that is watching closely as these events unfold and that is, unbeknownst to Jefferies, fully aware of his actions.

Through a Catholic Optic

Critics often find Hitchcock's films to be "deeply infused with anxiety, guilt, and existential angst, which they trace to his Catholic upbringing and education," as one writer explains.[40] Although Hitchcock rejected the label "Catholic" filmmaker, he once conceded, "One's early upbringing influences a man's life and guides his instinct."[41] Film critic Richard Blake attributes this to core Catholic beliefs leaving an "afterimage" on the filmmaker's imagination. The term *afterimage* refers to "the image that remains after a stimulus ceases or is removed." It is an involuntary phenomenon, something like when the light from a camera flash remains even after you close your eyelids and it temporarily alters your vision. Along with other filmmakers from a Catholic background, Blake finds traces in Hitchcock's movies of the director seeing "the world through a Catholic optic," he explains. "They are likely to carry with them the 'stories' of their childhood through which they have learned to situate questions of the ultimate meaning of life, and these in turn tend to shape the meaning of events in daily life, like love, community, loyalty, death, family, sex, conflict, violence, and sacrifice."[42]

Perhaps that's the reason characters in Hitchcock's movies represent an ambiguous view of human nature—more so than in typical Hollywood releases. They inhabit a world of moral complexity that blurs distinctions between innocence and guilt or good and evil. Their actions, along with the film's visual style, give expression to the moral and psychological mindset of the main characters, which culminates in "the transcendence of physical conflict over psychological and even moral confrontation with evil," as Sterritt puts it. Among the recurring themes in Hitchcock's films that are particularly apropos to *Rear Window* are a vagueness of guilt and innocence, equating acquired knowledge with increased danger, and a fascination with voyeurism.[43] Jefferies becomes *The Man Who Knew Too Much*, a film title Hitchcock used twice that alludes to the equation of knowledge and danger.

The storytelling itself in *Rear Window* mimics the nature of movie watching itself, the way a film opens a window on another world and we take pleasure in looking at other people's lives. "Rarely has any film so boldly presented its methods in plain view," Roger Ebert notes. "Jeff sits in his wheelchair, holding a camera with a telephoto lens, and looks first here and then there, like a movie camera would. What he sees, we see. What conclusions he draws, we draw—all without words, because the pictures add up to a montage of suspicion."[44] In the scene described above, the way that Jefferies and Stella watch the events transpiring in Thorwald's apartment across the courtyard resembles our watching the movie—including a collective sigh of relief with the characters as the police arrive to rescue Lisa. The bond between our point of view and that of Jefferies intensifies as we watch with him through a telephoto lens that Stella calls a "portable keyhole."

Critics admire Hitchcock for his technical use of point-of-view shots as an expressive device, a stylistic tendency that creates an emotional and even physical connection between viewers and the main character. Our being made to identify so intensely with Jefferies makes us complicit in some sense in his voyeurism. We share his irresistible temptation to watch and, with it, his unease, guilt, and anxiety about invading another's privacy. So, when Thorwald attacks Jefferies, as Ebert notes, "We can't detach ourselves, because we looked too, and so we share the guilt and in a way we deserve what's coming to him."[45] Moreover, the outcome of Jefferies's situation and his fate is not predetermined as is typical of a heroic protagonist displaying an inherent goodness. His moral complicity creates an uncertainty about his fate, which also heightens the suspense and elicits emotions of fear and concern for the well-being of the main characters. Again, this occurs largely because of the way the film limits the audience's vantage point to that of Jefferies—an adroit use of formal techniques to convey content and elicit matching emotions.

It is possible to see *Rear Window* as either a condemnation of voyeurism or an exploitation of it. But the film itself offers a moral posture that is "far subtler and more profound than either suggests," as Wood concludes. We are made to feel discomforted by Jefferies's prying, which eventually risks putting Lisa in danger, and yet we find satisfaction that it results in the capture of a murderer and, moreover, releases Jefferies from "the spiritual deadlock he had reached at the beginning of the film."[46]

The final scene recalls the opening one. A fade in from black on a tight close-up of the wall thermometer shows the heat wave (disruption) has passed, signaling that social and moral order has been restored. With the crime uncovered and solved, the community returns to a new normal—in many ways the same, but with new possibilities. In a single shot, the camera pans left, tilting up and down, surveying the apartments and courtyard. Miss Lonely Hearts and the struggling composer have found each other and celebrate the recording of his song; he puts the record on the turntable and we hear the soft ballad, "Lisa." Painters are putting a fresh coat of paint on the walls in the empty Thorwald apartment. Miss Torso welcomes back her Army sweetheart with an enthusiastic hug (Stanley!). The newlyweds show signs of coming down to earth, their honeymoon wearing off.

As in the opening sequence, we see Jefferies again asleep in his wheelchair, this time with a smile of satisfaction on his face. The camera moves down his body revealing with a bit of humor that he has two broken legs now. The breach between good and evil has been repaired. Thorwald will serve prison time, and Jefferies, Blake observes, "must continue to pay the price of his transgressions by enduring his own brand of confinement until his two broken legs are healed."[47] That Jefferies has two broken legs lets us hear the narrative "voice" of the filmmaker in an implied judgment of the character for his unethical behavior. Hitchcock is presumably not letting Jefferies off the hook, even though his actions uncover the murder. The camera pans right and along the body of Lisa, who is reclining comfortably in blue jeans and a plain blouse on the couch, reading *Beyond the High Himalayas*. Seeing that Jeff is asleep, she puts down the book and looks contentedly at *Bazaar* magazine, leaving us wondering who has the upper hand in their happily-ever-after relationship. Fade out.

6

Redemption American-Style

The Melodramatic Vision

> The oddity of melodramatic endings—the last-minute rescues, the surprising reunions of long separated families and lovers, the foiling of the villains' plots—were in their context metaphysical necessities.
>
> —David Grimsted

A consummate Hollywood blockbuster film, *Titanic* celebrates the magical quality of the cinema, transporting moviegoers around the world to the deck of the *Titanic* in all the grandeur of its maiden voyage. Writer and director James Cameron's blockbuster hit rivaled the popularity of *The Ten Commandments*, *Lawrence of Arabia*, and *Dr. Zhivago*, traditional Hollywood epics that drew vast numbers of viewers to theaters in search of romance, adventure, and spectacle. Reviewers especially noted the comparison to *Gone with the Wind*, since both films center on a woman's emotional experience and present the central romance against a catastrophic backdrop.

Although its core audience was female (60 percent), *Titanic* scored in all four audience quadrants (male and female, over and under age twenty-five) and managed a phenomenal 20 percent repeat audience in comparison to the customary 2 percent. Forty-five percent of all the women under twenty-five who saw the movie went twice, and 76 percent of all people who saw it at least twice planned on seeing it again. "A chick-flick period piece with a tragic ending is rewriting the Hollywood rules," *Newsweek*'s David Ansen wrote about *Titanic* during its initial theatrical run. "Why are we all sobbing with pleasure?" Audiences cried in Moscow, Tokyo, Rome, Slovenia, Mexico, and Hong Kong. In some towns in France, admissions topped the local population, meaning "the French are going to it three or four times—something the French are not supposed to do," Ansen remarked.[1] As people returned to theaters again, and again, and again, *Titanic* went on to become the first movie to earn $1 billion worldwide. It eventually took in over $2.1 billion, double the amount of the previous record holder, *Jurassic Park* (1993). It currently ranks second in worldwide box-office grosses, trailing Cameron's *Avatar* (2009), which earned over $2.7 billion. As a demonstration of its staying power, when *Titanic* was reissued on IMAX in 2012, it set a record for 3-D releases.

How is it that a conventional Hollywood movie that critics considered "no masterpiece" captured the collective imagination worldwide?[2] No doubt, the incredible popularity of *Titanic* stems in part from its supplying viewers with diverse pleasures. Female moviegoers were wooed by the tragic romance, while males were thrilled by the spectacle of the disaster. More importantly, the film represents a mythic affirmation of universal emotions, capturing widespread interests in love, sex, violence, heroism, wealth, and redemption.

As critics observe, *Titanic* is a pure old-fashioned melodrama. The story is contrived. The characters are class caricatures. And the tragic ending? Heartwrenching. "The formula at work here would have been right at home in silent melodramas," *Variety*'s Todd McCarthy writes. Gauging its box-office potential, he remarks, "The dynamic of the central love story, between a brash lad from steerage and an upper-class young lady bursting to escape her gilded cage, is as effective as it is corny, and *will definitely help put the picture over with the largest possible public.*"[3]

Among critics, use of the term *melodramatic* is almost always pejorative, indicating an artwork lacking subtlety and story and character development. Scholars, however, have begun recuperating the aesthetic functions and popular appeal of melodrama as a prominent and enduring feature of American culture.[4] Drawing on their work, I use the term *melodrama* to describe how an aesthetic mode and a particular outlook come together in movies that celebrate American ideals and values. Awareness of the melodramatic vision gives us a deeper understanding of mainstream Hollywood films: their patterns of meaning, the nature of their dramatic and emotional appeal, and what critics have long recognized as aesthetic shortcomings.

The Imagined World of Melodrama

A subtype of drama, melodrama is not a distinctly American story form. Its influence in Europe, England, and then the United States can be traced directly back to the start of the nineteenth century. Since then, scholar Andrew Horn argues, melodrama "has perhaps been the central mode of perception" reaching beyond the West to countries around the world.[5] Melodrama's mythic and archetypical elements have proven remarkably dynamic and adaptable, capable of transcending time periods, cultures, and genres.

Movies in the *melodramatic mode* function largely as metaphors that represent desires, fantasies, and aspirations as matters of personal choice. Film scholar Ben Singer observes, "People in all places, at all times, undoubtedly have gained psychological comfort from the belief that destiny rewards the virtuous and punishes the bad."[6] This is a key tenet of what I'm calling the *melodramatic vision*, a utopian worldview represented by inspiring stories about empowered individuals who inhabit a world of moral absolutes and poetic justice. Hollywood films express this outlook with an immediacy and straightforward emotional appeal, which no doubt contributes to their incredible popularity worldwide.

From the silent-era films of D. W. Griffith and Cecil B. DeMille, to those of contemporary moviemakers like James Cameron, Steven Spielberg, and others, the aesthetic conventions and outlook of melodrama have long formed the core of mainstream Hollywood storytelling. These movies rely on the assumption of the universe's moral order for story plausibility and stable characterizations, and they function to satisfy spectator desires to make sense of the world. They are evangelistic in a sense, aligning audiences with a system of cultural ideals and moral logic.

Melodrama is a type of story characterized by strong emotionalism and excessive expression; sentimentality and sensationalism serve as its dramatic mainstay.[7] At a basic level, it features extreme situations and actions, Pollyannaish heroes and heroines, and dastardly villains who always get "foiled again." A critic clearly uses jargon associated with melodrama when describing *The Legend of Zorro* (2005) as "a hiss-the-villain, cheer-the-hero kind of movie."[8] Tear-jerking scenes, suspenseful plots, high action, cliffhangers, comedy, music, dance, and lavish spectacle characterize the melodramatic mode.

By and large, melodramatic stories depict a polarized world of plainly black-and-white issues. Characters are simply drawn. Heroes and heroines exhibit moral integrity, natural talent, and the capacity for genuine love; virtue is the source of their strength. In contrast, villains are irredeemably corrupt and driven by all manner of wickedness. The conflict between good and evil plays out in sharp contrast: evildoers are destroyed, and the virtuous are rewarded with life happily ever after.

Melodrama's starkness in theme and characterization leaves little room for complexity and moral ambiguity. And that's the point. That justice prevails in these scenarios of emotional heartbreak and dramatic suspense represents the volatility and instability of life as well as a yearning for protection against forces beyond a person's control. Though convenient indifference to plausibility kindles critical derision, an important aspect of melodrama is its cultural expression of populist ideals and attitudes. Its enduring and emotional appeal is an effect of "the combined function of realism, sentiment, spectacle, and action in effecting moral legibility," film scholar Linda Williams observes.[9] These stories achieve *moral clarity*, she explains, by means of a combination of *pathos*, sympathy for another person's suffering, and *action*, the thrill and suspense afforded by heroic adventures and encounters with wrongdoers, monsters, or natural calamities.

Movies in the melodramatic mode—whether *Titanic* or *Rear Window*, a *Rocky* or *Harry Potter* film, or the latest superhero release—each in their own way elicit viewer sympathy for heroes caught up in formidable situations. Audiences vicariously share the fears of protagonists who face misfortune, loss, disaster, or life-threatening circumstances, or who confront a villain depicted as the embodiment of evil. Moreover, finding deep satisfaction in virtue triumphing, spectators leave the theater reassured of the existence of moral order and justice.

Melodrama offers "a utopian myth of divine protection," as Singer puts it.[10] It's what American studies scholar Alan Trachtenberg calls "some magical outside assistance," a fitting phrase that gives expression to the popular American adage: "God helps those who help themselves."[11] We find in the American melodramatic vision a peculiar cultural brew that interlaces self-sufficiency with finding God's favor. I like to think of it as a sort of sentimental nod, or courtesy perhaps, that reflects popular parlance congenially referring to the sovereign Lord of the universe as "The Big Guy Upstairs." In *Armageddon* (1998), a science-fiction disaster film, Harry Stamper (Bruce Willis) goes on a space mission to save the world from an impending asteroid strike. He puts it plainly in the film's climax: "Come on, God, just a little help. It's all I'm asking."

Trachtenberg's "magical outside assistance" is an enduring fusion of American individualism and Christianity that goes a long way toward explaining popular perceptions of the role of Providence in both the movies and life. Since the 1990s at least, Barna surveys have consistently shown that most Americans believe that the adage "God helps those who help themselves," attributed to Benjamin Franklin, can be found in Holy Scripture.[12] A writer in *Harper's Magazine* highlights the paradox. "The thing is, not only is Franklin's wisdom not biblical; it's counter-biblical," he observes. "Few ideas could be further from the gospel message, with its radical summons to love of neighbor." Putting it directly: "On this essential matter, most Americans—most American *Christians*—are simply wrong."[13] In comparison to people in other nations, Americans are far more likely to attribute success to hard work paying off than to "forces outside our control." At the same time, though, a much higher share of Americans—more than double the next highest nations—also believe that religion is very important in their lives.[14] More on this in a moment, but for now let it suffice to say that these attitudes can be taken as representing enduring convictions about basic human goodness and the sine qua non of individual initiative.

As metaphors, melodramatic stories point toward the notion that humanity needs to find its way back to some point of original innocence. As we saw in *Rear Window*, the basic narrative begins with a state of normality. An ideal situation (domestic bliss or an honest and decent community) is disrupted by an outside force or diabolical act. To thwart the evildoer, the main protagonist overcomes a series of seemingly insurmountable obstacles and difficulties. The story ends with the defeat of the villain and restoration of moral and social order. The similarity, if not in some measure the substance, of this narrative pattern to the Bible's overarching story (creation, fall, redemption) is unmistakable—and hardly surprising. The Judeo-Christian tradition contributes one of the central strands of American culture. What is more, the American setting itself is significant as a context for melodramatic movies: a mythic place of limitless horizons where the realization of anyone's dreams is possible

The melodramatic vision can be understood as a distinctly American appropriation of the biblical narrative, which of course renders any notion that humanity can restore an original state of innocence a humanistic ideal. As noted earlier, the restoration of creation to a paradisiacal condition is a future reality only to be achieved one day at the long-awaited return of Christ. Nevertheless, the melodramatic vision can be perceived as echoing Christian values—to a certain extent. Isolating key features for comparison with the biblical realities outlined in chapter 2 reveals starkly different views of God, the human dilemma, and redemption.

More Than a Feeling

A key feature of the melodramatic worldview is its insistence on the basic goodness of God, humans, and American society. This outlook rests on a sanguine view of the human condition. In a world of "virtuous and well-intentioned" people, theater scholar Jeffrey Mason maintains, "one who strays is not inherently vicious but rather momentarily wayward, and his innate goodness will inevitably re-assert itself."[15] It follows that the uncorrupted heart functions like an internal moral compass, letting a man know "what a man's gotta do," to borrow an old western cliché. That truths are self-evident and available "to every person of untainted heart," as historian David Grimsted puts it, serves as the great equalizer in a democratic society—the judgment of the person of pure heart is just as good as the next person's, regardless of wealth, social status, or education. Moreover, Grimsted explains, "The doctrine of natural impulses guiding the feeling heart left no room for moral ambiguity, nor did the melodrama's categorical imperative that good and bad must be vigorously segregated to make clear the workings of just Providence."[16]

This begs the question: If Americans are naturally good hearted and well meaning, then what's the problem? Or to put it more pointedly, what's the source of evil that clearly exists in the world (and provides dramatic conflict)? The answer is twofold: the "Other" and waywardness.

As to the first, evil is personified in the antagonist who threatens the well-being and progress of the community.[17] Hollywood movies depict evildoers as un-American and bent on destroying democratic society; the ensuing dramatic conflict represents an implicit clash of basic values, which we can see in all sorts of villains. Disney's animated antagonists are all irredeemably corrupted by their selfish desires. Criminals pursue the American dream by illegal means: Gordon Gekko in *Wall Street* (1987), Jordan Belfort in *The Wolf of Wall Street* (2013). A cyber-terrorist like Thomas Gabriel in *Live Free or Die Hard* (2007) is driven by pride, greed, and revenge. In defense of the free world, James Bond and Ethan Hunt frustrate the sinister goals of the heads of international crime syndicates or rogue agents. Superman, Batman, and Spider-Man battle Lex Luther, the Joker, and the Green Goblin, who threaten destruction of the established order. And of course, Darth Vader and grandson Kylo Ren embrace the dark side of the Force, seeking authoritarian rule of the galaxy by wiping out the freedom-loving resistance.

Evil is also depicted as an external threat: foreigner terrorists (the German brothers Hans and Simon Peter Gruber in the *Die Hard* films), monsters (*Jaws*), space aliens (*Independence Day*), or a supervillain like Loki (*Marvel's The Avengers*), for example. We could go on and on. The point is that presenting evil as something alien to or existing outside the normally harmonious community effectively preserves the notion of inherent human goodness. The ritual destruction of the evildoer serves dramatically to restore moral and social order.

The melodramatic outlook both personifies evil by isolating it in individu-als and externalizes evil by attributing it to the Other. At the same time, this outlook diminishes the power and pervasiveness of evil as part of the human condition by using *waywardness* as a flimsy attempt to acknowledge sinful-ness without compromising innate human goodness. It offers an insufficient concession to the reality of sin that makes individuals the font of their own redemption and that of society. The reasoning goes like this: If people are basically good and thus have a natural compassion for one another, then pursuing self-interest is equivalent to serving the common good. Whatever problems exist, then, are the fault of individuals and not the result of life circumstances, a corrupt society, harmful practices, or flawed public policies. This supreme faith in basic human goodness as a source of personal and social redemption results in a penchant for individual over corporate action. We need only increased personal responsibility, and not institutional reform, for right living and a healthy world.

From this vantage point it appears the world can be divided easily enough with clear lines that distinguish good from evil. While all this might make for a moral clarity that is immediate and easily recognizable, with time—even within the fictional world of Hollywood franchises—this outlook starts to look quixotic. Its dramatic appeal and related believability diminish, looking more and more contrived and superficial.

By giving an exaggerated place to emotion, the melodramatic mode makes human feelings universal and authoritative—the ultimate judge of any situa-tion. Sentimentality, the lynchpin of melodrama's appeal, can manipulate our emotions, however, by telling us how to feel. The story kindles our emotions, but there is nothing of depth or importance for us to consider—much to the chagrin of critics. The work invites viewers to give it emotional meaning, but it holds out little to imagine, and even less to think about, besides how it makes us feel when lovers are reunited, the heroine achieves her goal, the bad guys are blown up.

Sentimentality relies on excess to foster an "idealization of the good and a deceptive vilification of the bad," film scholar Carl Plantinga explains, so that it "encourages self-righteousness when it elicits allegiance for idealized characters."[18] The result makes for rather one-dimensional stories featuring stock characters, straightforward situations, and clean resolutions. Sto-ries like these "portray the human condition in an idealized state," story consultant Dara Marks maintains. "This means that characters who are 'good' were born good and characters who are 'bad' or 'evil' were born that way as well; neither have any capacity to grow and evolve."[19] While such films might have strong emotional appeal and entertainment value, they are really distortions of the human condition. And for that reason, they lack plausibility as a reliable map of reality—at least from a biblical vantage point.

Melodramatic endings can be contrived if not sufficiently justified by the course of events in the narrative. When this happens, they tend to trivialize human experience instead of enlarging it. The answers they provide have less value because they come too easily. In providing moral clarity, the happy ending assumes that all things work out for the best for "good" people. They fall in love with the right person and live happily ever after. Wrongdoers are always punished, and justice is secured for the innocent. In real life, however, love does not always find a way, justice does not always prevail, and even the best intentions can go awry.

All things considered, the melodramatic mode might lack realism in the sense of corresponding to reality, but in another sense, it "corresponds to an important aspect of reality," literary scholar Eric Bentley points out. "It is the spontaneous, uninhibited way of seeing things."[20] In other words, the melodramatic outlook is taken to be an unfiltered view, a sort of stripping of reality to the bone in order to reveal fundamental truths. These stories tap into deep human desires for poetic justice and function as rituals of wish fulfillment. They repeatedly assure audiences of the rightness of their cause and the inevitable triumph of their values and way of life. In that sense, the melodramatic outlook can be understood as mythic or idealistic, representing the way people want the world to be and, to some extent, may even believe that it is.

A Tale of Two Outlooks

As Oscar-winning actor Tom Hanks tells it, the late writer and filmmaker Nora Ephron once gave him some guidance about writing: "Tell people what you're going to tell them, and then tell them, and then tell them what you just told them."[21] Heeding that advice, let me summarize a bit before moving on.

In chapter 2, we saw that humans are flawed image bearers indebted to God for the breath of life and redemption of the whole creation. Sin is integral to the human condition, which creates an inescapable predicament leaving us with no other hope than to rely on God's love and mercy. God's incredible and amazing grace is unmerited, a divine initiative centered on the atoning work of the risen Christ. Humankind is accountable to God for the flourishing of life and the creation.

A biblical outlook exposes the complexities of the human heart and translates into characters that are amazingly complicated and believably flawed—

protagonists and antagonists alike. It creates expectations for stories and characterizations that portray the frailty of human experience and the need for a source of redemption outside of ourselves. It follows that character traits may not always be clear and unchanging; motivations are mixed and not entirely pure. Characters can be both confused and confusing, a tangled mix of social and cultural influences and inherited personality traits. Social identifiers like race, class, sex, gender, ability, and other factors can deepen already interesting characterizations.

How does the melodramatic vision compare with a biblical one? One easily sees how this influential cultural outlook runs against the grain of biblical realities. A common assumption is the existence of a fundamentally moral universe enforced by divine justice. Beyond that, however, these two perspectives represent different patterns of meaning for making sense of life and acting in the world.

Though the melodramatic vision conceives of humans as inherently good, the reality of sinfulness, so evident in life, culture, society, and history, dispels any notion of the human heart being untainted—and any notion that "feeling," intuitive natural impulses, can serve as a fail-safe guide and source of knowledge and virtue. This makes accounting for the reality of sin troublesome. The melodramatic outlook diminishes the totalizing effect of sin, and by carving the world up neatly into black and white, good and evil, it even sanctions a demonization of the Other. Ritualistic stories displaying such an overly simplistic view of human nature and the world can be seen as "concealing the fundamental contradictions of society and making the existing order seem to be both inevitable and desirable," as Horn points out.[22] This mythic construct renders class, race, gender, education, and circumstance irrelevant since anybody with enough determination can secure his or her own fate.

The belief in essential goodness means that every person has the internal resources and full capability to achieve success on his or her own in this life and, apparently, in the next. This is redemption American-style, conditioned upon fidelity to the tenets of our individualist culture. Here we have a faith in the power and capacity of an individual to "pull herself up by her own bootstraps," to use the popular saying. Humans are not indebted and accountable to God; rather, God, who is supposedly keen on self-reliance, is obliged to help those who help themselves. Ideology supersedes faithfulness to God, who is remade in the image of culturally defined values and relegated to handing out merit badges on Judgment Day.

The melodramatic outlook is grounded in long-standing popular American beliefs in human innocence and perfectibility. It bases values on self-interest;

corresponding ideals concern ambition, success, talent, and abilities. It dictates these attitudes: be independent, rely on no one, and expect others to do likewise. This belief links self-sufficiency with finding God's favor. Can you see how these features hang together as a perspective? What is more, this perspective conflicts in crucial respects with the essential biblical view of humans as divine image bearers, accountable to God in everything and called to live in accord with biblical norms of truth, justice, and stewardship.

It is crucial to see how the American individualist culture, at bottom, counters the theological tenet of salvation by faith alone that lies at the heart of Christianity: "For it is by grace you have been saved, through faith—and this is not from yourselves, it is the gift of God—not by works, so that no one can boast" (Eph. 2:8–9). Jesus tells the Pharisees that it's not the healthy but only the sick who need a doctor, adding, "For I have not come to call the righteous, but sinners" (Matt. 9:12–13). The melodramatic outlook also contradicts the biblical meaning of goodness, which measures a person's worth by what they do for others, especially the poor, outcast, and downtrodden—that is, the "least of these" (Matt. 25:31–46).

And what does God require of us? That we love our neighbors as ourselves: "Value others above yourselves, not looking to your own interests but each of you to the interests of the others" (Phil. 2:3–4). That we hunger and thirst for righteousness (Matt. 5:6) and give to Caesar the things that are Caesar's and to God the things that are God's (Matt. 22:21). That we love our enemies (Matt. 5:44), forgive those who sin against us, make laws that are just, love kindness, and walk humbly with our God (Mic. 6:8). Remember these are value-laden directives for both personal and public life and a reliable guide for thinking discerningly about our culture.

Arguably, aspects of the melodramatic outlook are beneficial to the extent that they encourage and provide opportunities for people to develop their skills and talents, promote inventiveness, and point up the value of an honest day's work. Gone awry, however, this outlook purports to be a recipe for success in both this life and the next, ultimately endowing individuals with everything they need to secure their own destiny and salvation. Think about it. What more do inherently good and well-intentioned people need with God than perhaps a little magical assistance in fulfilling their personal dreams? Humanity's relationship with God becomes simply a matter of wishing upon a star, which I hasten to add is an obvious allusion to a powerful cultural concept embedded at the heart of the world-famous Disney enterprise. And this concept undoubtedly, and with good reason, has universal appeal: we all want our deepest desires and dreams to come true.

Finally

Now it surely lies within the realm of the imagination to interpret melodramatic movies that emphasize moral clarity as expressing "Christian" values or metaphorical suggestions of religious redemption. We derive much satisfaction from happy resolutions. They can be understood as metaphors pointing to the ultimate triumph of truth and justice and, in that sense, have roots in Christian hope for the time when God "will wipe away every tear from their eyes" (Rev. 21:4).

In addition, instances of magical assistance can be taken as evidence of God's presence in human affairs. In the realms of fantasy or science fiction, for example, depictions of mystical beings or magic at work are as commonplace as characters bursting into song in musicals. And advances in CGI let filmmakers create worlds containing spiritual or unseen dimensions with such cinematic credibility: the magical London of *Harry Potter*, Middle Earth, or the *Star Wars* universe. As Rick Carter, production designer for *Star Wars: The Force Awakens* (2015) said, the Force is real "because it's actually something that can be expressed by us as artists through the cinematic form."[23]

It's more challenging for storytellers to intimate the "transcendent" in a fictional world composed of everyday realities and occurrences. Writing about Krzysztof Kieślowski, for example, film scholar Joseph Kickasola makes the point that the Polish filmmaker "constantly highlighted what might be dismissed as 'mere coincidence' and pondered whether they are not indices of extratemporal forces at work. Coincidence or Providence? Happenstance or a sign?"[24] As it is, in ordinary life it seems clear enough that we "see only a reflection as in a mirror," or in the King James Version, "through a glass, darkly" (1 Cor. 13:12). Life is filled with loose ends, unanswered questions, unsolved mysteries, and even times when no final victory seems sure. How we construe meaning and finally understand life's journey results from partial human understandings that are relative to perspectives that are conditioned by cultural and historical circumstances. The closest it may be humanly possible to get is perhaps captured with the well-known saying, "Coincidence is God's way of remaining anonymous."[25] To follow sensible expectations is a good rule for ordinary fictional realism to remain plausible.

Rather than close off possible interpretations, I want to suggest nevertheless that mainstream Hollywood films largely reflect their individualist culture and ought to be understood in that context. It is reasonable to ask then, At what point might an interpretation be stretching it too far in ascribing meaning beyond the filmmaker's intentions and what's available in the text itself? This question is about seeing the differences, however subtle, between movies

Christians think are "Christian" and those that might be seen as displaying Christian sensibilities.

It seems to me that a discerning Christian posture calls for more nuance in recognizing Hollywood heroes for what they are: Christlike figures or mini-messiahs whose independence, ingenuity, and basic goodness is sufficient to redeem themselves, rescue others (often using violence), and in the end, be extoled by fellow humans and receive deservedly a heavenly reward. They make up a cloud of witnesses, to use a biblical image, testifying to the promise of the American dream: By living virtuously and working hard enough, anyone of however humble origins can advance socially, materially, or otherwise. Self-sufficiency and the pursuit of wealth and upward mobility is valued and expected; character is based on individual ability, determination, and entrepreneurial spirit. Anyone—even you (yes you!)—can transcend heredity and circumstance to achieve your goals and desires, become whatever you want, and maybe while you're at it, even save the world. "Come on, God, just a little help. It's all I'm asking."

MOVIE MUSING

Titanic (1997) and the Melodramatic Outlook

Titanic is rated PG-13 (Parents strongly cautioned). It includes partial nudity, one brief sexual situation, mild profanity and the soul-shaking sight of a great ship going down.

—Janet Maslin, *New York Times*

Titanic is much more than a tear-jerking romance and cinematic spectacle. Its reception and record-shattering box-office performance became a worldwide cultural event. The movie won eleven Academy Awards, including Best Picture, and is on the list of the American Film Institute's 100 Greatest American Movies of All Time.

Most readers likely have seen *Titanic* or, if not, are familiar enough with the story and characters to make it an effective illustration. As noted earlier, *Titanic* is a quintessential American melodrama, an action-adventure love story given to exaggerated emotional expression in its portrayal of the different troubles of rich and poor. Its basic elements read like a melodramatic checklist. There is plenty of *action* with cliffhangers and chases, stock characters, and polarized situations (*moral clarity*). We feel sadness over lost love (*pathos*) and marvel at the spectacle of the ship sinking (*sensationalism*).

Titanic gives a conventional and predictable story a stirring inventiveness. Foreknowledge of the impending doom casts a sense of dread that heightens the immediacy and emotional impact of the story and especially the romance between Rose and Jack. Writer and director Cameron explains, "I figured the best way to get in touch with the emotion of the event would be to take one set of characters and tell the story as a love story—because only by telling it as a love story can you appreciate the loss of separation and the loss caused by death."[26] It works both dramatically and as an expression of the melodramatic outlook. Let's consider that as we look at the story's treatment of God, the human condition, and nature of redemption.

Are You Ready to Go Back to *Titanic*?

The film begins with a present-day framing story. A team of scientists led by Brock Lovett (Bill Paxton) have an expedition underway searching for the Heart of the Ocean, a priceless blue diamond necklace believed to be within the *Titanic* wreckage. The heart-shaped diamond has multiple meanings throughout the film. For Lovett and crew, it's a commodity—the prize in a pirate's treasure. It represents social status to Cal Hockley, who purchased it as an engagement present for his fiancée. The necklace belonged to Louis XVI, he tells her: "It's for royalty, Rose—we are royalty." Rose, however, views it as a degrading object and uses it to deny Cal's possession of her. In the end, she treasures it as a symbol of her eternal love for Jack.

In that present-day framing story, a CNN news report features a sketch of a young woman wearing nothing but the necklace, which Lovett and crew find in a safe. When Rose DeWitt Bukater (Gloria Stuart), nearly 101 years old, sees the televised report, she contacts Lovett, claiming to be the woman in the drawing, and is flown to the research vessel. Crew member Lewis Bodine narrates a computer-animated simulation showing the stages of the ship's sinking. "As her bow is going down, her stern is coming up . . . out of the water and the hull can't deal so it splits!" he says excitedly. "Right down to the keel, which acts like a big hinge. . . . Pretty cool, huh?" Bodine effectively gives viewers a logistical playbook that heightens anticipation and generates suspense when we finally watch the events unfold almost in real time. Cameron said that he "wanted to place the audience on the ship, in its final hours, to live out the tragic event in all its horribly fascinating glory."[27] Undeniably, the film's re-creation of the catastrophic sinking—the ship breaking in half, the giant propellers lifting out of the water as the aft section goes perpendicular and then plunges into the black, icy sea—is haunting, breathtaking, and unforgettable.

"Thank you for that fine forensic analysis, Mr. Bodine," Old Rose says. "Of course, the experience of it was somewhat different." And that's the story about to be told. Old Rose's face is reflected in a TV monitor as an underwater camera pans the ship's encrusted interior. Later in the film, as the young Rose and Jack embrace at the bow rail, their figures dissolve to a shot of the bow resting on the ocean floor. These powerful editing transitions effectively weave together past and present. The camera moves in for a tight close-up of Old Rose as the bow of the sunken *Titanic* appears in the background. A matching dissolve to the ship in port takes us back to 1912.

The juxtaposition of scenes with the young Rose (Kate Winslet), then Jack (Leonardo DiCaprio), boarding the *Titanic* cues spectators to their eventual meeting and shared destiny. Rose is beautiful, but also independent and intelligent, qualities that make it difficult for her to conform to established social rules and behavior. Her engagement to Cal Hockley (Billy Zane) represents a marriage not of love but of convenience, intended to insure her and her widowed mother's financial future and privileged lifestyle. Rose feels trapped and is even suicidal; her spirit is drowning.

As Rose is boarding the magnificent vessel with her mother and fiancé in a stately manner, Old Rose says in a voice-over that the *Titanic* was a "ship of dreams to everyone else." To her, though, "it was a slave ship, taking me back to America in chains. Outwardly, I was everything a well-brought-up girl should be. Inside, I was screaming." We hear and cut to a matching shot of the *Titanic*'s steam whistle blowing—signaling the ship's imminent departure. The next shot is a view of the *Titanic* several blocks away. The camera pulls back, revealing that we're looking out through a window of a smoky Southampton pub, and then moves around four young men at a table playing five-card draw poker.

Fabrizio leans toward his partner, "Jack, you are pazzo. You bet everything we have." Jack replies coolly, "When you got nothing, you got nothing to lose." It's a line of dialogue that introduces us to the free-spirited protagonist. Their opponents, Swedish card players Olaf and Sven (perhaps not coincidentally the names of the snowman and reindeer in Disney's *Frozen*), argue about having bet their tickets. We watch the tense game move on in a series of facial close-ups, intercut with extreme close-ups of disembodied hands drawing cards and the swollen pot on the table that contains bills and coins from different countries, a knife, a pocket watch, and two third-class White Star Line tickets.

Finally: "All right. Moment of truth," Jack says. "Somebody's life is about to change." And as the audience knows, indeed it is. Olaf and Fabrizio have nothing; Jack's full house beats Sven's two pair. "We're going to America!" Jack yells. It's the classic melodramatic event: an instance of chance (or outside magical assistance) that alters the protagonist's course. The *Titanic* sets sail in five minutes, the bartender announces. Jack and Fabrizio hurriedly gather their winnings. In a series of tracking and long shots we see them dash down the dock and through the crowds, reaching the ship just in the nick of time as the gangplank is being pulled away. On board, Jack shouts excitedly to Fabrizio, "We're the luckiest sons of bitches in the whole world, you know that!"

Jack repeatedly refers to the card game as a fortuitous event. "I won my ticket on *Titanic* here in a lucky hand at poker," he says at dinner, adding with a glance at Rose, "a very lucky hand." To which Col. Archibald Gracie remarks philosophically, "All life is a game of luck." To the contrary, Hockley insists, "A real man makes his own luck."

Conflicting outlooks. One about accepting life's circumstances, learning from them, and enjoying life's abundance; the other about control, self-determination, and superiority. Later, determined to survive the impending disaster, Cal fills his overcoat pockets with money and the diamond necklace. "I make my own luck," he says again, this time to his bodyguard, Lovejoy, who opens his coat to show his gun: "So do I."

Flying in the Face of God

Real-life *Titanic* survivor Eva Hart said that her mother refused to go to sleep while aboard the ship "because she had this premonition, solely based on the fact that she said to declare a vessel unsinkable was flying in the face of God."[28] In the movie, the arrogant Hockley asserts as much: "God himself could not sink this ship." Hockley's remark voices the hubris and unfailing confidence that characterized the Western world's entrance into the twentieth century—aptly symbolized by the ocean liner *Titanic*. When the ship's owner, J. Bruce Ismay, says he chose the name *Titanic* to "convey sheer size, and size means stability, luxury, and above all strength," Rose taunts him, suggesting that Freud's "ideas about the male preoccupation with size might be of interest to you."

As it is, there is nothing in *Titanic* to suggest that God is even remotely interested in the fate of those souls on board. The extreme long shots that make the gigantic vessel seem infinitely small while cruising alone in the vast darkness of the ocean suggest that if God is watching, it is only as a distant observer. Whether uncaring or impotent, God is irrelevant in the world of this film. Our foreknowledge of the impending disaster makes passengers singing a hymn about God's protection ("Eternal Father, Strong to Save") and the band playing "Nearer My God to Thee" as the ship fills with water seem empty and the prayers of those on board futile. As people race to the highest point of the ship to escape the rising water, a passenger recites a familiar passage from Psalm 23: "Yea, though I walk through the valley of the shadow of death, I will fear no evil." To which Jack sarcastically remarks, "You want to walk a little faster through that valley?"

Perhaps as film critic Stanley Kauffmann considers, "The disaster can be seen as an instance of the gods reproving hubris, or, if you prefer, of the self-deception of ego." As he sees it, it's the Atlantic Ocean that "seems enraged by the word 'unsinkable.'" The film contains a human-versus-nature theme: "Bursting through gaps in the hull, rushing down corridors, licking at rooms, triumphing over great ballrooms and tiny closets, down stairways and into elevators, the sea, in the hands of Cameron and his technical associates, becomes hungry, vindictive."[29]

If human arrogance and the desire for power are root evils that distinguish the main characters as good or bad, they pale dramatically in comparison to the central story of love and personal redemption. In melodramatic fashion, the meaning of this incredible tragedy as it relates to class, empire, and technology is overshadowed by the romance.

New York Times critic Janet Maslin describes *Titanic* as "ultimately a haunting tale of human nature, with endless displays of callousness, gallantry or cowardice."[30] These character traits point up the moral legibility typical of melodrama. As the passengers face the inevitable, an older couple comforts each other, the water rises around a parent holding her child, and musicians play hymns while passengers get into the lifeboats. Passengers on the lower decks struggle to escape in hopes of surviving. Ismay sneaks into a lifeboat with the women and children. The conniving Cal bribes a steward and enters a lifeboat under pretense of caring for a crying child. Meanwhile, the ship's captain and designer each wait separately with dignity for the inevitable to happen.

Looking briefly at the film's treatment of the human condition, *Titanic* displays a "faith in unconditioned individuals," as one scholar puts it.[31] In other words, Rose and Jack exhibit an inherent goodness that transcends their social status and background and is not derived from them. The haughty attitude Rose exhibits at first is not a true expression of her character; she shares many of Jack's traits, but they have been repressed by her upbringing.

Unlike Cal, who has been irredeemably corrupted by wealth and patriarchy, Rose is momentarily wayward, aware that she's trapped in a gilded cage. "This match with Hockley is a good one," Rose's mother tells her as she pulls hard, tightening the laces of Rose's corset—a garment symbolizing gender restraints. Clothing symbolizes Rose's increasing freedom. Rose slips on the hem of her dress on the ship's rail while contemplating suicide, kicks off her red-satin shoes at the party in steerage, and finally undresses, posing for Jack's drawing of her wearing only the priceless piece of jewelry. As it is, Rose only needs to be liberated from the confines of her high-class existence for her innate goodness to reassert itself.

While Cal is "all business and politics," Jack is a free-spirited bohemian artist who does not even have "a dark side," as film critic David Ansen notes. "How much more interesting the human drama would have been if Cameron had allowed his characters a shred of moral ambiguity."[32] When the "unsinkable" Molly Brown (Kathy Bates) dresses Jack up in her son's formal wear, even Cal admits that third-class Jack can "almost pass as a gentleman." It's a standard convention traceable to the Cinderella story. In the romance *Pretty Woman*, for example, the appearance onscreen of Vivian (Julia Roberts) wearing an elegant red evening gown complemented with white gloves visually transforms the heroine Cinderella-style from a Hollywood streetwalker into a "princess." Likewise, Jack is a prince in disguise, capable of transcending social barriers with a simple wardrobe change—and in doing so, rendering them hollow.

"Why Can't I Be Like You, Jack?"

Titanic's themes of trust, sacrifice, liberation, and triumph of the human will over adversity make it easy to think of the film as a redemptive metaphor. The movie, however, is part of a cultural system and can be understood as an epic version of the American dream centered on the self-realization of Rose. In a memorable line from the film, Rose declares that Jack "saved me in every way that a person can be saved." This gives testimony to love's redeeming power, which overcomes the stern class barriers that create the central tensions in the main narrative—both the romance and the sinking of the ship. The setting, the *Titanic* itself, is a microcosm of a class-structured society set sail across the Atlantic—the equivalent of the stagecoach in director John Ford's classic western *Stagecoach* (1939).

A large number of *Titanic* passengers are European immigrants bound for America, a mythic place where class is fluid, superficial, and finally, a relic of the past. For emphasis, the story features the exceedingly rich against third-class passengers who are checked for head lice; second-class passengers remain invisible in this, as well as in other *Titanic* films. Bluebloods, those of inherited privilege and European aristocratic distinctions, are locked in the strong social conventions of a patriarchal society. Men wield power; women are expected to remain passive and virtuous. The film depicts these attitudes as clashing with American values: freedom, equality, and opportunity.

In one scene, the film crosscuts between two evening parties to highlight the class disparity. Cal and company talk politics while sipping cognac and smoking cigars at a staid after-dinner party on the upper deck. Meanwhile, Rose whirls about in abandon, dancing to an Irish reel at a party in steerage. What they lack in material comforts, the poor make up for by enjoying the simple pleasures in life and knowing what true love is. They are the salt of the earth, and Jack introduces Rose to the vitality of the people in steerage.

The film nevertheless does not critique the pursuit of wealth. Whatever criticism it offers of class is "safely focused on the snobbery of a few loathsome first-class characters," as one scholar explains.[33] In that sense, *Titanic* only legitimizes wealth, social status, and the trimmings of the leisure class. Rose does not reject these, only the repugnant values exhibited by some, especially her fiancé.

Hockley does not need to twist the corners of an oily black moustache to be recognized as the villain. Heir to a steel fortune, his only concern is with the approval of his social set. He equates wealth and social status with worth and character. Aware of the limited lifeboat capacity, Rose says, "Half the people on this ship are going to die." The snobbish Cal responds, "Not the better half." Like everything else in life, he thinks he can buy Rose's love and sexual favors. When she refuses his sexual advances and does not return his love, he becomes frustrated, angry, and violent. He's also manipulative, deceitful, and a liar. No one in the movie theater wants Rose to marry him.

In contrast to Cal, the free-spirited artist Jack is the ultimate expression of pure independence. His character traits, luck, talent, and good looks easily identify him as the hero. Playful and energetic, Jack represents the unrestrained freedom of youth. He is completely mobile and unattached; his poverty is a matter of choice and not forced as the result of social circumstances. For Jack, economic insecurity is not painful but an adventure. "You don't know what hand you're gonna get dealt next," he tells his upper-crust dinner hosts. "You learn to take life as it comes at you. To make each day count." When asked where he lives, Jack replies coolly, "Well, right now my address is the RMS *Titanic*. After that, I'm on God's good humor."

In one scene, as Rose and Jack stand on the ship's upper deck, Rose says, "Why can't I be like you, Jack? Just head out into the horizon whenever I like it?" Salvation for Rose is really a matter of self-fulfillment. She desires what Jack has: independence and freedom to pursue her own American dream.

Jack wants Rose to trust him—to have faith in him. And she does, establishing a pattern. It's implied when they first meet, when he talks her down from the ship's railing as she's about to take her life by jumping overboard: "Take my hand. I'll pull you back in," Jack assures her. As their love grows, Jack encourages and inspires Rose to live her own life. Later Rose says, "I trust you," while stepping up on the rail on the ship's bow, her arms outstretched in an iconic and much-publicized image from the film symbolizing her freedom. "I'm flying, Jack!" she shouts excitedly (frame 16).

In her first-class stateroom, Rose disrobes. Wearing only the Heart of the Ocean diamond, she allows Jack to sketch her in an erotic scene that signifies more than her love and trust. The nude drawing, the one Lovett and crew discover, is Rose's declaration of independence. "The last thing I need is another picture of me looking like a porcelain doll," Rose tells Jack.

Afterward, the young lovers elude Lovejoy and make love on the lower deck in the backseat of a car. These scenes are intercut with others of Hockley finding the drawing and the Captain and crew discussing the ocean's calm that makes it more difficult to spot icebergs. The multiple story lines are converging. Standing on the ship's deck, Rose tells Jack she's going with him when the ship docks. "This is crazy," Jack says. "I know. It

Titanic © 1997 Paramount Pictures Corporation and Twentieth Century Fox Film Corporation

Frame 16. In *Titanic*, Rose desires what Jack has: independence and freedom to pursue her own American dream.

doesn't make any sense. That's why I trust you." The young lovers' kissing momentarily distracts two lookouts perched above, who turn to see an iceberg "right ahead." The ship's crew jumps into action. Rose and Jack are standing on the deck as the mountainous iceberg glides alongside, ripping into the ship's hull.

Finally, Rose clings to Jack's hand at the railing where they first met as the ship's stern plunges into the black ocean. "I trust you," she tells him again. Jack's good sense and sacrifice save her from sure death in the North Atlantic's icy waters. "Promise me you'll survive," Jack insists. "Promise me now, Rose, and never let go of that promise." She assures him, "I'll never let go." The line of dialogue refers explicitly to Jack's hand, implicitly to their love, and on a deeper level to her personal freedom and redemption.

As one writer explains, the film depicts romantic love "as a life-giving force, which gives back to Rose the will to live (which she had abandoned when the two lovers first met) and, more precisely, the will and confidence to live her own life, unrestrained by the social conventions of the day."[34] Adrift after *Titanic* has disappeared into the ocean, Jack says, "Winning that ticket, Rose, was the best thing that ever happened to me. It brought me to you." Otherwise, Jack and Rose defiantly take their fate into their own hands and survive the catastrophe (well, nearly) through the sheer force of will, resourcefulness, and bold determination. Jack sacrifices his own life to rescue this damsel in distress, passing on his will to live and zest for life and liberating her from the pretentiousness of the elite and the limitations of being a woman in a patriarchal world.

In a highly symbolic shot of Rose beneath the Statue of Liberty, she renames herself. Taking Jack's family name, she becomes "Rose Dawson," a survivor of the *Titanic* and freed now from family and social obligations to pursue her own American dream. Meeting Jack is pivotal in changing Rose's life. As one writer observes, "Through him she discovers herself as a sexual being and free spirit, abandons fiancée, mother, class for (bedside photos tell us) a long and exciting life as an actress, aviatrix, traveler, potter, mother."[35]

Finally, it's not just class barriers that the young lovers overcome—even in death, true love is victorious. Just before she dies, Old Rose dreams of heaven, symbolized by a white light. She and Jack are reunited for eternity on the grand staircase of the *Titanic*. As scholars observe, "The ship's dome has become the celestial sphere, while the grand staircase to the first-class dining room has become the stairway to paradise. Heaven is the upper deck."[36] True love is enough to secure one's place in a *Titanic*-inspired heaven where everyone travels first class.

A mythic affirmation of universal emotions, *Titanic* captures widespread interests in love, spectacle, and redemption, and celebrates the magic of the movies. As *Newsweek's* David Ansen puts it, "This is one grand, generous entertainment—old-fashioned film-making brought up to date with the most spectacular technology available."[37]

7

The Yellow Brick Road to Self-Realization

Classical Hollywood Cinema

Great stories never really end; they take up residence inside us and
live on in our thoughts, conversations, fantasies, and dreams. They
are also a powerful influence over our beliefs, values, opinions,
and perceptions.

—Dara Marks

Reflecting on "the state of the movies in our state of disunion," the *New York Times*'s chief film critics Manohla Dargis and A. O. Scott question "the old movies-for-everyone ideal." To what extent do American movies still provide a sense of national unity? "Conservatives have long railed against liberal Hollywood, and liberals have bemoaned the racism, sexism and militarism of Hollywood products, but through it all red and blue states have come together to produce plenty of box-office green," Scott remarks. "Movies are a common treasury for everyone to share. Is that still true? Was it ever?"[1]

Hollywood is by no means monolithic; there is no single American culture shared by all citizens. Yet we can talk about a mainstream American culture, not as simply the sum of existing subcultures, but as a cluster of core ideals and values that represent "the broadest dimensions of shared meanings and assumptions," according to media scholar George Gerbner. He argues that commercial media function to cultivate a common outlook through a process involving the homogenization, absorption, and "apparent convergence of disparate outlooks," which he calls *mainstreaming*.[2]

Along these lines, British film scholar Andrew Higson treats the cinema as playing a crucial role in the maintenance of a national culture as an "imagined community." This happens via the proliferation of certain kinds of stories that "narrate the nation imaginatively, narratives that are capable of generating a sense of national belonging among their audiences." This is not a straightforward process. National character is hardly "a fixed phenomenon," he explains. Consequently, as a cinematic construction, "the shared, collective identity which is implied always masks a whole range of internal differences and potential and actual antagonisms."[3] Nevertheless, Hollywood producers often take a lowest-common-denominator approach in order to maximize audience and box-office prospects, and it is generally understood that popularity largely depends on a movie's effectiveness in affirming dominant ideals and values.

In that light, this chapter highlights persistent and overarching patterns of content and meaning that are distinctive features of what scholars call the *classical Hollywood cinema*. Classical Hollywood filmmaking is a prolific mode for producing movies that are visually pleasurable and emotionally charged spectacles, making it the most influential narrative and visual style in the commercial cinema worldwide.[4] The classical Hollywood film blends the melodramatic aesthetic mode and outlook with a set of cinematic conventions linking narrative, character, and film style to ideals and values associated with American individualism: a goal-oriented protagonist, narrative causality, and complete story resolution.

The Classical Hollywood Cinema

Classical Hollywood filmmaking consists of a system of formal principles designed to make the most of film's unique capacity to manipulate space and time and to make screen storytelling as clear as possible. Of paramount importance in preserving the illusion of realism is creating and maintaining a sense of *continuity*. The aim is to make the story and flow of space and time seamless. To this end, editing patterns, camera placement and movement, lighting, sound, acting, and costume and set design all work together in nuanced ways to deliver story information and maintain unity within the world of the film.

The classical Hollywood cinema reins in traditional melodrama's reliance on incredible coincidences by emphasizing *narrative causality*, which refers to the way one event causes another to happen. The story advances in a tight cause-and-effect chain, with each scene flowing into the next. Classical narratives have a linear structure; the events are generally presented in the order they occur. The only exceptions are scenes that viewers recognize as flashbacks in time (well, except for the guy I met at the showing of *Manchester by the Sea*). Very little happens without reason. This is not surprising when you realize that Americans tend to think that most events have some "knowable, physical cause." The inexplicable may be vaguely attributed to "God's will," but as one writer observes, "most Americans have difficulty even comprehending the notion, so prevalent in many other parts of the world, that 'fate' determines what happens in people's lives."[5] Americans prefer to believe that individuals control their own destiny, even if they might need some occasional celestial help, as we've seen.

When a classical Hollywood film begins, we magically enter a fictional world where events are already in progress. During the first act, we receive initial impressions about the main characters that define them as individuals with a history. The most salient traits (surprise!) are self-reliance and goal achievement. These will hardly (if at all) change throughout the film. The story typically centers on one or two characters and emphasizes their external actions as an expression of internal feeling (the character's inward processing of events). In other words, the external journey corresponds with an internal one in which the protagonist discovers something about him or herself or the world at large. The film establishes the story's believability by reliably binding a character's mental makeup and outlook—clearly identified traits, desires, and motivations—with his or her choices and actions.

As we saw in *Rear Window*, usually the story has a main line of action with one or more related subplots. The first act ends with the main character starting off in pursuit of an identifiable goal. During the second act, the protagonist encounters an external opposition, more often than not an antagonist with contrasting traits, values, and aims. This confrontation creates conflict and obstacles that must be overcome to achieve the goal. In the final act, events and problems introduced in the beginning are fully resolved with the goal achieved: boy gets girl, hero/detective solves the crime, superhero saves the world, personal dreams come true.

The classical film designs narrative conventions and filmic techniques so they work together stylistically to preserve the illusion of reality by narrating the story without drawing attention to the film itself. The camera's recording of the action, the subsequent editing of shots, and the sound design constitute the primary *means* to convey the story; together they direct point of view and disclose story information—in essence, "telling" the story. The narrator remains more or less invisible, as it were.

A scene's opening establishing shot, for example, provides spectators with an overview of the space where the action is taking place (e.g., the aircraft hangar in *Top Gun*). The craft known as *continuity editing*, a process of linking different shots together with temporal and spatial consistency, routinely uses various matching techniques to make the transitions between shots smoother. Filming the action from one side of an imaginary line, known as the "180-degree rule," ensures consistency in screen position, movement, and direction. Or a shot-reverse shot sequence composed of a series of over-the-shoulder shots focuses the viewer's attention on the interplay of characters (actors) in conversation with each other.

Audiences are so familiar with these and other standard methods that they go unnoticed. The effect is to make classical movies seem even more real or natural, rather than artistically constructed—a key motif in this book. Classical films present the narrative in such a way that viewers are ideally placed to ensure they receive all the information necessary to understand the story. It is important to realize, however, that the conventions of continuity editing themselves "tend to imply a world that is ordered and comprehensible," as film scholar Geoff King stresses. "They offer the viewer in most cases a 'safe' and comfortable position from which to understand the world presented on screen."[6]

Movies produced outside mainstream Hollywood might use alternative designs, as we'll see in the Movie Musing about *Do the Right Thing*. Alternative-styled movies may feature protagonists with unclear traits and vague, confused, or even nonexistent goals. Their struggle might be more internal than external, like the ballerina Nina (Natalie Portman) in *Black Swan* (2010). A central protagonist might even be missing. Instead of a linear plotline, the story may be told with a nonlinear structure—that is, with events arranged out of logical sequence, rather famously in *Pulp Fiction* (1994). Film techniques, like jump cuts, freeze frames, or flash-forwards, can be used to break the pattern of continuity or to create some viewer discomfort and uncertainty. In addition, an ambiguous or open ending that leaves questions or events unresolved characterizes movies that deviate from the classical Hollywood style.

The Yellow Brick Road to Self-Realization

To illustrate, let's look at *The Wizard of Oz* (1939), the delightful children's musical fantasy about "a place where dreams you dream really do come true." The story is familiar enough, so I won't summarize it any more than to highlight the features that make it an archetypal classical Hollywood film.

The film's *inciting incident*, the event that sets the story in motion, actually takes place after the opening credits and just before the film begins: Dorothy's dog, Toto, has bitten Miss Gulch. "That dog's a menace to the community," Miss Gulch tells Dorothy's Aunt Em and Uncle Henry. "I'm taking him to the sheriff and make sure he's destroyed." Toto's mischief is the impetus (cause) that propels the narrative forward in a linear fashion. Dorothy (Judy Garland) starts out with the goal of saving poor Toto and runs away from home (the effect), which is (now cause) why she's not in the storm cellar with the rest of her family when the tornado strikes (effect), and is instead carried away (cause now) and left stranded in the Land of Oz (effect). Once in Oz, her goal is to return to Kansas, which creates a succession of short-term goals: to get to the Emerald City, to secure the Wizard's help, and then to meet his seemingly impossible demand intended to dissuade her—get the broomstick of the Wicked Witch of the West. The plot advances in a straightforward, orderly way until it reaches a complete resolution with Dorothy returning to Kansas having learned: "There's no place like home."

The story centers on the actions of the main characters who exhibit an innate goodness. Dorothy, Scarecrow, Tin Man, and the Cowardly Lion each display clear traits and desires, and have a distinct goal that is made clear in different variations of the same song ("If I Only Had . . ."). Dorothy's desire, initiative, confidence, bravery, and determination spur the others to fulfill their dreams. They pin their individual hopes collectively on the Wonderful Wizard of Oz, expecting him to give them "a brain, a heart, a home, the nerve!"

They encounter one obstacle after another during their journey on the Yellow Brick Road. The main impediment to their achieving their goal is the Wicked Witch of the West, an equally determined antagonist. Her goal is to get the powerful ruby slippers that Dorothy came to possess after her Kansas house landed in Oz, inadvertently killing the Wicked Witch of the East. The Wicked Witch is, of course, the personification of evil; her destruction restores order in the Land of Oz and makes Dorothy out to be a redeemer. She not only leads her companions on their quest but also, by destroying the Wicked Witch, delivers Oz from the scourge of fear. Even the Winkies, the Witch's castle guards, celebrate their boss's destruction: "Hail to Dorothy! The Wicked Witch is dead!" And with no questions asked, they happily give their liberator the Wicked Witch's broomstick.

The Wizard of Oz typifies classical filmmaking and the melodramatic outlook. The story also provides us with a useful image to describe them: the Yellow Brick Road to self-realization. Although they don't realize it, Dorothy and her companions have *within themselves* everything they need to secure their fate. For various reasons, they each have become disoriented, having lost their way. A large part of the story's enjoyment, however, is watching how each character utilizes the very trait they believe they lack. Their journey on the Yellow Brick Road serves to bring each of them to that realization, which spectators take delight in having known all along.

Ultimately, Dorothy and company have no real need of the Great and Powerful Wizard of Oz, a God figure whose unmasking from behind a pyrotechnical visage reveals him to be only a bumbling old man. He admits to being a "humbug," but when Dorothy calls him "a very bad man" for deceiving them, the Wizard responds, "Oh, no my dear, I'm a very good man. I'm just a very bad wizard." As to fulfilling his promise to give Scarecrow a brain, Tin Man a heart, and Cowardly Lion courage, the Wizard informs them, "You've had them all the time."

Dorothy too only had to make the journey on the Yellow Brick Road to "find out for herself" that "there's no place like home." Only then would she have believed Glinda, the Good Witch of the North, that with the magic slippers she had the power to whisk herself away from Oz. Glinda had earlier provided a little outside magical assistance by way of a snowfall to even things out and counteract a sleeping spell the Wicked Witch cast over a field of poppies. "You don't need to be helped any longer," Glinda tells her now. "You've always had the power to go back to Kansas." The movie's theme, or implicit meaning, is a testimony to innate human goodness and self-determination.

A Sense of Limitless Possibility

The redemptive journey to self-realization defines the protagonist's character arc—how the character changes over the course of the story. Mainstream Hollywood movies are populated with self-sufficient individuals who, from the start, have within themselves all they need to accomplish their goal. Overcoming self-doubt or other stumbling blocks provides the only key they need. The lessons learned in the course of the narrative result in the characters truly believing in themselves. The characters' internal self-realization occurs in tandem with an external line of action: pursuit of a worthy goal or a soul mate, investigating a crime or mystery, creating a new situation, restoring a desired state of affairs, or ensuring the destruction of a fierce threat or enemy.

If I am overgeneralizing here, it's not by much. This basic motif forms part of our cultural liturgy, given expression in countless American movies. What makes Hollywood protagonists heroic is the way they discover their innate potential. "This is the power of the climax," Dara Marks contends. "It is the fight for change, for liberation, for recognition, for reconciliation, and for connection. But more than anything else, it's always the fight for a *new and greater life*."[7]

Therein lies the appeal of the protagonist in *Erin Brockovich* (2000), a rags-to-riches story involving one of the biggest environmental crimes in history. Erin (Julia Roberts), an unemployed single mother of three living in the world of lower-middle-class suburbia, talks her way into a job in a law office. A transformation takes place when, on her own initiative, she begins an investigation of a suspicious real estate case involving the Pacific Gas & Electric Company. Erin discovers that the company is quietly buying land contaminated by a deadly toxic waste the company was dumping illegally. Area residents are being poisoned, their lives plagued by strange and debilitating illnesses and the death of loved ones. Her investigation leads the law firm into one of the largest class action lawsuits in history, involving a settlement of over $300 million.

In this story, a heroic individual exposes corporate corruption; change occurs initially and primarily as a result of individual ambitions, goals, and actions. The film title exalts the individual heroine—not the victims or the social cause. "She's a normal but very decent person at her core," screenwriter Susannah Grant explains. "She doesn't do anything that any one of us couldn't do if we decided to do the right thing. And what's exciting about that for people is that it's not alienating. It gives you a sense of limitless possibility and your own power by virtue (of) watching hers."[8] By implication, we are all—each of us—fully capable of doing the same if only we tap into a "sense of limitless possibility" and "do the right thing." This ideal of a pure individual with self-determining powers is a bedrock theme in the classical Hollywood cinema.

Individualism obviously has positive and negative aspects. We all need a measure of freedom, independence, and self-governance. Individualism can be a positive force in that it fosters creativity and initiative; the defense of personal liberty ensures respect for equal rights for all people. Living for yourself, however, is a diminished life and runs counter to the Christian calling to seek the kingdom of God and his righteousness above all else (Matt. 6:33–34) and to live accountable to God and responsible to one another (Phil. 2:3–4). Moreover, when taken to an extreme, focus on the self can be a negative force. Psychologist David Myers calls this "radical individualism"—when self-interest and self-indulgence outweigh social responsibility and moral obligation.[9] Radical individualism has led to a more fragmented society with greater isolation of individuals and a deepened distrust of social institutions that are themselves disconnected. Many commentators are now lamenting how much this hyperindividualism has come to characterize American life and society in the early twenty-first century.

"Your Business Is Politics, Mine Is Running a Saloon"

Mainstream Hollywood celebrates individual desires and goals in a way that downplays the import of institutions and collective action. As a rule, American movies tend to represent social, political, or economic problems as personal—a sign of *individual* weakness and not a flaw of any existing *system*. The resolutions to these stories then come by way of individual, not corporate or institutional, remedies. In this way, filmmakers can offer satisfying, if also sometimes superficial, resolutions to complex problems: the gunfight won, the boy gets the girl, the crime is solved, humans defeat the alien invaders. Here we see a long-standing pattern in the American cinema.

In the Warner Bros. classic *Casablanca* (1942), the love that Rick (Humphrey Bogart) has for Ilsa (Ingrid Bergman) is what finally shakes him out of his cynicism. At the beginning, Rick refuses to be involved in anyone else's affairs. "I stick my neck out for nobody," he says. "Your business is politics, mine is running a saloon." The dialogue cleverly blends personal and political independence. "I'm the only cause I'm interested in," Rick tells Captain Renault, who replies, "A wise foreign policy." Signor Ferrari, owner of the Blue Parrot café, tells him, "My dear Rick, when will you realize that in this world, today, isolationism is no longer a practical policy?"

Only after lovelorn Rick realizes the circumstances under which Ilsa left him in Paris and discovers that she still loves him is he motivated to help her and her husband, the underground resistance leader, Victor Lazlo, escape the Germans. In the climactic scene, Rick tells Ilsa, "I'm no good at being noble, but it doesn't take much to see that the problems of three little people don't amount to a hill of beans in this crazy world." Rick's character arc—from self-serving to risky involvement—becomes a metaphor for American skepticism and reluctance to become entangled in World War II. To ensure that Ilsa and Victor get away, Rick even kills the German Major Strasser in a conventional western shootout that clearly associates him with the traditional American hero.

A long history of movies features heroic individuals who weed out corruption in American institutions. In *Mr. Smith Goes to Washington* (1939), an idealistic small-town Boy Rangers troop leader single-handedly (well, with the help of an assistant/love interest) exposes and defeats the corrupt political machinations of long-term, experienced Washington senators. Betrayed IMF agent Ethan Hunt proves his innocence and uncovers internal treachery in *Mission: Impossible* (1996). Suffering from amnesia, Jason Bourne's quest to discover his identity exposes corruption within a covert CIA assassin program in *The Bourne Supremacy* (2004). The lone District Attorney Jim Garrison in

JFK (1991) is a rare exception: his investigation of a conspiracy to assassinate President John F. Kennedy ends without a conviction, even if the story leaves viewers persuaded that truth did not prevail in this case.

Focusing on a single protagonist can make storytelling more dramatic, but it can also distort reality, especially the role of collective action as an agent of social change. The struggle and sacrifice of ordinary people can be lost in the way we privilege the stories we tell. The historically based movies *Mississippi Burning* (1988) and *Amistad* (1997), for example, were faulted for giving too much credit to individuals instead of the groups of people who made up the civil rights and abolitionist movements. More recently, Dargis makes a similar charge, saying that *Detroit* (2017), a film based on events that took place during the city's race riots in 1967, "underscores personal rather than institutional white racism and largely omits black resistance."[10]

Though earning generally positive reviews, *42* (2013) also received some criticism for overlooking how much politics shaped Jackie Robinson's experience and lifelong pursuit to combat racism. The slice of life depicted in *42* focuses only on part of his baseball career. The story then conforms to "the classical Hollywood formula of Heroic individual sees obstacle. Obstacle is overcome. The End," Dave Zirin writes tersely in *The Nation*. "That works for *Die Hard* or *American Pie*. It doesn't work for a story about an individual deeply immersed [in] and affected by the grand social movements and events of his time."[11]

As Zirin explains, Robinson was affected deeply by marches to integrate baseball during the Depression, as well as by his court-martial trial during World War II, his testimony against singer and actor Paul Robeson amid the McCarthy-era communist witch hunting, his involvement and struggles with the civil rights and Black Power movements, and his support for the 1968 Olympic protestors. Robinson himself was dissatisfied with the way his own story was used to promote an individualistic approach to ending racism. "He wanted to shift the discussion of his own narrative from one of individual achievement to the stubborn continuance of institutionalized racism in the United States," Zirin reports. He adds, "To tell his tale as one of individual triumph through his singular greatness is to not tell the story at all."[12]

Ava DuVernay's *Selma* (2014) stands in sharp contrast. Unlike so many movies we've considered, the title of this treatment of the famous civil rights marches in March 1965 comes from the event and movement—and not its leader. It opens with an ordinary black woman, Annie Lee Cooper (Oprah Winfrey), heartbroken after her fourth failed attempt to pass an absurd test designed only to prevent her from registering to vote. Cooper's individual rights are what the movement—and story—is about, as director DuVernay makes clear: "This is

Frame 17. In *Selma*, institutional barriers have to be overcome via a political process and collective action.

a film that's about the people of Selma and the black leadership of Selma and the allies who came to the aid of black people who were being terrorized in Selma."[13] As the opening scene makes clear, it is an institutional barrier, a racist practice based on an unjust law, that has to be overcome collectively (frame 17).

The film centers on Martin Luther King Jr. (David Oyelowo), who is depicted "as a dynamic figure of human-scale contradictions, flaws and supremely shrewd political skills," Ann Hornaday writes.[14] But King is one among a cast of characters based on real-life players, all with something at stake as these events unfold and mark a turning point in civil rights history. Critics compared *Selma* to the behind-the-scenes maneuverings that drove the narrative in *Lincoln*. The film "is as much about the procedures of political maneuvering, in-fighting and bargaining as it is about the chief orchestrator of the resulting deals."[15]

Champagne, CDOs, and Subprime Mortgages

The Big Short (2015), a uniquely inventive film, effectively dramatizes a story largely about institutions, corporate behavior, and how social systems work. Based on Michael Lewis's bestselling book, the movie deals with the housing bubble that burst and sparked a worldwide financial crisis in 2008. The causes of the financial crash are multiple, complicated, and difficult to understand, which was one problem Lewis had in writing the book. The other involved how to make readers want to know about complex high finance. Director and coscreenwriter Adam McKay encountered the same difficulties in adapting the material for the screen.

Not being an economist, I have a hard time understanding the spiraling factors that came together to cause the crash: subprime mortgages, collateralized debt obligations (CDOs), hedge funds, and more. So, I turn to award-winning economist and *New York Times* columnist Paul Krugman. Although Krugman says he might "quibble over a few points," he insists that the movie basically got the story right and "does a terrific job of making Wall Street skullduggery entertaining."[16] How? The story is told by focusing on the personal drama of creatively drawn characters variously involved in what is happening. We lose the significance of these events and character actions, however, without some understanding of the confluence of financial, economic, and political factors underlying the crash.

To make complex high finance entertaining, *The Big Short* shifts into a self-reflexive mode with the actors speaking and looking directly into the camera, breaking the "fourth wall"—the conceptual threshold that screens the filmic world from the audience. The effect is to disrupt the narrative flow and make spectators aware they're watching a movie. The repeated scenes of "real life" people talking directly to the camera become a pattern within the film used to explain abstract concepts or debunk story events.

The beautiful Australian actress Margot Robbie explains subprime mortgage bonds to us while sipping champagne in a bubble bath (frame 18). Celebrity chef Anthony Bourdain explains how dubious home loans were repackaged into CDOs by showing how days-old fish is used to make seafood stew: "It's not old fish. It's a whole new thing." Sitting at a Las Vegas blackjack table, singer Selena Gomez explains how a synthetic CDO works by comparing it to people in a casino betting on the outcome of another player's hand. These cameo appearances function like "a series of footnotes" to help us understand the financial jargon, while also providing comic relief, one critic explains. "I'm still not ready to take the commodities exam, but these episodes

The Big Short © 2015 Paramount Pictures Corporation / Monarchy Enterprises / Regency Entertainment (USA), Inc.

Frame 18. Actress Margot Robbie breaks the "fourth wall" to help viewers understand the financial jargon while providing comic relief in *The Big Short*.

help break through the wall of verbiage that might otherwise prevent us from seeing *The Big Short* as a very human story."[17]

The fictional world depicted in *The Big Short* is driven by greed, self-interest, and material success. People have no more value than the commodities being bought and sold. The only ethical standard is what you can get away with. "Tell me the difference between stupid and illegal and I'll have my wife's brother arrested," Jared Vennett (Ryan Gosling) says. The story's poignancy centers on Mark Baum (Steve Carell), whose dismay and disapproval throughout lends the film a moral voice. "We live in an era of fraud in America," Baum says. "Not just in banking, but in government, education, religion, food, even baseball. . . . For fifteen thousand years, fraud and short-sighted thinking have never, ever worked. Not once. Eventually you get caught, things go south. When the hell did we forget all that? I thought we were better than this, I really did."

What started with financiers giving subprime mortgage loans to borrowers ended with the financial system tumbling down. And everyone did not live happily ever after. Millions of people lost their jobs and homes. US households lost on average nearly $5,800 and saw a combined loss in stock and home values totaling nearly $100,000.[18] No senior executives at any of the big Wall Street firms were charged, despite reports of possible criminal activity; only one investment banker was prosecuted and served jail time.[19]

The Big Short is an illustration of film as cultural criticism. One way to interpret it identifies the way it points up the harmful consequences of relegating virtue to personal life and letting power and wealth determine fairness and decency in politics or business. As noted earlier, Christian faithfulness not only concerns personal life but also addresses cultural patterns and social arrangements, all of which have to do with people's deep-seated beliefs about life and society.

MOVIE MUSING

A Classical Hollywood Film: *Rocky* (1976)

Rocky . . . is a Horatio Alger story about a struggling prizefighter, and it believes in values that most movies don't believe anymore. It believes in love. It believes in the American Dream. It believes in the essential goodness of people and in the almighty power of human will.

—Frank Rich, *New York Post*

Ingeniously, [Ryan] Coogler has transformed "Rocky"—the modern cinematic myth that, perhaps more than any other, endures as a modern capitalist Horatio Alger story of personal determination and sheer will—into a vision of community and opportunity, connections and social capital, family and money.

—Richard Brody, *New Yorker*

In many ways, boxing is the quintessential American metaphor: an individual who has to rely on skill, hard work, and internal fortitude is alone engaged in a fight to the finish. The slew of boxing films includes *Raging Bull* (1980), *The Hurricane* (1999), *Cinderella Man* (2005), and *The Fighter* (2010). In *On the Waterfront* (1954), a despondent Terry Malloy (Marlon Brando) utters those classic lines of dialogue that capture the American dream: "I coulda had class. I coulda been a contender. I coulda been somebody, instead of a bum, which is what I am, let's face it."

The *Rocky* movies have made an indelible mark on American popular culture. Media marketers still make use of the familiar theme song, "Gonna Fly Now," as a musical metaphor for training hard and winning against the odds. Even if you've never seen a *Rocky* film, you're probably familiar with the main character and story. In the original film, Apollo Creed, played by an African American actor, Carl Weathers, is the reigning heavyweight champion. "I'm sentimental," he tells a boxing promoter. "And a lot of other people in this country are just as sentimental. And there's nothing they'd like better than to see Apollo Creed give a local Philadelphia boy a shot at the greatest title in the world on this country's biggest birthday." With that, Creed both aptly summarizes the movie's

Rocky © 1976 Metro-Goldwyn-Mayer Studios, Inc.

Frame 19. *Rocky* celebrates American individualism with a determined protagonist who believes in himself and accomplishes his goal against all odds.

main story line and draws attention to the film itself as melodrama and an American rags-to-riches story.

As we've seen, countless American movies feature rugged individuals who on their own merit manage to escape their humble circumstances by exercising some exceptional gift to overcome obstacles and trials. Their climb from "rags to riches" becomes a filmic metaphor that affirms America as the land of opportunity. According to scholars, the American myth "exhorts us to shake free of the limiting past in a struggling ascent toward the realization of promise in a gracious future."[20] It's not hard to see how this cultural myth *is* the story of Rocky: a heroic individual who by believing in himself realizes his potential and accomplishes his goals against all odds (frame 19). This myth, with its associated ideals and values, informs the characterizations and the narrative structure of *Rocky*: act 1 (the setup) shows Rocky's limiting past; act 2, his struggling ascent; and act 3, the achievement of his goals.

Going the Distance

The film opens with "ROCKY" in huge white letters scrolling across the screen while a brass ensemble trumpets the arrival of a king. The opening image is a mosaic of a Byzantine Christ on the ceiling in what appears to be a church that has been converted into a boxing arena. The camera tilts down from Jesus to Rocky (the "Italian Stallion") Balboa (Sylvester Stallone); it takes no stretch of the imagination to see that this is designed to make us think of Rocky as a Christ figure. Shots during the fight make it look as if Jesus is watching over Rocky in the ring, further signifying a connection between religion, life, and boxing. Rocky not only redeems himself but also gives new life to those around him. Later, Rocky's manager, Mickey (Burgess Meredith), tells him, "You're gonna eat lightning, and you're gonna crap thunder!" It's as if Rocky were a god.

Rocky lives alone in a single-room apartment on the south side of Philadelphia and makes ends meet collecting money for a loan shark. His boxing career is going nowhere. He loses his locker at the gym, with owner and trainer Mickey making it clear that Rocky wasted his potential as a fighter. In the meantime, Apollo Creed has a problem: without a ranked contender available, Creed needs a gimmick or will have to cancel an upcoming scheduled fight. He decides to give a local unranked Philadelphia fighter a shot at the title. America is "the land of opportunity," the champ tells the promoter, who says, "I like it. It's very American." Creed replies, "It's very smart." Both know that "the media will eat it up," and they will profit handsomely.

Rocky is selected not because he is a competitive fighter—by all appearances he's not—but because of his nickname. "Now who discovered America? An Italian right?" Creed says. "What better way to get it on than with one of its descendants?" Despite Rocky being a southpaw, Creed is self-assured. "I'll drop him in three. 'Apollo Creed meets the Italian Stallion.' Sounds like a damn monster movie." It's also a classic melodramatic situation: the chance event is a fortuitous happening "rather than causal action on the part of the protagonists, that brings about the villain's demise and saves the day," Ben Singer explains. "Through chance, bad things happen to bad people, and good things happen to good people."[21] Apollo Creed might just as well have selected Rocky as been struck by a bolt of lightning. Creed's choice and the film's opening imagery suggest some outside magical assistance at work.

Rocky's training—both highly cinematic and visually graphic—depicts his personal transformation and "struggling ascent," aptly symbolized by the Philadelphia Art Museum steps. Rocky's first day of training starts with an early morning run. Wearing a plain grey sweat suit, he holds his side as he struggles to make it up the museum's steps. As the fight approaches, Mickey says that Rocky's got "heart," meaning willpower. And he "goes to the body like nobody you've ever seen," a strategy a boxer uses to attack his opponent's midsection and abdominal area instead of his head. This is visualized for us when, as part of his training routine, we see him breaking the ribs of huge slabs of beef hanging at the meat factory where his friend Paulie works. (Watch out, Apollo.)

Weeks of workouts culminate in a montage sequence that has become a staple in similar films and parody in others. The inspirational theme song acts as a sound bridge over a collage of shots showing Rocky preparing for the fight: exercising, hitting a punching bag, sparring in the ring at Mickey's gym, and gaining speed running along the docks. The sequence reaches a climax with a fit and confident Rocky now dancing atop the museum steps: with a panorama of the city in the background, the native Philadelphian raises his arms triumphantly, signaling the arrival of a champion.

Despite his intense training, Rocky realizes the unlikeliness of winning and sets his own goal: to become the first challenger to "go the distance" against Creed. And against tremendous odds he achieves his goal, a personal victory, in a fight described as "a mythic spectacle."[22] He also wins the love of his shy girlfriend Adrian (Talia Shire). Rocky can now get married, start a family, and reap the benefits of worldly success—the traditional American dream—all of which occurs in the sequels.

Reflecting Reality

Many writers have observed that *Rocky* implicitly captured the ambivalent mood of Bicentennial America. Released in the aftermath of the US defeat in Vietnam, Watergate, and the civil rights movement, and amid the decade's second recession, *Rocky* tapped into white working-class prejudices and fears, especially resentment of African Americans. Lower-middle-class and working-class whites believed America had been pushed around for over a decade, and they had personally been left out for the sake of progressive change. As Stallone said of audience response, "When they're cheering for Rocky, they're cheering for themselves."[23]

Rocky asserts a sociopolitical explanation: liberals and African Americans had stolen the American dream from its rightful heirs; the world had been turned upside down. One writer argues that the film uses a "scapegoating ritual" to symbolically resolve the crisis by directing ethnic anger toward African Americans.[24] Disregarding socioeconomic realities, the film shows working-class whites languishing while African Americans thrive and Apollo Creed (modeled after Muhammad Ali) reigns as the world's boxing champion. During the fight, the American flag looms large in the background, especially when Rocky stuns Creed by knocking him down in the first round. This image alone, of a white man defeating an African American, can be read as a metaphor symbolizing racial attitudes among some whites at the time.

The basic American myth provides a framework for the other films in the series. In *Rocky III* (1982), for example, Rocky loses a title fight to a fierce challenger, Clubber Lang (Mr. T). When Mickey dies of a heart attack, Rocky teams up with Apollo Creed to defeat Lang in a rematch. To get back "the eye of the tiger," Rocky trains at the Tough Gym in Los Angeles where Creed started; we realize now that Creed too is an American dream story. In the rematch, Rocky combines the finesse and speed he's learned from his former rival with his brute endurance to defeat Clubber Lang.

Creed (2015), the seventh installment in the series, is patterned after the original 1976 film. An aging Rocky, battling cancer, reluctantly agrees to train Adonis "Donnie" Johnson Creed (Michael B. Jordan), the illegitimate son of Apollo, who died in a bout with Soviet boxer Ivan Drago in *Rocky IV* (1985). Donnie, an orphan, grew up in foster homes and is serving time in a Los Angeles juvenile detention center when Apollo's widow, Mary Anne (Phylicia Rashad), offers him help. She takes him in and provides for his education, and soon enough Donnie is on the fast track with a brokerage firm. Though Mary Anne does not want him to box, Donnie's passion is to follow in the footsteps of the father he never knew, which takes him to Philadelphia in the hope that Rocky, his father's old friend, will train him.

Cowriter and director Ryan Coogler (*Fruitvale Station*, 2013; *Black Panther*, 2018) said that his father loved the *Rocky* movies and made him watch them when he was growing up. The twenty-nine-year-old black filmmaker's familiarity with the stories is evident in the way he seamlessly blends the gritty texture and character-driven narrative of the original *Rocky* with a contemporary feel, including a soundtrack with several hip-hop tracks. Coogler exploits conventions of Stallone's Oscar-winning melodrama—the Philadelphia setting, the art museum steps, Bill Conti's theme song, and training montages—right up to the predictable and implausible climactic championship fight. These traditional elements are recontextualized, however, through the African American male experience, evoked at the start with Donnie's release from the juvenile correctional facility. The story begins "with a cry for justice, for a society that would rescue every young Adonis from isolation, poverty, and brutality in order to foster their strength and cultivate their incipient spark of genius and originality," as film critic Richard Brody observes.[25]

Coogler transforms the original *Rocky* story by putting it in the context of the Black Lives Matter movement: its demand for basic human rights, freedom, justice, and an end to systemic violence and discrimination against African Americans and by extension all people. Coogler "might not believe in the reality of *Creed*," critic David Edelstein maintains, "but he puts every bit of faith and skill he has in the reality of the dream."[26] The film can be interpreted as a retelling of the mythic blueprint of its precursor, a cinematic metaphor less about the way things are than how they ought to be: to have opportunity regardless of circumstance, to cultivate your talents, and to realize your ambitions.

MOVIE MUSING

A Creative Alternative: *Do the Right Thing* (1989)

> Spike Lee's masterpiece could easily have come out yesterday—or in 1961 or in 1978—and it would pack the same cultural wallop.
>
> —Jon Friedman, *New York Natives.com*

Do the Right Thing, the masterpiece of writer, director, and actor Spike Lee, deviates from the classical Hollywood narrative style in key ways and provides a sharp illustration. I referred to this film earlier, pairing it with the original *Rocky* in part to set up the two Movie Musings. Race and ethnicity factor differently in their respective visions of American life—the one celebrates national ideals, while the other probes their realization for people of color.

Though both films have realistic settings, *Rocky* represents a mythic horizon of opportunity. *Rocky*'s tagline, "His whole life was a million-to-one shot," clearly identifies the film as an American dream story. Conversely, *Do the Right Thing* nestles an ethnically diverse community within contemporary sociopolitical realities that temper the basic optimism of the American myth (frame 20). Spike Lee's screenplay draws on real-life incidents, especially the deaths of Michael Stewart in 1983 and Michael Griffith in 1986. The self-determination that defines Rocky and drives the film's narrative meets with skepticism in *Do the Right Thing*. It's a difference in perspective. The one invests an individual with the power to control his destiny, while the other insists that people's lives are shaped by circumstances and "shows how communities affect their own lives, and how their lives are shaped by personal and impersonal forces," sociologist Michael Eric Dyson observes.[27]

We can see this difference in the way the two movies tell and resolve their stories. *Rocky*'s narrative follows a main plot (preparation for the championship fight) and a

Do the Right Thing © 1989 Universal City Studios, Inc.

Frame 20. *Do the Right Thing* is an alternative film that centers on a racially and ethnically diverse community and tempers the basic optimism of the American myth.

related subplot (the budding relationship between Rocky and Adrian). The film ends with complete closure: Rocky achieves his goal of "going the distance" against Creed and wins Adrian's love.

Do the Right Thing centers on a block in "Bed-Stuy" (Bedford-Stuyvesant) that is home to a racially diverse network of characters. New to the block is a not particularly welcomed Korean family that turned a boarded-up storefront into a fruit and vegetable store. A corner fixture is Sal's Famous Pizzeria, a remnant of the neighborhood's demographic shift from Italian to African American and Puerto Rican. The hardworking owner, Sal (Danny Aiello), takes some pride in having built the business from the ground up and remaining despite the changes. When his oldest son Pino (John Turturro), who is vocally racist, pleads with him to sell and set up another pizzeria elsewhere, Sal tells him, "These people have grown up on my pizza." Still, Sal seems rather overconfident in the way he perceives himself as part of the community and in understanding what real racial integration might require.

The story begins with radio DJ Mister Señor Love Daddy (Samuel L. Jackson) giving the day's forecast: "HOT!" That's confirmed in a crane shot of the neighborhood block that is saturated with yellow, orange, brown, and reddish hues and by constant references in actions and dialogue throughout the day. The sweltering heat is both a feature of the setting and symbolic of the tensions simmering just beneath the community's surface.

Mookie (Spike Lee) lives with his sister, Jade (Joie Lee), and works for Sal delivering pizzas. His work is half-hearted, and Pino keeps an eye on him. Sal is aware of that but likes Mookie and values his role in the business. Making deliveries, Mookie threads his way through the neighborhood wearing a Brooklyn Dodgers jersey with "Robinson

42" on the back. His personal interactions seem to lace together a community where everyone seems to know everyone else. Mookie has a young son and a Puerto Rican girlfriend, Tina (Rosie Perez), who lives with her mother. Tina clearly wants something more from Mookie.

Radio Raheem (Bill Nunn) struts around the neighborhood blasting Public Enemy's "Fight the Power" on his boom box, which irritates Sweet Dick Willie (Robin Harris) and two other older black men who spend this Saturday sitting in lawn chairs under a beach umbrella in front of a bright red wall, commenting on the neighborhood comings and goings. Then there is Da Mayor (Ossie Davis), an older black man with a drinking problem. The neighborhood youth disrespect him, and he tries to find ways to win the affection and approval of Mother Sister (Ruby Dee), a matronly figure who spends most of the day looking out her window. Da Mayor prevents a boy from getting hit by a car, uses money Sal pays him for sweeping in front of the pizzeria to buy beer at the Korean store, and advises Mookie to "always do the right thing."

Fight the Powers That Be

Power is a key motif in *Do the Right Thing*. The film's theme song, Public Enemy's "Fight the Power," plays over the opening credits and repeatedly throughout the film on Radio Raheem's boom box: "We've got to fight the powers that be." Power is a central dynamic in conflicts between father and son, mother and daughter, siblings, police and citizens, and different racial groups.

In one scene, Radio Raheem is on his way to get "a slice" at Sal's Famous. He stops to tell Mookie the story behind the "love" and "hate" brass knuckles he wears on each hand. Mookie steps back, and the camera moves into the space in front of Radio Raheem, who is talking directly to the audience now. "Let me tell you the story of right hand-left hand. It's a tale of good and evil," he says while shadowboxing to demonstrate the struggle between peace and violence that ends positively with "Left-Hand Hate KO-ed by Love."[28]

Other sequences also disrupt the narrative flow by design. In one, a handheld camera moves in quickly from a long shot to medium close-up of a character talking directly to the camera spewing stream-of-conscious slurs and insults at another racial or ethnic group: Mookie (African American), Pino (Italian), Stevie (Puerto Rican), Police Officer Long (White), and Sonny (Korean). By breaking the screen barrier, and by acknowledging the audience's presence, the sequence in some sense involves spectators directly in the film's events. It ends with a shot of DJ Mister Señor Love Daddy in reverse now, sliding on his chair toward the camera from a long shot to medium close-up: "Yo! Hold up! Time out! TIME OUT! Y'all take a chill! Ya need to cool that s—— out! And that's the double truth, Ruth!" The effect is to call attention to the film itself, interrupting the story as if to drag viewers across the threshold into the film's world and directly into the sights of vocalized racism.

Two slow-motion sequences serve to reveal characters' deep suspicions. In one, Sweet Dick Willie and friends glare back at the police driving by. In another, close-ups of Mookie and Pino show their displeasure at Sal flirting with Jade. And the film uses high- and low-angle shots throughout to suggest the power and intimidation that exists between characters.

The narrative builds toward a dramatic conflict, but not by tracing one direct line of action. Instead, the climax happens somewhat unexpectedly, a clash of flawed characters and their differing aims that took shape during the day—with unfortunate consequences now. The effect is to undermine the centrality of the goal-oriented protagonist and disrupt the pattern of narrative causation that typically leads to an anticipated and satisfying resolution to the problems presented in the story.

Instead of a story driven by a goal-oriented protagonist, *Do the Right Thing* tells the tale of a community besieged by racial conflict. Character motivations and goals are not clearly defined and appear in conflict with others. When we first see Mookie, for example, he's counting money, and he later entreats Sal to pay him in advance; yet it remains unclear what Mookie plans to do with it. Sal is determined to keep his pizzeria open despite growing racial tensions in the neighborhood and Pino's adamant opposition.

Buggin' Out (Giancarlo Esposito), who's been quick to take a stand and even pick a fight, sort of finds a goal, which ends up being pivotal: he notices that there are no pictures of African Americans hanging on Sal's Wall of Fame—only Italians. Becoming incensed, he tries to persuade others to boycott Sal's Famous until he adds pictures of African Americans: "Malcolm X, Nelson Mandela, Michael Jordan." Buggin' Out's demand might seem trivial, but it carries symbolic weight, adding a layer of meaning to the escalating tensions. Sal's Famous serves a mostly African American community, but it's Sal's establishment and he's proud of his Italian heritage.

No one's much interested, however. "Keep walkin', Doctor. I don't want to hear none of your foolishness," Da Mayor tells him. "Sal ain't never done me no harm." Sweet Dick Willie adds, "You either." Finally, Jade advises, "Buggin' Out, I don't mean to be disrespectful, but you can really direct your energies in a more useful way." Undeterred, Buggin' Out gets support from the disgruntled Radio Raheem and Smiley (Roger Guenveur Smith), who stutters and has a developmental disability. Smiley goes around the neighborhood selling photos of Martin Luther King Jr. with Malcolm X; he had a run-in with Pino earlier in the day. Radio Raheem is still irked that the no-nonsense Sal made him turn off his blaring boom box in the pizzeria that afternoon.

Just after closing, Buggin' Out, Radio Raheem, and Smiley enter Sal's with Radio Raheem's boom box blasting "Fight the Power." The high- and low-angle shots used throughout the film are often combined with Dutch-angle shots—the camera is tilted at an angle—typically used to suggest that a situation is off-kilter. This method is especially effective during the film's climactic scene, giving viewers an alarming sense of things quickly getting out of control and the world of the film losing its balance. Racial epitaphs fly as Sal smashes the boom box with a baseball bat, infuriating Radio Raheem. A fight ensues with their bodies crashing through the door and into the street. With a crowd gathering, Radio Raheem is killed in a policeman's choke hold and taken away in the police cruiser. Sal and his sons stand in front of the pizzeria; the Korean couple in front of their store across the street. The tensions mounting throughout the day threaten to explode, and for a long, tense moment we're not sure what's going to happen.

Then Mookie throws a garbage can through the window of Sal's pizzeria, igniting a riot with the neighbors-turned-mob now burning down Sal's place. Mookie's action has been debated considerably. In the scene just prior to Buggin' Out's arrival, Sal tells Mookie that he's "like a son" and that Mookie will always have a place working there. Some writers argue that by throwing the garbage can through the window of Sal's pizzeria Mookie did "the right thing," redirecting the mob's anger away from Sal and his sons. "I wanna clear up something once and for all," Spike Lee said pointedly, reflecting on this scene. "Mookie did not throw the garbage can through the window to divert the mob from jumping on Sal. [Mookie] threw the garbage can through the window because he just saw one of his best friends get murdered in cold blood by NYPD."[29]

The ending is ambiguous, and intentionally so, to provoke debate with more questions than answers. The morning after the riot, Mookie goes to Sal's, the pizzeria in ruins, concerned only with getting his week's wages—Sal can rebuild with the insurance money. The movie ends with the audience left wondering: After getting paid, is Mookie really going to visit his son as he tells Sal? And does that signal a change in his relationship with Tina? Will Sal rebuild or relocate? What does it mean to do the right thing? The most important question, of course, asks whether racial conflicts can be resolved peacefully or if violence is necessary. "Are we gonna live together? Together are we gonna live?" DJ Mister Señor Love Daddy asks. There's a gnawing sense that nothing's changed, that life just goes on—but without Radio Raheem in it.

The film concludes with onscreen quotations: one by Martin Luther King Jr. and the other by Malcolm X. The rhetoric of King and the civil rights movement advocated progress, nonviolence, and integration. It aimed to end racial injustice by appealing to conscience and building viable coalitions between those with and those without political and economic power. The Black Power movement, which drew on Malcolm X's teachings, then rejected these goals and values; the focus shifted from breaking down barriers of segregation to building strong African American communities as the way to achieve racial justice. The contrary quotations on the use of violence highlight the film's theme while demonstrating the complexity of securing racial justice.

Behind Its Time and Ahead of Ours

When it was released in 1989, *Do the Right Thing* was probably "the most controversial film of the year," Roger Ebert noted, describing it as coming "closer to reflecting the current state of race relations in America than any other movie of our time."[30] Spike Lee's film steers far from anything simplistic in its attitude and exploration of racial dynamics and perspectives. Much more could be said about this landmark film in African American cinema, which has endured as a masterwork and culturally important movie. Its ongoing significance testifies as much to the cultural sensibilities it exhibited at the time as it does to the persistence of the problem of racial divisiveness it addresses.

On its twenty-fifth anniversary, film writer Lee Weston Sabo observed, *"Do the Right Thing* wasn't ahead of its time. It was behind its time, and it's ahead of ours." He adds, "If you updated the soundtrack and the fashion a bit and released it next week, critics would praise its timeliness and how its depiction of police brutality and racial tension captures the angry zeitgeist surrounding the recent killings of unarmed black civilians by police officers."[31] That was written after the tragic death of Michael Brown, who was shot by a white police officer in Ferguson, Missouri, in 2014. In the summer of 2016, the nation was rocked by two gruesome killings of black men by police and a horrible attack by a gunman who killed five Dallas police officers during a nonviolent protest. "Day in and day out, we feel powerless to make our black lives matter," Michael Eric Dyson writes in an op-ed piece in the *New York Times.* "We feel powerless to make you believe that our black lives should matter."[32] This powerful sentiment renews the challenge for all of us to do the right thing and recognize our common humanity as image bearers of God.

8

A Man's Gotta Do
What a Man's Gotta Do

American Action–Adventure Movies

It is something of a paradox that American movies—a great democratic art form, if ever there was one—have not done a very good job of representing American democracy.

—A. O. Scott, review of *Lincoln* (2012)

Star Trek Beyond (2016) is the third film in a reboot of the Paramount franchise featuring younger versions of the original cast. Pondering a sense of unease, Captain Kirk (Chris Pine) records in the captain's daily log, "Things are starting to feel a little . . . episodic." Similarly, in *Die Hard* 2 (1990), New York police detective John McClane (Bruce Willis) asks himself, "How can the same s—— happen to the same guy twice?" As happens only in the movies, McClane continues to find himself caught up in one terrorist crisis after another in subsequent follow-ups: *Die Hard with a Vengeance* (1995), *Live Free or Die Hard* (2007), and *A Good Day to Die Hard* (2013). These self-referential lines of dialogue inject some inside humor for viewers familiar with previous installments in the series. They also lightheartedly underscore the formulaic repetitiveness of Hollywood franchises.

Every year, around ten movies known as *tentpoles* will make over $200 million in domestic box-office earnings (US and Canada). The term alludes to the pole that holds up the tent frame and canvas. These large-scale Hollywood productions are designed to reap maximum profits from worldwide distribution. Their outstanding success lets Hollywood studios spread their financial risk across their entire slate of annual offerings. The studios' tentpole strategies rely crucially on movies that I'm classifying broadly as *action-adventure films*.

Action and adventure are overlapping genres. The hybrid label is used simply to create an umbrella category spanning a range of distinct genres that intersect. Detective stories stress puzzle solving, for example. The sci-fi universe features alien worlds, and the high-tech gadgetry associated with sci-fi films also typifies espionage thrillers, like the James Bond vehicles, and superhero movies. Fantasy, like *The Lord of the Rings* trilogy, and traditional adventure films, like the *Indiana Jones* series, rely heavily on action-packed sequences. The same is true of apocalyptic, war, and routine action movies like *Rocky*. All feature characters caught up in exciting events and usually dangerous, life-threatening situations. My lumping them all together for a general treatment does not mean I'm unaware of their dissimilarities. These film genres, while distinctive, can still be seen as variations on a general story line that provides a common basis for analysis.

Adventure stories consist of "an event or series of events that happen outside the ordinary course of the protagonist's life, usually accompanied by danger, often by physical action," writer and critic Don D'Ammassa explains. In terms of narrative form, they "almost always move quickly, and the pace of the plot is at least as important as characterization, setting, and other elements of a created work."[1] Action-adventure protagonists have the key traits of ingenuity and combat skills, which explains how they always manage to survive against incredible odds. The central character's struggle might be against a nefarious antagonist, a menacing force of nature, or some other obstacle calling for customary scenes involving physical hand-to-hand fighting, death-defying feats, and wild chases.

Here I aim to create a broad framework by looking at a few specific films, and in doing so suggest another plank in developing a framework of expectations. Again, movie watching need not—and I would suggest, should not—be mindless. However entertaining, action-adventure movies explore ideas and themes worth thinking about more deeply and critically. The intent here is to provide some historical and generic context as way of outlining key elements with enough detail that readers can use them to examine other movies of their own choice. And it will come as no surprise that the American action-adventure film showcases the melodramatic aesthetic mode and outlook. If you've seen enough action-related genre films, all this may sound familiar—though I hope also organized in a way that perhaps you've not thought about before.

"Happy Trails, Hans"

Today's action-adventure films have especially strong ties to the traditional Hollywood western, which represents "America's foundational ritual," as film scholar Thomas Schatz puts it.[2] The western thrived for a long time as an enduring expression of America as an imagined community, providing a basis for national self-understanding. Moviemakers tested its central dynamics in different historical contexts as a way of talking metaphorically about politics (*High Noon*, 1952), race (*The Searchers*, 1956), and the Vietnam War (*The Green Berets*, 1968; *Little Big Man*, 1970). More recently, the melodrama *Brokeback Mountain* (2005) employed traditional western motifs and iconography to discuss sexual orientation.

In film and fiction, westerns are usually set in the late nineteenth century around the time of the closing of the American frontier. Literary scholar John Cawelti describes the western as a mythic version of the nation's history, "a timeless epic past in which heroic individual defenders of law and order without the vast social resources of police and courts stand poised against the threat of lawlessness or savagery."[3] The dramatic conflict centers on persistent tensions between the individual and community, between social order and lawlessness, and on the use of violence in the advance of civilization. Director John Ford's landmark *Stagecoach* (1939) revolutionized the genre—and made John Wayne a major movie star. It also became a prototype for cinematic stories depicting the pioneering experience as critical to the formation of the American character and institutions.

Movie westerns have pretty much all but become nonexistent now, yet their influence on the action-adventure genre remains. The genre's basic elements—its story formula, reluctant hero, and ritualized violence—have been recycled and amped up in today's action-adventure movies. *Star Wars* (1977), you will recall, is such an amalgam of movie types that a commentator dubbed it "Genre Wars." Lucas's blockbuster hit revived the science-fiction genre and codified the western "in a galaxy far, far away." Han Solo dresses like a frontier cavalryman and wields his blaster like a cowboy's six-gun. The Mos Eisley Cantina on the planet Tatooine looks like a frontier saloon, and key scenes, including the climactic destruction of the Death Star, are true to the classic western formula. You can find all these elements in the recent installments, *The Force Awakens* (2015) and *The Last Jedi* (2017). The original *Star Wars* trilogy set the pace for producers eager to cash in on Hollywood's new bread-and-butter audience: male adolescents under twenty-five whose repeated viewings of movies like *Jaws*, the *Star Wars* films, and *Raiders of the Lost Ark* compensated for the erosion of the general family audience.

The influential *Die Hard* franchise likewise established a pattern for action films that are all predictable in theme, character, and story line—and driven by a fixation on profit margins. The film title itself can be used as a descriptor for a bevy of imitations: for example, *Die Hard* on a plane (*Air Force One*), a battleship (*Under Siege*), a bus (*Speed*), or an island (*The Rock*); in a mall (*Paul Blart: Mall Cop*); or at the White House (*White House Down*). The *Die Hard* films and offshoots reimagine the mythic setting of the Great Plains in the western. The global village of today's transnational economy is cast now as a foreign "wilderness" inhabited by cutthroat corporate executives, corrupt political dictators, drug czars, mercenaries, and heartless terrorists. Their acts of cruelty, wanton violence, and destruction make them the new "savages." In the Old West, outlaws held up stagecoaches, trains, and frontier banks. Today, homegrown criminals and international outlaws hijack planes, raid corporate vaults and Federal Reserve buildings, and hack into government and commercial computer systems. The archvillain in *Mission: Impossible II* (2000) goes even further by demanding corporate stock options—the gift that keeps on giving. This became such a staple in the formula that the James Bond parody *Austin Powers: International Man of Mystery* (1997) makes fun of it as the time-traveling Dr. Evil holds the world hostage with nuclear weapons for "$1 million dollars. Sorry. $100 billion."

It's worth looking at the pacesetting original *Die Hard* (1988), both for how representative it is and for how self-aware it is in adhering to the western conventions. An unorthodox New York policeman becomes a reluctant hero when a group of German terrorists seize the Nakatomi Tower in Los Angeles. Led by Hans Gruber (Alan Rickman), they take the employees hostage at the Nakatomi Corporation's Christmas Eve party as a planned distraction while they break into the building's vault and steal $640 million in bearer bonds. Foiling their plan and destroying these heavily armed criminals is left to Bruce Willis's character, John McClane, who just happens to be at the party to meet his estranged wife before visiting with their children for the holidays.

McClane's name itself evokes that of John Wayne, and the film's dialogue is filled with overt references clearly identifying him as the classic western hero. "How 'bout you, cowboy?" an LA policeman (Reginald VelJohnson) asks McClane. "You got any kids back on the ranch?" Hans sarcastically calls McClane "Mister Cowboy" and lectures him on corporate greed. "Who are you?" Hans asks with contempt. "Just another American who saw too many movies as a child? Another orphan of a bankrupt culture who thinks he's John Wayne,

Rambo, Marshal Dillon?" (In Hans's mind, if not also the popular imagination, war and western heroes are one and the same.) McClane replies sarcastically, "I was always partial to Roy Rogers actually." He signs off with a trademark line, "Yippee-ki-yay," with an expletive added for effect. It's a line he repeats in *Die Hard 2* as he's about to blow up the Boeing 747 that a group of mercenaries are flying to escape from Washington Dulles International Airport.

In their climactic face-to-face shootout, Hans says, "This time John Wayne does not walk off into the sunset with Grace Kelly." McClane gives a snarky retort, "It's Gary Cooper, a———," and then outdraws and shoots Hans. Imitating legendary gunslingers, he blows imaginary smoke from the gun barrel and utters the classic cowboy farewell: "Happy trails, Hans." McClane destroys the perpetrators of evil, restoring law and order, saves his damsel-in-distress wife, and is reunited with his family.

In the fourth installment, *Live Free or Die Hard* (2007), the aging McClane gets some needed help from a young computer hacker, Matt Farrell (Justin Long). This time they're up against cyberterrorists who breach the nation's computer infrastructure. "You know what you get for being a hero?" McClane asks his untried and frightened sidekick. "Nothin'. You get shot at. You get divorced. Your kids don't want to talk to you. You get to eat a lot of meals by yourself. Trust me, kid, nobody wants to be that guy." Farrell asks, "Then why are you doing this?" McClane doesn't hesitate, "Because there's nobody else to do it right now, that's why." At bottom, his motivation is personal integrity. With a slight, knowing smile, Farrell replies, "That's what makes you that guy."

And "that guy" is the reluctant hero willing to sacrifice life and limb to do "what a man's gotta do." The movie dialogue conversation between McClane and Farrell seamlessly articulates both the gendered ideal man (which we look at in the next chapter), and the classic American hero depicted in myriad Hollywood movies. As another example, *Captain America: Civil War* (2016) ends with Steve Rogers estranged, a fugitive, having relinquished his Captain America identity. Nevertheless, he leaves a voice message for Tony Stark (Iron Man): "I promise you. If you need me, if you need us . . . I'll be there." The sentiment is the same as McClane's and affirms that Rogers too, with the rest of the action-adventure protagonists, is "that guy." What American moviegoer would expect anything else?

The Epic Moment or What a Man's Gotta Do

Scholars show how American action-adventures, from traditional westerns to comic-book superhero movies, adhere to a distinctively American *monomyth*, a term that refers to a narrative template for the hero's journey. Here's how Robert Jewett and John Shelton Lawrence describe the central character and story line: "A community in a harmonious paradise is threatened by evil; normal institutions fail to contend with this threat; a selfless superhero emerges to renounce temptations and carry out the redemptive task; aided by fate, his decisive victory restores the community to its paradisal condition; the superhero then recedes into obscurity." This distinctive pattern, which derives "from tales of redemption," in effect "secularizes the Judeo-Christian redemption dramas," they explain. "The supersaviors in pop culture function as replacements for the Christ figure," but with a crucial difference: the way these selfless and reluctant heroes "save" a community of "good" people is via an act of regenerative violence, which is a key metaphor in the mythology of the American West.[4] Characters like Neo in *The Matrix*, for example, replace "the ineffectual baggage of the Sermon on the Mount" with "a duffel bag full of pistols, guns, and explosives needed to destroy the command center of political evil."[5]

A staple in action-adventure films is the "epic moment," a violent confrontation of apocalyptic proportions drawn from the classic convention of the western shootout.[6] It is the anticipated—if also utterly predictable—climactic scene when the hero, who alone can save the imperiled community, destroys the villain in spectacular fashion. Afterward, the hero-redeemer rides off into the proverbial sunset, presumably on to the next humanity-saving adventure.

Furthermore, narrative events entirely justify the hero's actions. Dramatic escalation makes viewers more and more upset and outraged at the evildoer's excessive hatred and victimizing of innocent characters. The course of the narrative makes clear that the use of violence is necessary, and indeed, is the *only* possible resolution to the story's problems. The supervillains must all be stopped; nothing less than the future of civilization is riding on their destruction. The same holds for James Bond, who encounters one megalomaniac after another, all bent on world domination. And let's not forget the shape-shifting Sumerian god, Gozer the Gozerian, who wants to destroy humanity and arrives in the form of the giant Stay Puft Marshmallow Man in *Ghostbusters*.

Apocalyptic or disaster films give another slant to the epic moment motif. The classic shootout is replaced with the hero facing off against some cataclysmic event endangering the future: an impending asteroid strike (*Armageddon*), a pandemic (*Contagion*), irreversible climate change (*The Day After Tomorrow*), a massive earthquake (*San Andreas*), or alien invasion (*War of the Worlds*). As you might expect, human ingenuity, bravery, and determination are enough to avert these potentially world-ending threats and save humanity from final destruction (perhaps with some magical assistance). The looming disaster serves to bring out the best in people: whatever differences existed previously seem petty now. Waywardness is overcome and new potentials realized, suggesting that harmony is possible among members of a community unified in the face of a much greater menace.

As a variation on the American monomyth, apocalyptic movies also secularize Jewish and Christian apocalyptic literature. Humans, and not God, are ultimately in control of human history and the future of the planet.[7] In contrast, Christian eschatology looks beyond history and time to the return of the Christ, a messianic figure who will triumph over evil and suffering and usher in "a new heaven and new earth" (Rev. 21:1). Rather than live faithfully and wait in anticipation of a new and perfected world to come, in apocalyptic films this world is periodically renewed via human agency. These movies can be understood as ritualistic, repeated metaphors pointing to an ongoing and optimistic movement toward final human power and perfectibility.

In one way or another, which is what makes the inevitable ending interesting, the action-adventure hero eliminates the imposing threat in a hair-raising, last-minute rescue. This decisive action "saves" or redeems the community, restoring its fortunes and ensuring the preservation of its values. In doing so, the movie provides audiences with cathartic pleasure. Spectators empathize with characters in distress who suffer under threats and violence, and they feel as much disdain and repulsion for the despicable antagonist. Consistent with the melodramatic outlook, there is nothing ambiguous about good and evil in this fictional world, which, as we've seen, is simplified and makes the moral status of every character definite.

Superpowered Gunslingers

On the frontier in the Old West, the gunslinger is a law unto himself. Cast in the same mold, action-adventure heroes exhibit an eccentric individuality; they are certain, self-reliant, and unattached, "that guy" we recognize as the Hollywood ideal. Action-adventure heroes variously display their independence in some measure of disregard for authority and official procedures that might interfere with their quest, resulting in clashes with employers or other higher-ups. At one time or another, they become introspective and express doubts about the life they've chosen, or that has been thrust upon them, and its effect on their souls. Wisecracking NYPD detective John McClane, for example, is pure of heart and immune to any corruption, but can't seem to make his marriage work and is always on the verge of losing his job. James Bond works for British Intelligence, Ethan Hunt for a fictional agency, IMF.

The amnesiac Jason Bourne was trained and began his career with Treadstone, a top-secret CIA black ops program. Others, like Batman and Spider-Man, operate in tandem with or outside official law-enforcement agencies.

Whether in an official capacity or not, the protagonists in action-adventure stories exist in the murky territory of vigilantism, which creates dramatic—and legal and ethical—complications. That they're doing much more than a local neighborhood watch committee by taking the law into their own hands casts suspicion on their activities and motivations. It's a motif probed seriously in the *Batman* movies directed by Tim Burton and Christopher Nolan. Aware of their ambiguous status, Batman and Spider-Man, for example, routinely do the heavy lifting and leave the evildoer bound and incapacitated for easy arrest by the police. That's more difficult when confrontations with the archvillain happen in broad daylight. Loki wants to rule the earth and enslave its population (*Marvel's The Avengers*, 2012). The Joker's mad destructive shenanigans imperil Gotham's citizenry (*The Dark Knight*, 2008). Zod vows to destroy the Earth and its inhabitants (*Man of Steel*, 2013). The Green Goblin terrorizes New Yorkers (*Spider-Man*, 2002). In the face of these supernatural-like threats, the public cowers in fear, while government institutions appear powerless, leaving only the superpowered to save civilization.

The resulting CGI-enhanced climactic battles leave Gotham, Metropolis, and Midtown Manhattan, respectively, in devastation (and taxpayers and elected officials none too happy about having to foot the bills for reparation). I have in mind especially the battles between Superman and Zod and between the Avengers and Loki's hoard of hostile extraterrestrials—those cybernetic serpentlike Leviathans(?) were awesome! The extraordinary powers of these crime fighters, combined with their extreme individualism, make them both admired and feared by bureaucrats and the public. Afterward, public anxiety is fueled by the realization that civilization needs the protection of superheroes who are, and must be, even more powerful and cunning than whatever supervillains might be on the horizon.

It's easy enough to see the superiority of action-adventure protagonists, especially the superpowered ones, who might well say of the community they vow to protect, "I'm not one of us." They are superhumans after all, partly human and partly divine, we might say. This motif is particularly pronounced in the *X-Men* series, in which difference is a main source of dramatic conflict. A troubling question apparently besets those characters bent on regulating superheroism: Who's to say these altruistic supersaviors will not become frustrated in dealing with bureaucratic guidelines and public anxiety, or simply go rogue, and set up their own authoritarian world order—just like the supervillains?

In the Marvel Cinematic Universe, SHIELD functions as a secret, high-tech, quasi-military agency under the vague jurisdiction of the United States government and the United Nations. The agency relies on its strong bond with Captain America, the Avengers, the Fantastic Four, and others, who are independent agents of sorts called upon to subdue threats. In *Captain America: Civil War* (2016), the superheroes are divided over the Sokovia Accords the United Nations is preparing to adopt—117 countries signed on. The clear intent of the agreement is to regulate activities of the superpowered by bringing them and their organizations under the auspices of a United Nations panel.

Techno wiz and entrepreneur Tony Stark/Iron Man thinks oversight is reasonable, even necessary, and supports the idea: "If we can't accept limitations, we're boundaryless, we're no better than the bad guys." Patriotic super-soldier Steve Rogers/Captain America refuses to sign the accord. The United Nations is "run by people with agendas and agendas change," he argues. "If we sign this, we surrender our right to choose. What if this panel sends us somewhere we don't think we should go? What if there's somewhere we need to go and they don't let us? We may not be perfect but the safest hands are still our own." Again, the conflict centers on a clash of values, ultimately resolved in favor of the power of the individual over that of the group, which makes these films recognizably American (frames 21a, 21b). A terrorist threat interrupts ratification of the accord, but the implications for what it means to be a superhero remain a central thread in the narrative.

Like other fictional "registration acts," the Sokovia Accords are designed to curb the autonomy of those possessing superpowers. As narrative events, these actions on the part of government officials highlight tensions existing in these fictional worlds: individual action versus communal responsibility, vigilantism versus institutions of law and law enforcement, and authoritarianism versus

Captain America: Civil War © 2016 MVL Film Finance, LLC

Frames 21a, 21b. Iron Man and Captain America are at odds in *Captain America: Civil War*, a film that centers dramatically on tensions between the individual and community and hints at misgivings about the basic altruism of superheroes.

democratic values. That they also suggest a measure of distrust in the basic altruism of these supersaviors—if we think about it in terms of the underlying melodramatic vision—in some sense signals doubts about the collective belief in innate goodness as sufficient to ensure "truth, justice, and the American way" (the mantra of Superman).

In the battle to maintain law and order, protect civilization, or ensure world peace, the action-adventure protagonist knows instinctively "what a man's gotta do" and relies on an internal moral compass. The hero or heroine's gut instincts (remember the doctrine of feeling?) always prove the wiser, making those representing institutions of government appear not nearly as sharp, even weak and incompetent or a step or two behind, hampered by laws and bureaucracy. Ironically, the story treats the community the hero saves and the democratic values it represents as themselves insufficient to the task; the institutions of law and government are usually portrayed as corrupt or in-effectual. Violent solutions supersede legal processes; the more powerful the weapon and the more spectacular the evildoer's destruction, the better.

Finally

Two crucial issues at the heart of the American action-adventure film merit further consideration. The first has to do with the use of violence, ever more extreme and boosted with CGI effects, to maintain world peace and the humanitarian values of civilization. The inevitable ending in action-adventure stories happens in accord with accepted moral and legal boundaries. That the hero always acts in self-defense, killing only as a means of justice and retribution, legitimizes the use of violence. But the contradiction remains, as does the ambiguity surrounding the action-adventurer, who is at home in both the civilized world and the world of violent evildoers. Herein lies the central paradox of the American action-adventure film and its hero: the use of violence as a necessary evil to preserve the greater good.

The second issue centers on the tension between the individual and community, widely recognized as a persistent theme in American movies and culture. Again, movies I'm calling action-adventure recycle and amp up the themes, formulas, and conventions of established American genres, especially the western. As they have evolved, these cinematic spectacles, predictable in story and characterization, have come to express a radical individualism infused with religious overtones. *New York Times* chief film critics A. O. Scott and Manohla Dargis took up this line of thinking in their dialogue about the state of movies that I referred to in chapter 7 (in the section "Your Business Is Politics, Mine Is Running a Saloon").

Now Scott is not a huge fan of Hollywood's superhero blockbusters. He found *Wonder Woman* (2017) to be a refreshing throwback of sorts to the early years of the genre and "the jaunty, truth-and-justice spirit of an even older Hollywood tradition." That is, "until the climax, which reverts, inevitably and disappointingly, to dreary, overblown action clichés." In his review of *Wonder Woman*, he derides superhero installments as "an endless sequence of apocalyptic merchandising opportunities."[8] It's not just their unashamed commercialism that bothers him, but the apparent lack of originality in the way they succumb ad nauseam to the worn conventions of the genre. Just as important, however, is "the glowering authoritarianism that now defines Hollywood's comic-book universe" that he observes of *Marvel's The Avengers* (2012)—a review, by the way, that ignited a firestorm of protest from Marvel fans and actor Samuel L. Jackson.[9]

How ironic that superhero movies, "the dominant genre of the 21st century," display an outlook that is "fundamentally anti-democratic," he asserts in the dialogue with Dargis. Without disagreeing, she points out that much of what Scott describes, "the individual hero, the anti-democratic spirit and the failed, at times corrupt government institutions—have given us some of the greatest American movies ever made." As it is, contemporary action-adventure movies, especially the superhero franchises, descend directly from traditional American genres that have long glorified individual action supremely over communal or institutional resolutions. They suggest in no uncertain terms that the salvation of America comes "from a messianic superhero, not democracy," as Dargis puts it.[10] Nor, I might add, from the Lord God Almighty.

MOVIE MUSING

A Biblical Blockbuster in the Making: *Noah* (2014)

> My best understanding of the Jewish tradition of midrash is that it is filling in a story with details from your imagination—staying true to the source where it says something, while imagining what's between the lines.
>
> —Alissa Wilkinson, *Christianity Today*

Press reports leave little doubt that *Noah,* a big-budget Hollywood epic drama, was conceived as a variation of sorts on the American monomyth. The film uses conventions of action-adventure films that put human agency front and center, and it employs the commercial imperatives of the Hollywood blockbuster, designed to attract the largest possible global audience.

With comic-book superheroes in a bit of a box-office rut, studio heads were apparently ready to take a gamble in the hope of starting a trend that might add some luster to their tentpole releases. "The demand for blockbusters is bigger than ever, but there are only so many comic books to mine for characters and stories, and you can't reboot the Spider-Man franchise or churn out Iron Man sequels forever," according to one reporter. "The Bible, meanwhile, has chapter after chapter and verse after verse of (to put it crassly) action-packed material—Moses, David, Job, Jesus, Revelation, and so on—plus a 'fanbase' that's even larger and more avid than Marvel Comics.'"[11] Talk about the commercialization of religion! And since the Bible is in the public domain, the studios don't have to haggle over licensing fees. Ka-ching!

Writer and director Darren Aronofsky pitched his concept to Paramount executives by calling attention to the fact that Noah's ark is "the only boat more famous than the Titanic."[12] A brief shot in Noah of the empty and abandoned ark on a ridge, broken in half, recalls the sunken Titanic resting on the ocean floor—an intertextual nod perhaps. Anyway, maybe studio heads thought they were green-lighting Titanic meets The Passion of the Christ.

Skepticism about a Hollywood-produced Bible epic embroiled Aronofsky's adaptation in controversy from the start. It was widely reported that the director referred to Noah as "the first environmentalist" and boasted that his screen adaptation was "the least biblical biblical film ever made."[13] With a production budget upwards of $125 million, nervous studio executives arranged test screenings with preselected audiences (Christian, Jewish, general moviegoers) that generated some "troublesome" reactions.[14]

To calm the tempest—and protect its investment—the studio agreed to include an explanatory note in future marketing materials: "While artistic license has been taken, we believe that this film is true to the essence, values, and integrity of a story that is a cornerstone of faith for millions of people worldwide." Added for good measure: "The biblical story of Noah can be found in the book of Genesis."[15] As this suggests, much of the hullabaloo had to do with frameworks of expectations and the fictive stance commentators took in balancing concerns about art and biblical correctness. Amid the storm, Paramount executive Rob Moore remained confident the film would be embraced by "the vast majority of the Christian community."[16]

Responses to the director's visionary film diminished Paramount's hopes that churchgoers would boost the film's box-office prospects. Turnout among North American Christians was disappointing; the film was banned in a number of Muslim countries as being anti-Islamic and in China purportedly for being too religious. Even so, Noah still earned $362 million worldwide, with over 70 percent of its theatrical revenues coming from foreign box-office income.

The American Noah: Neolithic Superhero

Film critics were quick to notice the way Bible stories were being repackaged with familiar figures cast in the mold of Hollywood superheroes—characters possessing divine-like qualities. *Son of God* launched what was being ballyhooed as Hollywood's "Year of the Bible" with a straightforward rendering of the Gospels and Jesus casually performing miracles "in a manner befitting a superhero,"[17] as *USA Today*'s Claudia Puig notes. And only a superhuman being could possibly endure the incredible torture that Roman soldiers inflict on Jesus in *The Passion of the Christ*. Bob Berney, who directed the marketing of *The Passion*, makes the connection transparent: "If you're doing big, epic effects films, you're going to run out of flying superheroes. These are superheroes of the ancient time."[18]

In comparison to the more literal approach of *Son of God*, *Noah* "has a lot more creativity to it," Paramount's Moore said. "And therefore, if you want to put it on the spectrum, it probably is more accurate to say this movie is inspired by the story of Noah." Still, he thought *Noah* reflects "the key themes of the Noah story in Genesis—of faith and hope and God's promise to mankind."[19]

"First and foremost, it's about entertainment," Aronofsky said. "My job is to make something entertaining and thrilling and exciting. What I always try to do is do something different, and I think this is very different from the normal blockbuster."[20] That includes smashing preconceived notions about Noah. Russell Crowe (*Gladiator* and *Master and Commander: The Far Side of the World*) was cast in the lead. The director told reporters, "You're going to see Russell Crowe as a superhero, a guy who has this incredibly difficult challenge put in front of him and has to overcome it."[21] Aronofsky's Noah emerges not from a phone booth or bat cave but from an antediluvian ark as a Neolithic superhero

Noah © 2014 Paramount Pictures Corporation / Regency Entertainment (USA), Inc.

Frame 22. In the Bible-based epic *Noah*, the central character resembles the American superhero who has to overcome an "incredibly difficult challenge."

every bit the classic action-adventurer. He's stoic, fearless, determined, adroit with the weaponry of the day, and skilled in hand-to-hand combat; faith serves as Noah's super-power (frame 22).

To broaden the film's appeal, while still making a movie for those "who take this very, very seriously as gospel," Aronofsky and cowriter Ari Handel created a "fantastical world a la Middle-earth that they wouldn't expect from their grandmother's Bible school."[22] That explains the inclusion of the Watchers (pulled from the book of Enoch), powerful earth-encrusted angels that look like Neolithic transformers fighting off the hordes when the rain comes. (Paramount's next-scheduled release, by the way, was *Transformers: Age of Extinction*.) And in a special-effects instant, geysers erupt and the skies unleash a torrent of rainfall for forty days and nights, submerging the earth in an apocalyptic deluge. Environmental destruction gives this big-budget, special-effects film an apocalyptic setting and contemporary relevance, while also highlighting a central biblical motif: human responsibility for the welfare of God's creation.

Noah is an inventive mix of American motifs, biblical themes, and current preoccupations that certainly shook up expectations. Matt Zoller Seitz, a critic at *RogerEbert.com*, for example, could only describe *Noah* as a "bizarre movie." It has the extravagant look we associate with a big-budget spectacle, but it's not "the latest Marvel Comics epic. Nor is it a standard-issue messianic sci-fi film along the lines of *Star Wars* or *The Matrix*." He concludes that *Noah* is really "more of a surrealist nightmare disaster picture fused to a parable of human greed and compassion, all based on the bestselling book of all time, the Bible, mainly the Book of Genesis."[23] I guess that about sums it up.

Back at the Ark

God's presence pervades the world of the film. In several sequences, we see a blend of images, sounds, and music meant to suggest God is communicating with Noah via dreams enhanced by hallucinogens. "Noah's visions of the flood and the ark, the gathering of the animals, the flood itself and the rainbow are all from God," Catholic critic Steven D. Greydanus observes. "God's existence is taken for granted by everyone, even the villain."[24] At the beginning, reverence to God pits the protagonist and antagonist against one another in an implicit clash of values over—get ready—the meaning of the *cultural mandate*! Remember, from chapter 2 (in the section "Your Mission, Should You Choose to Accept It")?

Several scenes refer to the account of creation, variously reiterating the divine command and core human purpose. It is written on Noah's heart; he recites the story in a ritualistic passing of the torch to future generations. "The Creator made Adam in His image, and placed the world in his care. That birthright was passed down to us," Noah tells his family. "This will be your work, and your responsibility. So, I say to you, be fruitful and multiply and replenish the earth." Noah understands the Creator's charge to have "dominion" in terms of creational caretaking. His archenemy, the wicked Tubal-Cain, who in the movie version killed Noah's father when he was a teenager, treats it as a license to exploit others and the creation. "The Creator does not care what happens in this world," Tubal-Cain declares. "Nobody has heard from Him since He marked Cain. We are alone. Orphaned children, cursed to struggle by the sweat of our brow to survive."[25]

According to coscreenwriter Ari Handel, "The story says that we all have goodness and wickedness in us, and it's up to us to pursue goodness and resist temptation."[26] If the characterizations in Noah are more complex than typical of Hollywood blockbusters, the dramatic conflict still plays out starkly with "good" characters having moments of waywardness. In other words, good and evil are still sharply demarcated for dramatic purposes.

It's an understatement to say that Noah takes original sin, including his own, with utter seriousness. Early on, however, one of the Watchers perceives "a glimmer of Adam" in Noah. More than a wistful allusion to pre-fall innocence, the insight will yield a payoff in the movie's climactic scenes. The stress Naameh (Jennifer Connelly) places on goodness, mercy, and forgiveness strikes a counterbalance to her husband's mounting pessimism. Noah remains steadfast in his belief, though, that he is chosen by God not because of his "goodness" but because he will complete the "task," which he tells his son is "much greater than our own desires."

While still taking the film on its own terms as an imaginative story of Noah and the great flood, we can gain insight nonetheless from how it departs from the original biblical source material. In the Genesis account, God establishes a covenant with Noah, his family, and the creatures that board the ark—a remnant to be preserved from the wrath of the flood. God instructs Noah, "Go into the ark, you and your whole family, because I have found you righteous in this generation" (Gen. 7:1). The Genesis flood typifies God's gracious provision for his people and the restoration of the creation: a cover-to-cover theme in Scripture. That Aronofsky's Noah, who has put the creation story to memory, does not understand this seems farfetched. "I'm guessing that Aronofsky's Noah is meant to be a tragically wrong-headed figure like Shakespeare's Lear or Melville's Ahab, but even insane pride must have a logic of its own, lest the hero come across as just plain stupid," Commonweal's Richard Alleva writes. "What kind of God would save a few humans temporarily only to have them promote their own extinction?"[27] It's not just a theological question but gets at the story's plausibility.

Noah believes and builds the ark, and his faith is confirmed spectacularly by the ensuing flood. But for some mysterious reason, he has determined that he and his family will perish "like everyone else." In other words, Noah believes that God intends to destroy humankind entirely, or as Time's Richard Corliss puts it, "Noah now accepts his and the world's mortality."[28] That motivation propels the narrative in the second half of act 2 toward the film's expected climactic epic moment—two climactic epic moments, actually. The narrative seems to be trying to serve dual masters: the action-adventure template and the biblical meaning of the flood, with the one fitting the other like an idiomatic square peg in a round hole.

Noah kills the stowaway Tubal-Cain in a fierce hand-to-hand battle on the ark, thereby avenging his father's death. Remember: everything gets resolved in a classical Hollywood film. Here we have epic moment number one. But that's not all. Recall that in apocalyptic movies the future of humankind rests in the hands of the main protagonist. Sure enough, at the decisive moment, the screenwriters bestow on Noah the power to determine the future of God's image bearers and creation: epic moment number two. And in this regard at least, it is an exaggeration to contend that this screen adaptation is "the least biblical biblical film ever made."[29] As it is, *Noah* falls in line with the traditional epic Bible drama. Hollywood adaptations have always turned Old Testament stories "about the covenant between God and the people of Israel into narratives about larger-than-life personalities whose actions change the course of history forever," religious scholar Adele Reinhartz explains. "To be sure, these personalities have their sources in Old Testament narrative, but the movies provide a much more intense focus on the individual, and, by implication, attribute primary and often more redemptive agency to them than do the biblical stories as such."[30]

Of course, there is never any doubt that Noah will do the right thing. But why? What is his motivation? And how might we understand his action?

Despite what the faithful ark builder believes the Creator demands of him, at the climactic moment Noah has "only love in his heart." So much for character ambiguity. And like every other American hero, in that moment of self-realization, Noah ultimately learns to trusts his intuition, those natural impulses key to the melodramatic outlook. He now knows instinctively "what a man's gotta do" and acts accordingly. Noah's statement at the decisive moment, that he has "only love in his heart," can perhaps be interpreted as a comment on both the divine and human nature. I suppose some theological hay can be made of this. From the vantage point I'm pursuing, however, it serves the purpose of drama more than theological reflection—though not exclusively. To be fair, the filmmakers had this to say.

In turning the four-page account in Genesis into over two hours of intense drama, Aronofsky and Handel came up with the idea of creating a character arc for God and transplanting it in Noah. "We were trying to dramatize the decision God must have made when he decided to destroy all of humanity," Aronofsky said in separate interviews. "He goes from a place of wanting justice—it's an angry God who is willing to destroy his creation even though it grieves him in his heart. And he gets of course to a place of mercy, to the first rainbow . . . and forgiveness and grace."[31] Is Noah to be likened to the Creator, then, who punishes sin and demonstrates his love and faithfulness by preserving a remnant of humanity? That may be what the scriptwriters implicitly had in mind. But there is no getting around the way this makes the Neolithic "superhero" Noah, and not God, redeemer of the cosmos. Now, as to the eternal, unchanging God having a character arc? I'll leave that to theologians.

Perhaps spectators are to think that Noah's self-realization results from learning a lesson though all this, a test like that of Abraham having to prepare to offer his son Isaac as a ritual sacrifice. Or maybe Noah has seen enough devastation and now refuses to complete what he believes is his "mission." Either way, and regardless of whether Noah rightly understands the Creator's intent, the effect of the scene is still to elicit viewer empathy for the tried and tormented hero whose individual autonomy and apparent goodness trump faith—that is, in this instance, what he *believes* God expects of him.

Finally

Let me remind you that considering the influence of the action-adventure mode and melodramatic outlook in the making of this biblical drama provides only one way of looking at this screen adaptation. Taking this slant does not preclude other viewpoints and interpretations. As it is, *Noah* had self-identified religious critics juggling concerns about artistic license and religious orthodoxy. Their differences of opinion on the merits of the movie became a story itself that added a level of discourse to the movie's reception that does not always occur. Writing in *Variety*, Justin Chang draws an important conclusion: "The invaluable lesson of *Noah* is that a sincere and authentic film about religious faith need not be strident, heavy-handed or unimaginative; nor must it cleave to the very letter of Scripture, timidly and reverently, in order to get at its deeper truths and insights."[32] Whether spectators find the movie brilliant or muddled storytelling, theologically provocative or insane, this cinematic representation of a familiar Bible story makes for a worthwhile conversation about film as popular art and theological speculation.

9

Stop Taking My Hand!

Gender and Mainstream Hollywood

> Women—long expected to internalize myths of exaggerated male
> potency as their own—finally have a symbolic universe that feels, if
> not entirely corrective, at least imaginatively in keeping with their
> own hopes, dreams and realities.
>
> —Ann Hornaday, review of *Wonder Woman* (2017)

Despite superhero fatigue in the summer of 2017, all the hype about *Wonder Woman* being the best superhero film since Christopher Nolan's *The
Dark Knight Rises* (2012), along with reports that box-office revenue for the
first superhero blockbuster directed by a woman (Patty Jenkins) was breaking
the "superhero glass ceiling," were enough to get me to the theater.[1] *Wonder
Woman* ended up outpacing its superhero rivals at the box office, taking in
$821 million worldwide.

As we've seen, the action-adventure universe is almost exclusively a male
domain. The traits that define these protagonists as heroic have been gendered
masculine, which complicates characterizations of action-adventure heroines.
Superpowered heroines have to be drawn according to cultural standards,
gender stereotypes, and genre requirements, while keeping in mind that it's
mostly adolescent males who drive the box office for action-adventure films.
With much more flair, *Los Angeles Times* critic Justin Chang captures these
dynamics in his description of the central character in *Wonder Woman*:

"Equally inspired by the women's suffrage movement, the pacifist movement and the pin-up movement, Wonder Woman herself has always been a welter of contradictions—sculpted from clay and filled with the breath of Zeus, perhaps, but no less profoundly shaped by market imperatives and feminist influences."[2]

Diana (Gal Gadot), princess of the Amazons and daughter of Queen Hippolyta and Zeus, has given her life to training to become an invincible warrior. She rescues an American pilot, Captain Steve Trevor (Chris Pine), when his plane crashes off the Themyscira coast. The remote island is invaded by Germans in pursuit of Trevor. After learning that the outside world is consumed in a global conflict, World War I, and coming to believe that Ares, the Greek god of war, is responsible, Diana sets out with Trevor determined to destroy Ares. If her gradual discovery of the human capacity for cruelty and evil makes her appear rather naive, it lends the character an "innocence," Chang points out, that "ultimately feels like a tonic, a bracing relief from the brooding psychological torment that has come to pass for character depth in the male-dominated superhero universe."[3]

What makes *Wonder Woman* an even more intriguing phenomenon are accounts of women being unexpectedly brought to tears during fight scenes, especially a scene at the battlefront in France. Frustrated with being told "no" by powerful men at each step along the way, with supreme confidence Diana bravely climbs a ladder out of the trenches and storms into "no man's land." Deflecting bullets with her shield and arm bracelets, she inspires and leads the dispirited British troops to a victory over the Germans, saving a nearby village. This scene encapsulates the movie's key themes. "It's compassion, determination, inspiration, and love rolled into one moment: Diana is taking

Frame 23. *Wonder Woman* has been perceived as a metaphor for female empowerment.

Wonder Woman © 2017 Warner Bros. Entertainment, Inc. / Ratpac-Dune Entertainment, LLC

fire and protecting those who can't protect themselves," *Vox* critic Alex Abad-Santos maintains. "And she's doing it with a small smirk that sharpens on her lips, as if she knows she's got this."[4]

Wonder Woman has been taken as a metaphor for female empowerment (frame 23). "It was tremendous," commentator Meredith Woerner writes. "The world had embraced characters like Captain America and Superman who are compelled by their sense of duty, honor and morality," she explains. "It took 75 years to make a movie about a female superhero motivated purely by love."[5]

The chemistry between actors Gadot and Pine lends the story's gendered scheme additional complication. Gadot displays a "mix of curiosity, sincerity, badassery, and compassion that has undergirded Wonder Woman since the beginning," a critic at *RogerEbert.com* observes. "Pine matches her hopefulness with a world weariness and sharp sense of humor" and brings "an emotional complexity to a character most aptly described as a dude-in-distress."[6]

Diana believes that ridding the world of evil is her sacred destiny, which is "essentially the core of every superhero movie in recent memory," as Abad-Santos notes. "Bit by bit, *Wonder Woman* pecks away Diana's and our general superhero fantasy." It does this by showing the cost of war "to people whose bodies aren't invulnerable," and more importantly, "plays with the idea of there being indomitable joy in seeing our heroes exert their power, by also questioning the strange trust we put in those heroes and the way we dehumanize our villains."[7] All the more disappointing for critics, then, was the way the movie ends by reverting to the tried, overblown spectacle fight scene.

All this, and especially the gender-laden discourse surrounding *Wonder Woman*, provides a useful transition from the previous chapter on action-adventure movies to one on gender types in the Hollywood cinema. Remember that we navigate within and by way of existing cultural conceptions, as exploration of gender and sexual identity takes place largely within traditional categories. As we've seen, the melodramatic outlook tends to oversimplify. As a result, it has created stock characters based on traditional gender ideals and expectations. Let's consider four gendered categories that are staples in the mainstream Hollywood cinema.

Gendered Cultural Patterns

Routine Hollywood films represent a polarized view of men and women that is riddled with contradictions. Film scholar Robin Wood gives us a perceptive overview. He describes the *ideal man* in American movies as a virile, strong, unrestrained, and unattached man of action and adventure. His *shadow*, or opposite, is the "settled husband/father, dependable but dull."[8] These images associate masculinity with emotional restraint, dominance, aggression, and the capacity for violence: globe-trotting adventurers like photographer L. B. Jefferies (*Rear Window*) or archeologist Indiana Jones, international spies like James Bond or Jason Bourne (and the parodic Austin Powers). They're simply not the marrying type. "This job of yours—it's murder on relationships," a dispirited Paris tells Bond in *Tomorrow Never Dies* (1997). And if they do marry, they don't make good husbands, the relationship doesn't last, or their work is a threat to loved ones, as in the case of John McClane in the *Die Hard* films or Ethan Hunt in the *Mission: Impossible* series. Independence marks the ideal man; love, marriage, and family represent the end of freedom and complicate the hero's calling and encounter with the forces of evil.

The *ideal woman* is to some extent the opposite of her male counterpart; a "wife and mother, mainstay of hearth and home," who stands in contrast to her *shadow*, the woman who is "erotic . . . fascinating but dangerous."[9] Hollywood often depicts women as needing a man for complete happiness. In that sense, their role, as we saw in *Rear Window*, is to be the domesticator of rugged adventurers who tend to be unrestrained in love and life. The male protagonist is typically active, while the female one may be spirited but is ultimately submissive, largely taking part in the man's adventures—think Pepper Potts in the *Iron Man* series, for example, or any of the women in Bond films. However talented and beautiful, the female protagonist's identity largely depends on a man. Let's see how this gendered framework plays itself out in the mainstream Hollywood cinema.

The Christmas favorite *It's a Wonderful Life* (1946) is a classic affirmation of the dominant view. The story centers on contrasting worldly success, individualism, and adventure with an ordinary life, community, and domesticity in the character of George Bailey (James Stewart). Mary (Donna Reed) plays the ideal woman who plots with George's mother to get him to marry her; the sultry and seductive Violet (Gloria Grahame) fulfills the role of her shadow. These gendered conceptions persist in time-honored movies like *Casablanca* and *Rear Window*, the action-adventure films mentioned in the previous chapter, and in Disney animated features from *Snow White and the Seven Dwarfs* (1937) to *Tangled* (2010) to infinity and beyond. The incredibly popular *Frozen* (2013) provides an exception of sorts in that it "shakes up the hyper-romantic 'princess' formula," film critic Stephen Holden notes. "As always, love is the solution to everything. When nothing can thaw the icy heart of the frightened Elsa, love does the trick, but in this case it is sisterly loyalty and devotion rather than romantic attachment."[10]

Contemporary films don't always adhere simply to the four gendered types that Robin Wood has identified. But awareness of them lets us see more clearly the ways story lines and characterizations affirm, clash with, or run against the grain of the traditional system. As one quick example, a *Christianity Today* critic describes Rey (Daisy Ridley) in *Star Wars: The Force Awakens* as "strong and sensitive and confident and caring" and "really good at fixing things." He points out, "She is the antithesis of what've come to be called Strong Female Characters, who make up for Damsel In Distress stereotypes by doing a 180-degree turn and just aping the qualities we admire in male characters."[11] When Finn (John Boyega) keeps grabbing her hand while they run from storm troopers, Rey literally fights off the stereotype, yelling, "Stop taking my hand!" This reviewer assumes a common cultural understanding: that readers are familiar enough with these gender types to appreciate his description of Rey as something different and refreshingly so.

By reworking these cultural patterns, writer and director Nancy Meyer questions their viability in *It's Complicated* (2009), an enjoyable romantic comedy about middle-aged couples. The movie stars Meryl Streep as Jane, a devoted mother of three, baker, and owner of a successful restaurant. Married for nineteen years and then divorced for ten, Jane finds herself unexpectedly entangled with her ex-husband and attorney, Jake (Alec Baldwin), who left her and remarried a much younger woman. While in New York at their son's college graduation, their relationship is rekindled.

Take notice how the following dialogue conversation can be read in terms of Wood's categories: "You had drunken sex with a married man in New York when you went back for Luke's graduation?" Jane's friend Trisha asks, astonished. "Turns out I'm a bit of a slut," Jane says with a smug smile. When she tells her girlfriends it's Jake, "Agness Adler's husband," they scream in delight. "That. Is. Genius," Trisha says, justifying the affair as an act of revenge. "Well, it's also sort of wrong," friend Joanne adds. "This is the most out of control thing I've ever done. Literally," Jane says. They try to rationalize it. "He was yours first," Joanne notes. But when Trisha says, "You can do better than Jake," Jane is a bit offended. "I mean you've outgrown him," Trisha clarifies. "Just please, don't let him talk you into saving him." No way, Jane insists, adding, "But girls, what about the fact that I'm now the other woman? I'm the one we hate." Doesn't matter. Jake's current wife remains "the one we hate," Trisha says.

Jake is unrestrained, aggressive, and emotionally clueless. "I have figured it out," Jane tells him. "I no longer feel alone or divorced. I just feel normal. You know how long it took me, to get that balance back?" Jake answers simply, "No." Still, the illicit affair is tantalizing, and the warm feelings of reawakened love confusing, which throws middle-aged Jane's self-perception for a loop. But being out of her comfort zone, as she comes to realize, "if you're honest with yourself, isn't all that comforting." Things get even more complicated when this talented baker, family provider, and now the "other" woman starts to fall for Adam (Steve Martin), a recently divorced architect she hires to design and remodel her kitchen.

If Jake represents the ideal male in Wood's scheme, the gentle and reserved Adam is his complete opposite (shadow). He's struggling to get over the pain of his wife leaving him for his best friend. Fearful of becoming emotionally vulnerable again, Adam is reluctant to start a new relationship. While driving, he listens to a self-help audiobook offering "a few basic rules" on dealing with a divorce: The most important is learning to forgive. Discovering he's part of a love triangle, Adam admits—with characteristic light humor—at first, "You know I'm not as macho as I appear. And I think it's best for us not to get any more involved because your relationship with Jake isn't really done, and I know you're saying it is, but he's in love with you and for everyone's sake, that should probably get resolved." Jane is overwhelmed by his insight, honesty, and expressiveness, which is not something she's accustomed to with Jake. She can only reply, "Wow. So that's how grown-ups talk." It is a heartfelt response and moment of self-realization that draws our attention to how much the gender types we're talking about here shape this story and characterizations, and not without an implied critique. In the end, Jake drives off into the sunset in his Porsche, alone, while Jane and Adam walk into her house laughing together about her chocolate croissants as her home remodeling project begins.

Welcome, and Happy Hunger Games!

The four-part gender scheme helps illuminate the cultural landscape of *The Hunger Games* (2012), which can be read as running against the grain of these familiar gender stereotypes. The Capitol's absolute power looms large in this fictional world, a chaotic dystopia showcasing the brutality of human nature. The Games themselves symbolize the struggle to survive in a repressive regime that plagues the characters populating Panem. The story's focus on Katniss Everdeen, a young woman in a do-or-die competition with her peers, inter-weaves elements of both war and romance—traditionally gendered genres.

The resolute heroine does not represent a simple gender reversal. That is, Katniss does not merely take on masculine qualities to survive in the arena. She is drawn instead as a complex and intriguing blend of gendered characteristics that together prove essential to accomplishing her goals. This process of discovery weaves through Katniss's character arc, informing her actions and her internal processing of events and shaping the course of the narrative (frame 24).

The Hunger Games © 2012 Lions Gate Films, Inc.

Frame 24. That Katniss transcends gender stereotypes is key to her character arc and the narrative in *The Hunger Games.*

Once becoming aware of the gender types, it's easy to see Gale Haw-thorne (Liam Hemsworth) and Peeta Mellark (Josh Hutcherson) as fitting the two male categories. Gale, Katniss's hunky best friend, hunting part-ner, and apparent love interest, is the ideal man. The "shadow" is Peeta, who is nothing if not "dependable but dull," and becomes Katniss's fellow District 12 tribute. Under the circumstances they each find themselves in, however, Peeta becomes more complicated throughout the series, blending traits from the two male categories, while Gale's course fulfills expectations for an action-adventurer. The way the series finally resolves the love triangle affirms this view.

Actress Jennifer Lawrence is perfectly cast, able to bring Katniss to life on screen by "combining formidable strength of will with convincing vulner-ability," as *Los Angeles Times* critic Kenneth Turan notes.[12] Transcending gender stereotypes is key to understanding Katniss's character arc. And the way the person changes over the course of the narrative inextricably involves the character's internal processing of external events based on three basic questions: What does the character want? Why does the character want it? What does the character need?[13] This line of analysis provides another way of getting at the connection between a story's explicit and implicit meanings.

Katniss *wants* to survive the Hunger Games. *Why?* Self-preservation ob-viously, which has been the mode of her existence growing up in Panem's poorest district. The way Katniss has dealt with her life circumstances proves to be both a strength and an impediment for her in the arena. She's doggedly self-reliant, knows how to manage hunger, and is an ace archer—a skill she's acquired by hunting illegally. And after years of watching the televised Games, she's able to anticipate—and exploit to her benefit—what the Gamemakers are likely to do to keep viewers tuned in: develop personal story lines, maintain story continuity, and enhance the competition's entertainment value.

It's evident that Katniss is also motivated by a strong paternal sense of duty. When her mother is left completely devastated by her husband's death, Katniss fills the void. At the Reaping, when first-timer Primrose's name is drawn against all odds, the determined guardian selflessly volunteers to take her sister's place. "You can't tune out again," Katniss tells her mother afterward. "No, you can't. Not like when Dad died. I won't be there anymore, and you're all she has. No matter what you feel, you have to be there for her. Do you understand? Don't cry." All this suggests that her display of typically masculine traits at least partly results from Katniss's having to assume her father's role as a strong provider for the family. Life's eventualities shake Katniss out of any preconceived gender roles and set her on a new and unexpected hero's journey, one partly thrust upon her, partly chosen.

A dramatic montage sequence that occurs while Katniss is in the arena visualizes her internal thoughts and feelings in such a way as to provide background exposition and link family dynamics to her motivation. Subjective shots showing Katniss feeling the effects as she succumbs to the hallucinogenic tracker-jacker poison are edited together with others serving as a flashback that reveals her father was killed in a coal-mine explosion. Images of the fireplace in their home—her father's picture on the mantle—exploding expresses the devastating impact his death has on the Everdeen family.

When she finally awakes from the tracker-jacker-induced nightmare, Katniss discovers that Rue (Amandla Stenberg), a District 11 tribute, has camouflaged and watched over her. They forge an alliance, which is an external event signifying Katniss's internal character development. With the survival skills she's acquired, Katniss's engendered poverty has fostered deep feelings of isolation, anger, and resentment. Her indifference toward and distrust of others are impediments to be overcome by learning to trust and realize the value of selflessness and kindness, which she does through her alliances with Rue and then Peeta.

At first Katniss seems detached from others; the only people in her life are Gale, her mother, and her sister, Prim. And even these relationships seem out of sorts with Katniss in the traditional role of the dominant male. In Katniss's perception, hers and her family's survival depends on her being able to exhibit traits coded "masculine"—that is, self-reliance, toughness, and coldness. When asked about getting sponsors, Katniss admits to Cinna, "I'm not very good at making friends."

Her stoicism comes just as much, however, from a sense of futility in the face of the Capitol's abject authoritarianism. "What if everyone just stopped watching?" Gale asks Katniss. "What if they did? What if *we* did?" Katniss is dismissive, "Won't happen." But he persists. "No one watches and they don't have a game. It's as simple as that." The conversation marks the heroine's resignation, but also gives an early indication of a budding political dissent that grows more evident in actions leading up to the film's climax. Repeated references to her as "the Girl on Fire" aptly symbolize her passion. It's a catchphrase with a touch of irony since the Capitol's Caesar Flickerman invented it as a way of promoting the Games. In the films that follow, Katniss's defiance and hunger for freedom and justice eventually blossom into a zealous revolt against tyranny.

And May the Odds Be Ever in Your Favor

What Katniss *needs* is to overcome her indifference and resignation in order to become a complete woman. This entails acquiring both an emotional self-awareness and a political consciousness for her to eventually lead a revolt against Panem's system of deep social, political, and economic injustice.

In preparation for the Games at the Capitol, Katniss starts out determined not to appear "weak"—that is, feminine—but to project instead a masculine image of strength, aggression, and fearlessness. In the scene of her last training session, she needs to impress the Gamemakers with her archery skills; a high-performance score is critical to getting sponsors and their gifts while in the arena. Seeing the Gamemakers helping themselves to food at a banquet table instead of watching her, the District 12 tribute makes a daring move. She fires an arrow at the Gamemakers, spearing the apple in a roasted pig's mouth in the center of the table and pinning it to the wall behind them. It's a bold display of courage and defiance that earns her the top mark going into the arena.

Peeta complicates Katniss's quest to emerge victorious from the arena and her own emotional limitation. "I have no chance of winning! None! All right? It's true. Everybody knows it," Peeta admits to Katniss and others. "You know what my mother said? She said, 'District 12 might finally have a winner.' But she wasn't talking about me. She was talking about you." A subjective flashback inserted here shows the only meaningful interaction Katniss and Peeta had prior to their selection as tributes. We see Peeta come out of the family bakery holding two half-burnt loaves of bread, his mother shouting, pushing, and hitting him before going back inside. Peeta breaks one loaf and throws the halves into the pig pen when he sees Katniss, half-starved, sitting in the pouring rain. Their eyes meet. He looks over his shoulder to be sure his mother's not watching and then throws the other loaf in the direction of Katniss. It's an act of kindness she clearly has not forgotten, and the memory runs against her stoicism.

Peeta, it turns out, far surpasses Katniss in playing to potential sponsors. He takes her hand, raising them together as a brilliant sign of solidarity during the tribute's parade. While Katniss is nervous and apprehensive during her interview with Caesar Flickerman on the eve of the Games, Peeta is charming and personable. When asked about having a girlfriend back in District 12, Peeta admits there's a girl he's "had a crush on forever, but I don't think she actually recognized me until the Reaping." Winning the Games won't matter, he explains, "Because she came here with me." Is this confession to having been secretly in love with Katniss genuine, or a survival strategy? Regardless, Katniss is furious. "What the hell was that?" she yells at him afterward. "You don't talk to me and then you say you have a crush on me? You say you want to train alone? Is this how you want to play?" Haymitch (Woody Harrelson), their mentor and a former District 12 survivor of the Games, however, sees an opportunity. "He made me look weak," Katniss insists, to which Haymitch replies, "He made you look desirable, which in your case can't hurt, sweetheart."

Pitching the District 12 tributes as "star-crossed lovers" furnishes a way to get wealthy Capitol sponsors to provide supplies while they are in the arena. The need to feign a romantic interest in Peeta, however, clouds their relationship, with Katniss having to sort out her true feelings. After that, Peeta's sincere late-night soul searching inspires Katniss with a payoff to come in the film's climax. "I just keep wishing that I could think of a way to show them that they don't own me," he says.

When the Gamemakers revoke an earlier rule change allowing two victors from the same district, Katniss comes up with the idea of them both taking Nightlock, poisonous berries. "Trust me," she says, betting the Gamemakers will not let them ruin the show with a double suicide. "Together?" Peeta asks. "Together," she replies. To her adroit combat skills, smarts, and decisiveness, the heroine has learned to add empathy, trust, and kindness—traits associated with Rue and Peeta. It harkens back to Peeta's earlier act of kindness to Katniss back in District 12 as well as to his wish for "a way to show them that they don't own me." Their decisive action contains more than a hint of rebellion. With its suggestiveness of human bonding and community, the District 12 tributes ultimately give expression to the binding ideals of unity and collaboration—the very values the Capitol seeks to squash in containing future rebellion. Haymitch understands that.

Back in the Capitol, Haymitch lets Katniss know that having "showed them up" does not play well with government officials, which sets up the ensuing drama in the sequels to follow. A bookending interview with Caesar Flickerman completes a pattern with Katniss saying that she and Peeta "saved each other." The audience gives a collective "aah," and as if officiating at a wedding, Flickerman says, "Ladies and gentlemen, the star-crossed lovers from District 12," pronouncing them, "this year's victors of the 74th Annual Hunger Games."

Finally

Katniss Everdeen evolves from a stoic, self-reliant, and indifferent individual to a more full-orbed, emotional human being. With the perfection of a Greek goddess, in mind, body, and spirit, Katniss emerges as an ideal combination of traits and motivations that are themselves culturally conceived as either masculine or feminine. The way she comes to embody gender-mixed traits challenges the viability of underlying cultural assumptions. Her bold independence, self-sufficiency, competitiveness, emotional restraint, and capacity for violence are traits traditionally identified as "masculine." These are balanced with others typically labeled "feminine," such as caring, compassion, vulnerability, and intuitive ways of thinking.[14] This characterization also adds a layer of meaning to themes in the film series centering on personal and social revolution—for example, equality, appearance versus reality, the individual and community. Katniss's character arc progresses strikingly like that of Rick Blaine in *Casablanca*, who as we saw earlier moves from being self-centered and an isolationist to becoming selfless, politically committed, and engaged. This similarity, of course, associates her in some sense with a long line of heroic American protagonists, but in a most inventive way.

MOVIE MUSING

There's No Magic in Boxing:
Million Dollar Baby (2004)

Frankie likes to say that boxing is an unnatural act, that everything in boxing is backwards.

—Eddie "Scrap-Iron" Dupris, *Million Dollar Baby*

Million Dollar Baby won four Academy Awards, including Best Picture. It's a story about an aging boxing manager, Frankie Dunn (Clint Eastwood), who reluctantly agrees to train Maggie Fitzgerald (Hilary Swank), a scrappy, spirited hillbilly girl from southwest Missouri. Frankie has a mysterious past. We know he's overly cautious and loses his best prospect by waiting too long to get him a championship fight. He's also alienated from his daughter for some unknown reason; he keeps a box of letters that were returned unopened.

Frankie's partner, Eddie "Scrap-Iron" Dupris (Morgan Freeman), narrates the film. Frankie was Eddie's manager back in the day before his boxing career was cut short by a blow that cost him his sight in one eye. Writing in *Christianity Today*, Jeffrey Overstreet describes Freeman's voice-over as a "Greek chorus with a sense of humor as dry as a leather punching bag."[15] Scrap tells this tale displaying a worldly wisdom that lends insight into the other characters' thoughts and feelings. Not until the very end do we discover that Scrap's third-person narration is actually a letter he is writing to Frankie's estranged daughter: "I thought you should know what kind of man your father really was."

For Maggie, boxing is "the only thing I ever felt good doing." She is a natural fighter, ready and determined to become a champion and escape a life waiting tables that began when she was thirteen. Otherwise, she tells Frankie, "I might as well go back home and buy a used trailer and get a deep fryer and some Oreos." Maggie, Scrap's voice-over informs us, "grew up knowing one thing. She was trash." She also believes that boxing offers "her one shot at a life better than the lives of her welfare-grubbing trailer trash mother and siblings," *Variety*'s Todd McCarthy observes.[16] She and Frankie develop a professional relationship that also fulfills the other's familial need. Maggie says, "I've got nobody but you, Frankie." He replies with a slight warm smile, "Well, you've got me."

Million Dollar Baby starts out as a typical American underdog story set in Los Angeles, the city of dreams. The narrative is propelled by an individual fighting to make something of herself and achieve a deep desire. "If there's magic in boxing," Scrap says in a voice-over, "it's the magic of risking everything for a dream that nobody sees but you." Not until the movie's midpoint do we discover this is not a conventional genre film, but "a movie about a boxer," as Roger Ebert puts it, a story that takes us "into the deepest secrets of life and death."[17]

We see this divergence expressed in the unusual cinematography. In the boxing matches, the arena is brightly lit, with a flat, uniform pattern called high-key lighting. There is very little contrast between darks and lights. Most of the movie, however, and especially the most intimate scenes, is filmed using a low-key lighting scheme that makes dramatic use of sharp contrasts between light and dark. Large areas of blackness appear sharply separated from illuminated spaces. Characters appear as fleeting shadows, moving in and out of darkness; sometimes we can't see them, or see them partly, even while they're speaking. They are here (temporarily?), then gone. The lighting scheme evokes a sense of transience (frame 25).

In one scene, for example, after a troubling visit with her family, Maggie and Frankie are driving at night. "Instead of using the usual 'dashboard lights' that mysteriously seem to illuminate the whole front seat," Ebert describes how precisely cinematographer Tom Stern "has their faces slide in and out of shadow, how sometimes we can't see them at all, only hear them. Watch how the rhythm of this lighting matches the tone and pacing of the words, as if the visuals are caressing the conversation."[18] The scene ends with a fade to black that A. O. Scott describes as "a subtle, simple and chilling harbinger of the greater darkness to come."[19]

The cinematography adds a layer of meaning to the movie's themes. Life is precarious, and human existence is temporary. It suggests, moreover, that characters inhabit a

Million Dollar Baby © 2004 Warner Bros. Entertainment, Inc.

Frame 25. The cinematography in *Million Dollar Baby* evokes a sense of transience.

morally ambiguous world. Good deeds, hard work, and effort are not inevitably rewarded. Success is fleeting. The cinematographer "establishes a relationship between metaphorical light and darkness," as critic Katherine Frumin notices, "producing an atmosphere where good and evil are in conflict."[20]

The training montage in *Million Dollar Baby*, a staple of the genre, echoes many of the same shots as the one in *Rocky*, for example, but with a different slant that gives the sequence another meaning. Maggie improves slowly, even cautiously. Her development being so tenuous, we wonder how far she might be able to go with her abilities; final victory is not certain. Instead of *Rocky*'s heart-pumping music, this sequence is held together with gentle guitar and Scrap's unassuming voice-over: "Frankie likes to say that boxing is an unnatural act, that everything in boxing is backwards." The sequence ends with Maggie asking Frankie, "You think I'm ready for a fight, boss?" Frankie just keeps walking away. It's nothing like the parallel scene in *Rocky* that ends with the Italian Stallion at the Philadelphia Art Museum, his arms raised triumphantly and the film's theme song blasting on the soundtrack. In contrast, the understated, haunting musical score matches the tone of Morgan Freeman's voice-over throughout the film.

Frankie eventually does schedule a fight. Maggie wins it, and those that follow—decisively, most with first-round knockouts. The two establish a father-daughter bond. Frankie gives her a Gaelic nickname that means "my darling, my blood."

With Frankie's help, Maggie gets her shot in a title fight against a German boxer, Billie "the Blue Bear," who has a reputation for being a dirty fighter. Maggie starts to dominate her opponent; it looks like Frankie's timing of the title fight was perfect. Maggie's talent and hard work are about to pay off, as she's on the verge of reaching her goal. Then, after a round ends, Billie throws an illegal sucker punch from behind Maggie, knocking her out. She falls, landing hard on the corner stool and breaking her neck. We see her lying on the canvas in an extreme long shot from above, sometimes called a "God shot," then cut to a subjective shot from Maggie's point of view. Frankie and medical staff appear in a tight-framed close-up gathered around and over her. Then the lights above start swirling around, unrealistically, but becoming a visual metaphor as if her life is spiraling out of control, before we fade to black.

We fade in with the camera closing in on Maggie in a hospital bed on a ventilator. The injury has left her a quadriplegic. The film connects a series of scenes at a hospital and then a rehabilitation center by using mostly dissolves and fades to black. The style of editing dramatically slows the pace of the film while also signifying that a long, difficult period of time has passed. Maggie's body begins to deteriorate until a leg infected with gangrene has to be amputated. Finally, she implores Frankie to help her die. And eventually he does, but not without some painful soul searching.

The pacing and uncharacteristic style of *Million Dollar Baby* prepare viewers for an unexpected turn of events. But the narrative makes it look like we're watching a straight-forward boxer melodrama—right up to the moment of her disabling injury. Now it suddenly feels like an altogether different story. Or is it?

Always Protect Yourself

One way to understand *Million Dollar Baby* is to look at how it uses the conventions of the boxer film to cast doubt on human autonomy. This film speaks as much about self-determination as typical boxer movies, like *Rocky*, but might well be interpreted as offering a glimpse into what the world looks like when faith in self-reliance fails. The effect is to turn the melodramatic world upside down. If Frankie and Maggie appear to be basically good and well intentioned, their actions do not produce the expected moral legibility. Frankie reluctantly does "what a man's gotta do," but his decisive action is fraught with inner turmoil and leaves him even more isolated and alone—the dark side of the classic American hero's fate. The fictional universe of this film is indeed a lonely place. Characters can only rely on their own resources with a little help from friends—if they can find and keep them.

From the start, Frankie insists that the most important rule is "to protect yourself at all times. Now, what is the rule?" Maggie repeats it: "Protect myself at all times." After the title fight, however, while lying in the hospital bed, a distraught Maggie tells Scrap: "I shouldn't have dropped my hand. I shouldn't have turned. Always protect myself. How many times did he tell me that?" Maggie blames no one. She takes complete responsibility for what happened and wants to remain in control of her fate. Maggie, Frankie, and Scrap believe deeply in themselves as the only bulwark against whatever circumstances life presents. Maggie's injury strikes an inverse of the classic melodramatic situation—the chance event. Whether it's fate, luck, or the mysterious will of God remains open to interpretation. Her unfortunate accident, resulting from a dastardly deed and an inexperienced cornerman putting the stool out too soon, suggests a world indifferent to the talented and hard-working heroine: terrible things can happen to good people.

Frankie remains committed to Maggie. He researches breath-activated wheelchairs and college programs, charting one future, but the way Maggie sees it, she'll be "frozen like this the rest of my life." For whatever reason, she has no interest in finding a new dream to replace the one she's lost. Some critics found this to be entirely consistent, and others, completely out of character. "Maggie has exhibited far too much courage and tenacity throughout the film for us to buy the fact that she's giving up now," a *Plugged In* reviewer maintains.[21] Ebert sees it differently: "I believe the character Maggie is such a fighter that she could learn to deal with her disability and enjoy her life. But here is the important point: She doesn't believe that."[22] Paralysis ends Maggie's short-lived dream. "I got what I needed. I got it all," she pleads with Frankie. "Don't let 'em keep taking it away from me. Don't let me lie here till I can't hear those people chanting no more." A limited horizon encloses her—at least as she envisions it. No longer able to box, which is all she "ever felt good doing," Maggie can find no reason to carry on in life.

We don't know anything about what Maggie believes about God other than her telling Frankie that, according to him, she'll be thirty-seven "before I can even throw a decent punch, which I have to admit, after working on this speed bag for a month getting nowhere, may be God's simple truth."

Frankie is a different story. Frankie trains boxers; his own life has been one long bout with God. His priest, Father Horvak (Brían F. O'Byrne), is weary and even irritated by Frankie's persistent and seemingly pointless theological questions about the Trinity and Immaculate Conception. He knows they serve as a distraction and "that what Frankie really needs is not catechism classes, but to make peace with God," as Catholic critic Steven Greydanus points out.[23] For twenty-three years, Frankie's rarely missed attending daily mass. Horvak says pointedly, "The only person comes to church that much is the kind who can't forgive himself for something."

Frankie believes in God, even as he's battling his own demons over an estranged daughter. The reasons remain unknown, but his past weighs heavily on him now as he contemplates his dilemma. "I swear to God, Father, it's committing a sin by doing it. By keeping her alive, I'm killing her. Do you know what I mean? How do I get around that?" Father Horvak advises him to "step aside, Frankie. You leave her with God." Not satisfied, he replies, "She's not looking for God's help. She's asking for mine." Is Frankie willing to play God? "Whatever sins you're carrying, they're nothing compared to this," the priest warns. "Forget about God or Heaven and Hell. If you do this thing, you'll be lost, somewhere so deep, you'll never find yourself." Frankie looks as if he has no doubt it's true. His struggle concerns this life as much as it does eternity.

The conversations between Frankie and Father Horvak linger in the background and refuse to go away. That Frankie is filled with doubts, regrets, skepticism, and confusion about God's presence in human affairs makes his decision all the harder and consequential. He realizes he is risking his eternal salvation. Film critic Peter Chattaway suggests that abandonment, an experience that marks the lives of the central characters, is a key theme, with Frankie finally feeling forsaken by God.[24]

The story's events lead to a personal crisis that results in a deeply emotional and spiritual loss. Whether or not viewers are sympathetic with his character or agree with his actions, there seems little doubt that he makes his decisions knowing full well that he is accountable to God. But on what basis does he finally decide? Faith in God or in self? What values ultimately drive his actions? These questions linger long after we leave the world of *Million Dollar Baby*.

Multiple Interpretations

It's not surprising that *Million Dollar Baby* was embroiled in controversy over its ending. The debate sparked conflicting concerns about free expression, representation, and the public good. Some disability activists organized demonstrations, and advocacy groups released statements criticizing the film as "thinly disguised propaganda for euthanasia."[25] The executive director of the National Spinal Cord Injury Association stated that Eastwood was using "the power of fame and film to perpetuate his views that the lives of people with disabilities are not worth living."[26] There were accusations that Eastwood was biased against people with disabilities after his highly publicized battle in a lawsuit over accessibility at his Carmel resort.

In response to the criticism, Eastwood emphasized the film's open point of view. The movie itself does not lend its approval to the characters' final actions but allows viewers to decide for themselves. "The film is supposed to make you think about the precariousness of life and how we handle it," he said. "How the character handles it is certainly different than how I might handle it if I were in that position in real life. Every story is a 'what if.'"[27] The motif of human vulnerability permeates the stories of the three main characters. The film gets high marks for coherence, intensity of effect, complexity, and originality. *Million Dollar Baby* follows the typical narrative pattern, but according to Frumin's assessment, "Eastwood creates a conflict that exists on so many levels, in so many characters, that the film moves from being cliché to innovative."[28]

Even so, plenty of speculating about those "what ifs" followed. Some reviewers argued that Maggie could have received better care, counseling to deal with her depression, and help in thinking about how she might lead a full and productive life. "All true in another world, or another movie," Roger Ebert wrote, adding, "It is not movie criticism to say Maggie needed better counseling. We might as well say Hamlet needed a psychiatrist."[29]

Ebert was upset that conservative critics and commentators who morally objected to euthanasia tried to "sabotage" the movie by revealing its shocking ending. "The outcome of the movie does not match their beliefs. They object to it. That is their right," he insisted. "To engage in a campaign to harm the movie for those who may not agree with them is another matter."[30] Eastwood was not happy either and could only try to defuse it: "Knowing the ending certainly didn't hurt 'The Passion of the Christ.'"[31]

Lennard J. Davis, a professor of disability and human development, agreed with Ebert that "freedom of expression and creative license are valuable things and every right-minded person should fight to preserve this right." He served a reminder, however, that movies do influence "how we think about ourselves and the world." Citing inaccuracies in the film's portrayal, Davis charged Eastwood with "dealing in the grand myths and legends that surround the idea of disability rather than the reality of living with a disability." Most of what people know about people with disabilities comes from the popular media. "So, it's only when such art forms begin to reflect the real lives of people with disabilities, will most folks get a better understanding of the 15 to 20 percent of Americans who live and cope daily with disabilities," he maintained.[32]

Million Dollar Baby is clearly open to multiple readings—all revealing the crucial role of a framework of expectations in film interpretation. "This is an honest portrayal of what the world looks like to those whose faith in a benevolent God fails," *Christianity Today*'s Jeffrey Overstreet writes, adding that "even a misguided tale can create opportunity for rewarding discussion."[33] David DiCerto, a Catholic critic, found the film's ending "morally problematic," but "not a polemic in favour of assisted suicide. The pain and devastation of those involved is achingly evident."[34] Jeff Shannon, a Seattle film critic and a quadriplegic, wrote a thoughtful and insightful article on the whole affair. He concluded: "While *Million Dollar Baby* is seriously flawed and disturbing from a disability perspective, it's also true to its characters, rich in humanity, and daring enough to let viewers think, in Eastwood's words, 'about the precariousness of life and how we handle it.'"[35] There's no way to resolve this controversial debate with the wave of an interpretive wand. The movie confronts viewers with a difficult and complex issue that does not lend itself to simple answers.

MOVIE MUSING

Boy Meets Girl in *La La Land* (2016)

Los Angeles is filled with dreamers, and sometimes it takes a partner to make your dream come true.

—Brian Tallerico, *RogerEbert.com*

La La Land is a self-reflective musical that pays homage both to its Los Angeles setting and to its genre. If you're familiar with sound stage musicals during their heyday from the 1940s through the 1960s, you'll enjoy noticing all the intertextual winks, nods, and references to some of the classics, only a few of which I'm able to mention here.[36]

In ordinary fictional realism, characters might sing or dance to music that is diegetic—coming from a source within the world of the film—like a radio or a live band performing. Typically, characters can't hear music coming from a source outside the world of the film: Rocky, for example, remains unaware of "Gonna Fly Now" playing while he's training. With musicals, however, we have different expectations.

A movie musical integrates song and dance into the narrative in ways that advance the story and express the emotions of the characters. The genre violates the rules of classical Hollywood realism with an apparent blurring of two different modes of reality: the "normal" world of the film and the characters' internal thoughts and feelings that are expressed through song and dance. We're not surprised that characters can hear, and then dance, and sing along with nondiegetic music that does not emanate from the world of the film. How does that work? Movie magic, of course. Aware of the nature of the genre, we simply suspend our disbelief and take delight in how it all happens.

La La Land adheres to screenwriting guru Syd Field's "classical paradigm structure," a dramatic form long recognized as the basis of Hollywood screenwriting. Briefly, in Field's scheme the story begins with an *inciting incident*—a life-changing event that confronts the main character(s) and propels the story forward toward plot point 1. A *plot point*, according to Field, is "any incident, episode or event that 'hooks' into the action and spins it around into another direction."[37] Plot point 1 marks the end of act 1 (setup) with a dramatic turn of events that creates a new situation and starts the main character(s) on a journey. Act 2 (confrontation) begins at the end of plot point 1 and is divided into two parts by a *midpoint*. Act 2 develops the main conflict with escalating tension showing the protagonist(s) confronting and overcoming obstacles, most often toward achieving an external goal. This dramatic unit concludes at the end of plot point 2, which spins the action in another direction and moves the story toward its climax and into act 3 (resolution).

La La Land follows the conventions of both the classical paradigm and the musical, but with a gendered twist on the formula that happens in an inventive way cinematically. One critic refers to it as some "alternative-reality reverie" that makes for a "killer punch in the film's ending."[38] The award-winning film fits the melodramatic mode and outlook of a classical Hollywood film, while reworking it in ways that make for an interesting analysis. Sebastian "Seb" Wilder (Ryan Gosling) and Mia Dolan (Emma Stone) are basically good characters, each in pursuit of a separate goal: Sebastian opening his own jazz club and Mia becoming an A-list movie actress. The story is driven as much, if not more, by Mia's and Seb's individual dreams as by their romance. The key question is this: Can Mia and Seb both fulfill their life passions by realizing their individual dreams and still maintain their deeply affectionate relationship?

The Setup

La La Land opens with a scene on the I-105/I-110 interchange in Los Angeles where a routine traffic jam in LA's sweltering heat has brought cars to a standstill. The gridlock sparks a rousing song-and-dance number, "Another Day of Sun," which announces the movie's genre. A graphic of the movie title appears, recalling those of the glittery MGM Cinemascope productions during Hollywood's Golden Era—as does the film's bold, vibrant, primary color scheme. Another graphic appears over an extreme long shot of the freeway and the city in the distance on this hot, sunny day: "Winter." The use of graphic titles to denote the seasons of Mia's and Seb's love affair nods to the MGM musical *Meet Me in St. Louis* (1944).

A single moving crane shot visually connects the two main characters and sets up their destined meeting to come later. Sebastian sits in a vintage 1982 Buick Riviera convertible rewinding a cassette tape player, listening repeatedly to a jazz piano riff. An impractical mode of transportation, the Buick accentuates his equally outdated view of jazz music. In a Toyota Prius hybrid in front of him—the apparent car of choice for Hollywood wannabes—Mia is preoccupied, rehearsing lines for an audition. She doesn't realize traffic has started moving. In a moment of road rage, Sebastian lays on his horn—a sound motif repeated throughout the film—and shoots out around her. We see a quick exchange of unpleasantries from Mia's viewpoint. Cut to Mia working as a barista in the coffee shop on the Warner Bros. studio lot. She and her manager stand awestruck when a famous actress comes in—her coffee is on the house. Mia scrambles, leaving in a rush for the audition that doesn't pan out.

A night out with her roommates ends with Mia's Prius being towed from a "no parking after 9:00 pm" zone. It's been a dreadful day. Walking past a restaurant, Mia is captivated by the piano music she hears ("Mia and Sebastian's Theme Song"). She goes inside, and as she stands there mesmerized by Sebastian's playing, the lighting changes, darkening around her as if Mia is the only one in the restaurant listening. The camera moves in to a medium close-up of her as a car horn overwhelms the sound of the piano—a sound bridge—and we cut back to the unpleasantries exchanged on the I-105/I-110 interchange, this time from Sebastian's point of view.

That the narration now jumps back in time to retrace Sebastian's actions breaks the linear flow of the narrative. Viewers learn about Seb's backstory in anticipation of his meeting and ensuing relationship with Mia. It also sets up the device used in the film's much-discussed ending. In conversation with his sister at his apartment, we learn that Sebastian is a pianist who won't even go out with someone who does not share his love for pure jazz, which he believes is dying. He wants to play nothing else and dreams of opening his own jazz club someday.

Cut to the restaurant prior to Mia's arrival. The manager gives Seb a sharp warning to stick to the assigned set list of Christmas music this time and not play the "free jazz."

With no one paying attention to his playing, and only a few measly dollars in the tip jar, Seb can't help himself. "Deck the Halls" morphs into the tender and moving, "Mia and Sebastian's Theme Song," as the lighting changes again. This time a single spotlight isolates Sebastian, alone in his own musical world, a visual expression of his passion for the fiery jazz refrain he plays ending the song. He sees Mia and their eyes lock. She witnesses him being fired by the restaurant manager. As he walks toward her, she starts to tell him how much his music moves her, but Sebastian angrily storms past, brushing her shoulder. The restaurant scene is their second encounter and a key moment in the narrative—the inciting incident. (That we see the inciting incident twice—first from Mia's and then Seb's point of view—also sets up the narrative device used in the film's surprising ending.) We hear the sound of a door close—an audio symbol—as the film cuts to black, and then we see a series of medium close-ups of Mia at various failed auditions.

Confrontation

A graphic: "Spring." At a pool party, Mia sees a bored-stiff Sebastian dressed in bright polyester playing keyboards in a 1980s retro band. Just to irritate him, she requests the Flock of Seagulls' hit "I Ran." During the band's break, Sebastian admits to being worse than "curt" that night at the restaurant, but her song request went "too far" for a "serious musician." It's clear Mia and Seb are both frustrated, having to work at jobs clearly beneath their talent just to survive; both harbor a nostalgia for their respective art that finally serves each in different ways.[39]

After the party, Seb walks Mia to her car. "Pretty strange that we keep running into each other," Mia tells him. "It is strange," he says. "Maybe it means something." She replies, "I doubt it," although everyone in the audience knows better. Overlooking the Los Angeles cityscape, they dance together, at first tentatively, expressing their suspicions,

La La Land © 2016 Summit Entertainment, LLC

Frames 26a, 26b. *La La Land* is filled with intertextual references to classic movie musicals like *Singin' in the Rain.*

and then suggesting real feelings for one another. It begins with Sebastian smoothly swinging around a streetlight pole in an obvious allusion to Gene Kelly doing the same in *Singin' in the Rain* (frames 26a, 26b). The dance sequence is filmed in a single long shot using a crane, more typical of the Studio Era mode of filming than of other recent musicals, and it recalls the breezy style of Fred Astaire and Cyd Charisse in *The Band Wagon* (1953). A call on her cell from Mia's beau interrupts the moment, and they part ways—Seb looking a bit disappointed.

Soon after, he shows up unexpectedly on the Warner Bros. lot. Outside the coffee shop, Mia points to the facade of a Parisian apartment across the street: "That's the window Ingrid Bergman and Humphrey Bogart looked out in *Casablanca*." As they start to stroll the lot, in a scene copied from *Singin' in the Rain*, Seb asks about Mia's current boyfriend: "What's your Bogart's name?" The question connects them with the couple in *Casablanca* and foreshadows their fate. This is one of several intertextual references to movies with ill-fated lovers. Mia's apartment, which she shares with her girlfriends, is decorated with an oversized wall poster of Ingrid Bergman and other movie posters, including the film noir classic *The Killers*, with Burt Lancaster and Ava Gardner in a one-sided romance that ends in betrayal.

Seb tells Mia she's more than "just an actress" and that instead of auditioning she should write her "own roles. Write something that's as interesting as you are." Mia decides it's time, and confesses, "I hate jazz," which the love thereof, we know, is a condition for him dating someone. He takes her to the Lighthouse Club, where famous jazz musicians played. "It's conflict," he explains to her over close-ups of the musicians playing their instruments. "And it's compromise. And it's just, it's new every time. It's brand new every night. It's very, very exciting. And it's dying." Seb shares with her his dream of becoming a club owner. In contrast to his current gigs, "We're gonna play whatever we want, whenever we want, however we want, as long as it's pure jazz." Mia is drawn to his passion and is thrilled when she gets an audition callback—finally. Before she leaves they agree to meet at the Rialto Theater to see *Rebel without a Cause* (more ill-fated lovers) for "research" in preparation for her audition.

When the time comes, however, Mia had forgotten about a dinner date with her Bogart, but then ditches him when the restaurant music magically transforms (from diegetic to nondiegetic music) into "Mia and Sebastian's Theme Song." It grips her and swells into a full orchestral score as she races to the Rialto. Standing on the stage with the film projected on her face, looking almost as if she's crossed the threshold into the world of the film, she searches the audience for Sebastian. Sitting together, they hold hands and are about to kiss when the film gets stuck in the projector, the celluloid melting onscreen during a scene at the Griffith Observatory. The house lights come on. Mia has the idea of driving to the observatory.

There they improbably sneak in through an unlocked door. In a moment of pure movie magic, Seb and Mia are lifted up among the stars and dance across the galaxy like Fred

Astaire and Eleanor Powell in *Broadway Melody of 1940*. The scene ends with their first kiss, an iris into black, then out to an extreme close-up of Mia's hand as she's starting to write her one-woman play—Seb's suggestion in the earlier scene on the Warner Bros. lot. The now familiar, loud sound of Seb's car horn signals he's arrived and is outside waiting.

The Midpoint

A graphic: "Summer." A montage sequence shows their growing romance. Seb sits in on piano with the band at the Lighthouse Club, and afterward, Keith (John Legend), an old schoolmate, asks if he's interested in playing "keys" in his new combo. Seb turns down the offer. That night, after he reads Mia's stage play, she shows him a logo she designed with a different name for his jazz club: "SEB'S" (the apostrophe a musical note), instead of the unappealing "Chicken on a Stick." She returns the favor now, each helping to inspire the other's dreams.

The next morning, Seb overhears Mia on the phone telling her mother she's confident but doesn't know how Seb can afford to open his own jazz club. It gives Seb pause. Afterward, he decides to accept Keith's offer to join his jazz-fusion band in a concession that can be read as Seb yielding his autonomy. He's thinking not just of himself but also, in gendered terms, of becoming the provider in his relationship with Mia (Wood's "shadow"). Though unhappy with the pop-style music they make for young listeners, he plans to use the money he'll be making to eventually bankroll his club.

We reach the midpoint with Seb and Mia pursuing their career ambitions at the expense of their relationship. It starts with a montage sequence with the song "City of Stars" serving as a sound bridge. Mia quits her barista job to focus on self-producing her one-woman stage play. She and Seb have moved in together. He's getting ready to go on tour. A series of dissolves connect shots of them alone in bed or in their apartment suggesting that time is passing by and they're not seeing much of one another. The band is successful, but it's clear to Mia that Seb's heart's not in it. Tension mounts between them.

A graphic: "Fall." During a rare meal one evening at their apartment, Seb suggests that Mia join him on tour. She can't, obviously, with her play scheduled to open in two weeks. Seb explains the cycle of recording, then touring, then recording and touring again, which means he's expecting to stay in the band for "the long haul." This comes as a surprise to Mia, who has come to like jazz now "because of you," and thinks he's abandoning his dream. But Seb says that's what he thought she wanted—for him to have "a steady job." She's confused and insists, "This is not your dream." To his frustration about the odds being against the success of his jazz club, she argues, "People are passionate about what other people are passionate about." A jazz version of "City of Stars" playing on an old vinyl LP stops for dramatic effect. "Maybe you just liked me when I was on my ass because it made you feel better about yourself," Seb tells

Mia. "Are you kidding?" Mia asks, clearly hurt by the remark. We see a close-up of a phonograph needle going round and round at the end of the vinyl LP, as if to signal the same for their relationship. The shrill, piercing sound of a smoke detector goes off—the dessert burned in the oven. It's Seb who goes into the kitchen and Mia who storms out of the apartment—actions that might be gendered otherwise. But here they seem to affirm the gist of their argument: neither one is ready yet to give up their dream for love.

Mia's one-woman show, "So Long Boulder City," which Mia tells Seb "feels really nostalgic to me," turns out to be an opening-night disaster with few people in attendance. Even Sebastian misses it because of a photo shoot that he forgot about, which recalls their first date. Mia has hit bottom in terms of both her career and her romance with Seb. Feeling a failure and doubting her aspirations, Mia makes the long drive home to Boulder City, Nevada.

The story takes another turn (plot point 2) when Seb gets a call for Mia from a casting agent. She was one of the few at Mia's devastating opening night and invites her now to audition for a starring role in a film. Seb drives to Boulder City and lays on the car horn to get Mia out of her parent's home. "It hurts too much" to continue, she says, but she is ready when he comes to pick her up bright and early the next morning.

At the climactic audition, Mia starts telling a story about her aunt, an aspiring actress herself, living in Paris (another *Casablanca* reference), where the film will shoot. Talk turns into song, "Audition (The Fools Who Dream)." We see the same lighting motif as before. The camera fixates solely on Mia, who stands alone in an otherwise darkened room. She performs as if it's her last shot, with a gentle sincerity we've not seen in her previous auditions. The camera slowly moves in for a close-up and circles around her, the effect intensifying her internal world of swirling emotions. It's Mia's moment of self-realization that completes her character arc. Writer and director Damien Chazelle says, "The visuals of it were stemming from that idea, and trying to call back also to earlier moments in the movie where we'd done this sort of light gag, just that simple idea of the room going darker and everything dissolving into a spotlight." He continues, "It represented some kind of a journey to one's self. So I think the idea here was to have the audition number be a climax for that and have everything else really fade away and fall away, and you're just left with her."[40] As the song ends, the lights in the room come on again, followed by a dissolve to Mia and Seb sitting on a bench beneath the Griffith Observatory (frames 27a, 27b).

Sebastian is sure she'll get the part; Mia is uncertain. "Where are we?" she asks him. Seb doesn't know but tells her there's nothing they can do. "'Cause when you get this, you gotta give it everything you've got. Everything. It's your dream." As for himself, Seb doesn't waver. "I've got to follow my own plan." There's "good jazz" in Paris, he tells her, noting that she loves jazz now, right? "We're just gonna have to

Frames 27a, 27b. A lighting scheme expresses the two modes of reality in the conventional musical and sets up a "magical do-over" sequence with a gender twist in the end of *La La Land*.

wait and see." It's a key dialogue conversation with Seb proposing they part ways in pursuit of their lifelong dreams. In a poignant exchange, Mia says, "I'm always going to love you." He replies the same. "I'm always going to love you too." Boy gets girl, boy loses girl. Now what?

Resolution and Epilogue

A graphic: "Winter." The blue sky and palm tree in the background turns out to be on a huge matte being wheeled across the Warner Bros. lot. Another graphic appears: "Five years later . . ."

A crosscutting sequence at first teases viewers with a customary ending. Completing the pattern at the start of the film, Mia is the movie star now who gets her coffee on the house in the shop on the Warner Bros. lot. Cut to a scene showing Seb performing duties as manager at a jazz club. Back to Mia, arriving at home and greeted by her husband (not Seb) and young daughter. What? Cut to Sebastian who is living alone. Now, the editing creates anticipation that we're about to see their paths cross again.

That evening Sebastian walks by a building with a huge billboard on its side advertising a movie starring Mia; her face recalls the pose of Ingrid Bergman on the oversized wall poster that once hung in her room. Cut to Mia and her husband caught in a traffic jam—recalling the one in the opening scene. At Mia's suggestion, they abandon their plans, get off the freeway, and find a place to have dinner. Afterward, while walking down a street, they hear music coming from a club and decide to go in.

Mia sees the neon "SEB'S" logo that she designed, and she freezes. Inside, Sebastian gets up on stage and spots Mia in the audience. They lock eyes. There's a moment. "Welcome to Seb's," he says, and sits down at the piano. He starts playing a song we recognize immediately—a haunting version of "Mia and Sebastian's Theme Song." The same lighting motif darkens the room around them while he plays, the song becoming a sound bridge over what one critic calls "a magical do-over."[41] The phrase describes, in a less cumbersome way, a five-year fantasy flashback/flash-forward montage-like sequence in Technicolor—a visual throwback to movies like *An American in Paris* and others, as writers observe.

The sequence starts with a cut to Seb finishing the same piece at the restaurant and being fired—the inciting incident revisited. The sequence serves as a "what if" scenario of what their lives would have been like. Instead of brushing past her, this time Seb takes Mia in his arms, kissing her passionately as the camera swirls around them, the song swelling on the soundtrack (nondiegetic). They have their own place, Seb declines Keith's offer, attends Mia's play, which is a hit and plays to a full house, goes to Paris with her while she shoots her film, and plays in jazz clubs there. Seb and Mia watch 16mm home movies showing they start a family and are living happily together.

We see Seb and Mia now in the car getting off the freeway to avoid the traffic jam and stopping in a jazz club. The camera pans around the room, settling on Mia and Seb sitting close together. (In the same shot earlier, a small table with a light on it between Mia and her husband visually puts some emotional distance between them; they seem happy enough, but the passion's not there.) Seb and Mia kiss. Cut to a close-up of Seb's hand on the keyboard striking the final notes of the song (diegetic). The camera tilts up to a close-up of Seb at the piano; cut to a two-shot of Mia and her husband, who applauds and then leans over and asks, "Do you want to stay for another?" She replies, "No, we should go."

As they are leaving, Mia stops, turns around, and looks back. She and Sebastian exchange a look, the camera cutting back and forth until he gives her a knowing nod and they smile at each other. It's a bittersweet and poignant moment that film critic Peter Bradshaw aptly describes as "heart-wrenching, romantic, unbearably sad, yet in such a way that a retrospective glow of something like joy and hopefulness is projected on to the events that led up to it."[42] Does their nonverbal exchange signal love, regret, nostalgia, happiness for the other? Or all this and more? It remains intentionally ambiguous but does give "you that sense that even if the relationship itself might be over in practical terms, the love is not over," Damien Chazelle said.[43]

The "Whoa, I Didn't Expect That!" Ending

That's how a *Variety* critic describes the way *La La Land*'s departure from the conventional Hollywood musical surprised audiences.[44] There are many ways to understand the film's resolution, which Chazelle has talked about in speeches and interviews. The writer and director said the scenario was inspired by a 1927 silent film, *7th Heaven*, starring Janet Gaynor and Charles Farrell. After receiving word that her lover, Chico (Farrell), has been killed in a war, Diane (Gaynor) refuses to believe he's dead. In the final scene, as Chazelle describes it, "There's an abrupt cut back to the battlefield. [Chico] Charles Farrell is suddenly alive, inexplicably, and makes his way back home. The last scene, he comes home, they kiss, swell of music, fade to black."[45] The way Chazelle interprets the ambiguity of the ending, the Farrell character is both dead and alive. It's a contradictory view that nonetheless points toward the two realities that exist in the musical genre itself: the "real" world and the inner realm of human emotion. "He died, but he is alive, because of how deeply she loved him," he said. "It's an idea that speaks to only what movies can do—that emotion can override everything, override the reality reflected onscreen."[46]

The "magical do-over" also plays off the "Broadway Melody" number in *Singin' in the Rain*, a parenthetical fantasy sequence that reflects on the career of the main character (Don Lockwood) and explores that film's illusion-versus-reality theme. In this sense, the *La La Land* sequence offers a condensed fast-forward version of the movie itself as if it adhered strictly to the genre's conventional formula and ending. "Let's give them the old-fashioned musical version of their story, where there's no real conflict and we can be left to reflect, is that actually better than what happened? Or are they actually in an even better place in real life than they would be there?" Chazelle explains. "That's the question the audience can be left with."[47] The director's intent, in other words, is to let spectators decide for themselves between the fantasy and the reality.

There is some question about viewpoint in the fantasy sequence. Those critics who consider it tend to write as if it's Mia's imagining. Jennifer Vineyard suggests several alternatives: "He shares all of this with her through his song, or she imagines it while hearing him play, or perhaps they share this bittersweet dream together, before they have to accept reality once again."[48] Ambiguity seems intended, and in some sense, viewpoint doesn't matter all too much. But it's still interesting to think about the sequence in this regard.

Perhaps others will disagree, but I want to suggest that as a matter of narrative structure—a resolution to the two points of view in the inciting incident—the "magical do-over" fantasy represents Seb's moment of self-realization. As noted earlier, Mia's character arc is completed at the last audition when she finally stops the fakery and becomes more than "just an actress," as Seb had encouraged her to do. In the movie's climax, she reaches inside herself now to tell a story that reveals how "interesting" she really is, something the casting agent sensed at her short-lived play. It's what makes Mia stand out from all the others in the waiting room who are "prettier and better at this because maybe I'm not good enough," as she admitted to Seb the night before.

Seb detests having to compromise his love for "pure jazz" and could not be satisfied with just being a successful jazz musician; he wants to own his own club, which was reportedly actor Ryan Gosling's idea.[49] Keith lectures Sebastian about reinventing the musical genre to keep it alive for the next generation. "How are you gonna be a revolutionary if you're such a traditionalist?" he asks. "You're holding onto the past, but jazz is about the future." As film critic David Sims notes, "Nostalgia has propelled Mia to stardom; it's given Sebastian his artistic integrity, but little else."[50] The way the "what if" sequence is tinged with a hint of regret suggests this is Seb's self-realization—if occurring too late. That said, insofar as they magically share the musical moment between them, it's also a feeling Mia seems to experience as well.

In the MGM classic *Singin' in the Rain* (1952), Don Lockwood (Gene Kelly) and Kathy Seldon (Debbie Reynolds) together find both love and movie stardom. The romance Mia and Seb have involves the same kind of partnership; each has a noteworthy impact in helping the other achieve success—but not without a cost. In the end, Sebastian is the owner of a thriving jazz club, but lives alone. Mia is a bona fide movie star with a husband and daughter. She seems happy enough. There is warmth between her and her husband, but not the passion she shared with Seb as the final scene in Seb's club suggests.

As to the story's key question, it seems that Mia and Seb could have had it all with a different choice here and there. Given the subtle gender twists in the story, what's interesting is the way the "magical do-over" shakes up even more the usual story line. The premise of the sequence is that Seb turns down Keith's offer and goes with Mia to Paris, playing in the jazz clubs there. In other words, Seb alters *his* dream to be with Mia, settling on becoming a successful jazz musician instead of a club owner to fulfill his passion to save jazz. And as a result, both appear happier together than either does in their current life, which makes the film's ending even more bittersweet. And that's what makes consideration of the sequence's point of view so interesting. Is this Seb's regret? Mia's wish? Or both?

Whichever way, the ending does resolve the real tension in the film, which is between personal ambition and romantic love. "*La La Land* ultimately is not about Mia and Sebastian's romance," as one critic puts it. "The real romance was with the shimmer of dreams."[51] After all, Mia's toast in her big number is: "Here's to the ones who dream, foolish as they may seem."

MOVIE MUSING

Narrative, Character, and Perspective
in *The Blind Side* (2009)

Ah, Hollywood. It has always "enhanced" reality for the sake of a good story.

—Deirdre Donahue, *USA Today*

Deirdre Donahue interviewed Michael Oher, then a Baltimore Ravens offensive lineman, for a piece in *USA Today*. The occasion was the publication of Oher's coauthored memoir, *I Beat the Odds: From Homelessness to "The Blind Side" and Beyond*, written in part to "help separate fact from fiction."[52] *The Blind Side* is a fictional film based on a nonfiction bestseller by Michael Lewis, *The Blind Side: Evolution of a Game* (2007). Lewis uses the changing NFL's offensive left tackle position to tell the remarkable story of now former NFL lineman Michael Oher.

Oher grew up in Hurt Village, a rundown public housing project that was notorious as a haven for drugs and criminal activity in North Memphis, Tennessee. Built in the 1950s, it was originally occupied by poor white families. They began leaving when black families started moving in as a result of school desegregation and unfair housing laws. When the federal courts ordered desegregated busing to integrate the Memphis public schools in 1973, white residents took flight to the city suburbs. That's when Stanley Roberts, a US marshal, moved his family "as far east as you could get and still be in Memphis," Lewis writes.[53] Daughter Leigh Anne (later wife of Sean Tuohy) was in the first graduating class at the new Briarcrest Christian School, which, like Hurt Village, represents part of a legacy of racism.

Abandoned by his alcoholic and drug-addicted mother, Oher ends up in and out of foster homes with spans of homelessness. He meets his best friend while playing basketball in community leagues. In 2002, his friend's father, Big Tony Henderson, was enrolling his son at Briarcrest and persuaded the coaches there to also enroll "Big Mike," who was living with him at the time. A black teenager, penniless and without a home, he was embraced by Leigh Anne and Sean Tuohy—wealthy, white, southern evangelicals, and Republicans who put the compassion in "compassionate conservatism." Michael benefited enormously from the Tuohys' unreserved love and considerable wealth and generosity. Providing him with a safe, loving, and comfortable home, the Tuohys helped him pursue his education, develop his athletic talents, and navigate NCAA college football recruitment. He earned a football scholarship at Ole Miss and went on to become the Baltimore Ravens' 2009 first-round draft pick.

The movie *The Blind Side* earned almost $256 million in domestic box-office income against roughly $30 million in production costs. It is an entertaining and touching story about human connection and healing.

Reviews of the film were generally favorable, with most critics agreeing that "as a fable about the power of giving, it hits pretty hard," as one put it.[54] What disappointed critics more or less was the way this crowd-pleaser glosses over the penetrating real-life circumstances. "*The Blind Side*, while inspiring, is a little myopic," *USA Today*'s Claudia Puig writes, for example, for "never delving into the ramifications of [the Tuohys'] actions or exploring more complicated socioeconomic and racial issues." Despite strong performances, the lack of character exploration "keeps it from being the moving story it could have been."[55]

Others were sharper, faulting the film as a depiction of white paternalism. A *Village Voice* critic contends that "the movie peddles the most insidious kind of racism, one in which whiteys are virtuous saviors, coming to the rescue of African-Americans who become superfluous in narratives that are supposed to be about them."[56] Then again, *The Blind Side* might well be taken as "another White Man to the Rescue flick," a *Christianity Today* critic notes, adding, "While not necessarily exempt because of it, a film based on real events complicates this dynamic."[57]

As to be expected, the real-life events that Michael Lewis chronicles do not neatly fit the structure of the classical Hollywood film. While looking at movies like *Lincoln* and *The Big Short* (based on another Lewis book), we've seen how much artistic license is part and parcel of a screen adaptation. In various interviews, writer and director John Lee Hancock explains that in dramatizing Lewis's account, he did not envision *The Blind Side* as a sports drama, "any more than you'd call *Jerry Maguire* a sports film." He also insists the story is not about race. "Any time you have people of different races in a movie that's about America, there's going to be a racial component," he said.[58] Nor is it about religion. "It would have been an also amazingly charitable act had the Tuohys been atheists. A good deed is a good deed," he said.[59]

Rather, the story's dramatic underpinning is the importance of family and "a discussion of haves and have-nots and nature versus nurture." Oher's "story goes to prove what having a safe bed to sleep in, having a family unit, having loving, interested parents can do."[60] According to one report, Lewis had an interest in "the *Pygmalion* aspect of the Oher-Tuohy relationship," and specifically how Leigh Anne and Sean were "not just giving him a home," the writer said, but "trying to assimilate [him] into the lives of rich, white Evangelical Christians."[61]

Hancock saw two "equally involving" story threads in Lewis's book, "one about Michael and the Tuohys, the other about the left tackle position, but they both turned around the same question—how did the stars align so brightly around this one kid from the projects?"[62] That's the movie "about America" he decided to make. As it is, the film has two closely related story lines, each with its own obstacles to achieving a goal with that key question in mind.

The main story line has to do with Michael and the Tuohys becoming a mutually reconstituted family. The problem in this scenario is Michael's lack of family. The narrative is organized as a variation on the romantic comedy formula: Michael gets a family, loses a family, and then gets a family back again. These key plot points lead to a climax and resolution with his becoming an adoptive member of the Tuohy family. Oher's path to Ole Miss and then on to the NFL is the secondary story. Even though Michael Oher provides the story's raison d'être—that is, the reason for its existence—the movie does not center on him but rather on the formation of a family that provides an environment to nurture his journey.

As a classical Hollywood film, *The Blind Side* focuses on key individuals whose goal-oriented actions resolve the story's problems. While it celebrates ideals, values, and assumptions associated with individual achievement, this movie differs in crucial ways from traditional American success stories. As we've seen, these films feature a self-reliant protagonist whose exceptional abilities, hard work, and determination are the means to overcoming a limiting past in a struggling ascent that ends in a personal triumph.

On balance, the film depicts Oher's achievement as much less about his own efforts than those of the Tuohy family. Their love, generosity, and ample financial resources uniquely position them to help Michael by affording him the privileges of the white upper class—a system of racial advantage the film does not question. His rags-to-riches story line then comes across as largely a by-product of their good fortune. In the slice of the story told in the movie, Sean and Leigh Anne testify to the American success myth.

The film denies Michael's character a measure of agency that struck *Boston Globe* film critic Wesley Morris as unrealistic: "I can't imagine that he would have gotten as far as he had gotten were he not—were he just sort of a passive bystander to his success."[63] That the source of Michael's self-realization and eventual success is rich white folks on the other side of the tracks creates an "odd predicament"—to borrow the NCAA official's phrase in the film—that complicates story construction and characterizations, even as it provides a key dramatic moment in the film.

Many dynamics here can complicate study of *The Blind Side*, but in a beneficial way. The film itself, the circumstances of its production, and the surrounding discourse draw attention to many of the concerns of this book, especially the role of perspective in both storytelling and life. *The Blind Side* provides an opportunity to see how a writer and director's intent influences a film's design in two ways. First, we can examine how this amazing real-life story is reimagined within the conventions of the classical Hollywood film. And second, we consider the way it brings a specific outlook to representing the events, people, and issues it addresses. All this lends itself to an interesting film discussion that helps us make sense of varying interpretations. It also provides a springboard for considering the perspective the film offers on race and religion.

Leigh Anne: The Good Samaritan

The Blind Side is a star-centered narrative. Sandra Bullock provides the main attraction; playing Michael Oher was Quinton Aaron's first lead role. The opening prologue with Leigh Anne's voice-over privileges her point of view. The film then mediates Michael's voice through Leigh Anne's, which provides its overarching perspective. The prologue also gives the story its sports context and marks its fictive stance as "based on a true story."

We see documentary footage of New York Giants' linebacker Lawrence Taylor making a blindside tackle that ends the illustrious career of Washington Redskins' quarterback Joe Theismann. In a voice-over accompanied with breezy nondiegetic music, Leigh Anne gives a breakdown of the four-second flea-flicker play and how it changed the game by increasing the importance of the offensive left tackle position—the second highest player in the NFL. "The left tackle's job is to protect the quarterback from what he can't see coming. To protect his blind side," Leigh Anne explains, which is the side opposite his throwing arm. The ideal left tackle "is wide in the butt and massive in the thighs. He has long arms, giant hands and feet as quick as a hiccup."

A visual connection to Michael Oher comes with a quick fade out and in to a long shot of him walking in slow motion toward the camera. In the background, young children play in a rundown neighborhood (Hurt Village). Leigh Anne says that Taylor "not only altered Joe Theismann's life, but mine as well." Two short blue-hued flashbacks, the first of many, are inserted between medium shots of Michael as he moves even closer to the camera, suggesting these are his memories of a disturbing childhood.

"Mr. Oher." A woman's voice is a sound bridge over a cut to an upscale conference room surrounded with windows. "Do you understand? Do you know why I'm here?" she asks Michael, who's being "investigated," we learn later, by this NCAA official because of his "odd predicament." The use of high and low angle shots makes the NCAA official look powerful looming over Michael, who, despite his size (six foot two and 350 pounds), now looks small and trapped. The insert of a close-up of his huge hands as he dries them on his pants suggests he's nervous. The scene ends with a "God shot" of the conference room and a graphic: "Two Years Before." It signals to viewers that the backstory we're about to see will get us up to speed about the nature of Oher's "odd predicament."

Over the opening credits we see Michael crowded in the back seat of a Ford Taurus driving with "Big Tony" Hamilton and his son Steve through the impoverished streets of North Memphis to the city's wealthy suburbs on the east side and Wingate Christian School (fictional name for Briarcrest). The trip visually establishes the film's setting, represented by the familiar phrase "the other side of town," which signifies class and racial divisions in Memphis (frames 28a, 28b).

Coach Cotton (Ray McKinnon) is amazed at Michael's size, quickness, and athletic potential, but the admissions board is reluctant to admit him given his dismal academic record. Pointing to the school seal on the wall behind him ("Neighborly, Academic,

Frames 28a, 28b. *The Blind Side* visually establishes class and racial divisions in its Memphis setting.

Christian"), the coach argues, "Christian! We either take that seriously or we paint over it. You don't admit Michael Oher because of sports. You admit him because it's the right thing to do." The purity of Coach Cotton's own motives aside, his speech introduces the theme of loving your neighbor. Enter Leigh Anne Touhy.

Film critic Steven D. Greydanus rather vividly describes Leigh Anne as "a red-state, family-values, guns-and-religion Erin Brockovich," associating her with another gutsy, strong-willed female protagonist. "Righteous, indomitable, unflappable, glamorous in plunging necklines and thigh-hugging skirts, she's also a pistol-packing mama, a happily married homemaker and mother of two, a Bible-belt Evangelical and a dyed-in-the-wool gridiron junkie."[64] The no-nonsense Memphis interior designer is married to Sean (Tim McGraw), a successful entrepreneur who owns "about a million Taco Bells," as their youngest, son S.J. (Jae Head), tells Michael. Teenage daughter Collins (Lily Collins) is a cheerleader and volleyball player at Wingate Christian School.

Leigh Anne has primary agency throughout the film; the Oher character plays a subordinate role, however much he is at the center of the story. We learn about what Michael thinks, feels, and has experienced through and along with Leigh Anne, which has the effect of aligning viewers with her character. She exemplifies the character traits we normally associate with American heroines. Her actions drive the narrative; few scenes don't include her.

Leigh Anne wants to help Michael. Why? Presumably for the reason Coach Cotton gave the admissions board: it's the right thing to do. She is the Good Samaritan. Though Leigh Anne is the main protagonist, her character arc is flat; her "need" is no more than hinted at, perhaps in a scene with her girlfriends, who function like a Greek chorus commenting on the action. Realizing that Leigh Anne is seriously considering adopting Michael, Sherry asks, "Is this some kind of white guilt?" Elaine adds, "What will your daddy say?" Leigh Anne responds sharply, "Before or after he turns over in his grave?" Nothing more is said, but Lewis's book, as NPR's Michel Martin notes, "makes clear that part of why Leigh Anne has a chip on her shoulder is that her father is . . . a thoroughgoing bigot."[65]

Michael: Ferdinand the Bull

Michael has the perfect physique for the new NFL left tackle position. The problem in the secondary story line is that he sorely lacks the requisite aggressiveness both on and off the gridiron. In the movie, he's depicted as having no real interest in football and little understanding of the game.

As Leigh Anne and Michael are entering a Big and Tall Shop on the north side of town, she says, "I've lived in Memphis my whole life and never been anywhere near here. You're going to take care of me, right?" Michael assures her, "I got your back." It's a first sign of his internal drive. Michael scores off the charts (the 98th percentile) in "protective instincts" on a career aptitude test. Then in a car collision, he instinctively reaches across to protect S.J. from an airbag releasing at two hundred miles per hour—practically a superhuman feat. Watching him on the football practice field, it dawns on Leigh Anne that Michael is like the gentle bull in the children's book *The Story of Ferdinand*.

In a memorable scene, Leigh Anne strides onto the field and instructs Michael to think of his teammates as his family and to "protect them" from the defensive players. "Tony is your quarterback," she says. "You protect his blindside." Piecing together Michael's background and temperament, Leigh Anne taps into a wellspring of willpower that puts a fire in the belly of Oher. As it is, by awakening his innate abilities, Leigh Anne becomes the catalyst for Michael's self-realization. Further, the scene ties together the two story lines. "This team is your family," she explains. "And you have to protect them." S.J.'s personal training of Michael lightens up the obligatory training montage sequence, focusing its meaning on their budding brotherly relationship instead of building strength and confidence, as is typical, we've seen, in sports dramas.

The story line portrays Michael as a diamond in the rough. His transformative arc goes from him being a six-foot-two, 350-pound child, withdrawn and undeveloped in every way, to him being a capable young man and stellar athlete with a promising future in the NFL. At first, he barely speaks, which makes him seem stupid, as does the infantile drawing on the back of a quiz he fails. Oher took exception to the film's depiction of him as "dumb instead of as a kid who had never had consistent academic instruction." He was especially miffed by scenes with middle schooler S.J. moving condiment and spice bottles around to teach him the fundamentals of the game and of Leigh Anne lecturing him on the practice field about the basics of blocking. "I know stuff like that makes for a good story on screen, but in reality, I already knew the game of football inside and out," he maintains.[66] He had always been interested in sports, idolized Michael Jordan, and played football at a Memphis high school before enrolling at Briarcrest.

Film critics liken Michael's depiction to that of the "black saint," a filmic type that can be traced back to Sidney Poitier films in the 1950s and 1960s. "Though raised in Memphis housing projects, he uses no slang and dislikes the taste of malt liquor," cultural historian Thaddeus Russell writes. "His table manners are impeccable. He exhibits virtually no sexual desire. He is never angry and shuns violence except when necessary to protect the white family that adopted him or the white quarterback he was taught to think of as his brother."[67] The portrayal of Michael as a gentle giant, however, diminishes his self-determination, which, as we've seen, is a chief trait of American protagonists. But it fits with the story conception of Michael becoming the Tuohy's third child.

Focus on the Family: Narrative Design

Will the Touhys become Michael's new family? That question drives the main narrative (frame 29). The secondary story line tackles the question, How will Michael shake free of his limiting past, get in touch with his innate abilities, and join the ranks of the NFL?

The Blind Side © 2009 Alcon Film Fund, LLC

Frame 29. The main story line in *The Blind Side* is about Michael Oher becoming a full-fledged member of the Tuohy family.

Shortly after Michael is enrolled at Wingate, the Tuohys are driving home after a middle-school Thanksgiving pageant. Dressed in costume as "Indian #3," S.J. talks about "some multicultural bias thing going on" during the auditions as the reason he lost the role of Chief to a Chinese student. Leigh Anne spots "Big Mike" walking aimlessly alone in the cold rain wearing a short-sleeved shirt and shorts. "Do you have a place to stay tonight?" she asks him, adding sternly, "Don't you dare lie to me." He shakes his head "no." Leigh Anne tells him to get in the car. Michael spends the night at the Tuohy home, a suburban mansion on Memphis's east side. "Sleep tight, honey," she says, after setting up the couch for him to sleep on. A book on the coffee table, *Norman Rockwell's Four Freedoms*, catches Michael's attention. A close-up of the book cover shows the "Freedom from Want" painting, also known as "The Thanksgiving Picture."

The next morning Leigh Anne finds the sheets folded on the couch. She goes after Michael, who's walking down the driveway, and invites him to join them for Thanksgiving dinner. Michael sits alone at the dining room table, barely eating, while the rest of the family enjoys their Thanksgiving meal in front of football games on two TVs. Inspired, Leigh Anne breaks the family's holiday gridiron tradition and turns off the televisions. Everyone moves into the dining room and takes a seat around the table. They hold hands while Leigh Anne offers a prayer of thanks for "bringing us a new friend." She adds, "Never let us forget just how very fortunate we are. Amen." That the shot is designed to look like Rockwell's "Thanksgiving Picture" cannot be missed (frames 30a, 30b). It marks plot point 1: Michael gets a family and is freed from want. Afterward, Leigh Anne invites Michael to stay long term.

The main narrative unfolds like a detective story. That Michael has never had his own bed piques Leigh Anne's curiosity. "We have to find out more about his past," she tells Sean and sets out working through Michael's defenses, trying to unravel the mystery of this young man who apparently by divine intervention has become a part of her life. She investigates Michael's past, starting with Child Protective Services and then a series of events requiring trips across town to Hurt Village. Through it all, she comes to see the poverty, drug addiction, family dysfunction, gang rule, and violence in Hurt Village, where Michael grew up.

Marking the film's midpoint, Leigh Anne tracks down Michael's mother, seeking her permission to adopt him. "You a fine Christian lady," Denise Oher tells her. Meanwhile, with the help of tutor Miss Sue (Kathy Bates), Michael's grades improve, as does his performance on the football field. A video S.J. posts online attracts college recruiters from across the country, resulting in a fun parade of cameos by NCAA Division I coaches. At Michael's high-school graduation ceremony, Leigh Anne has him give her "a proper hug."

Plot point 2 (Michael loses family) occurs in an extended replay of the earlier scene with the NCAA official. She confronts Michael now with the possibility "that the Tuohys, they took you in, they clothed you, they fed you, they paid for your private education. They bought you a car and paid for a tutor, all as part of a plan to ensure that you played football for the University of Mississippi." The idea that their love and generosity was all just a ruse, that their real intent was to manipulate him, had never occurred to Michael. He storms out of the room and confronts Leigh Anne. "Don't you dare lie to me. I'm not stupid," Michael says, echoing their first conversation. Michael's world is turned upside down. It sends him reeling and, not knowing where to turn, back to Hurt Village. That night he gets into a brawl with Hurt Village gang leader, Alton (Irone Singleton), who threatens to rape Leigh Anne and Collins—pivotal for Michael, who protects his family.

The Blind Side © 2009 Alcon Film Fund, LLC

Frames 30a, 30b. Shots drawing a comparison of the Tuohy family to Norman Rockwell's iconic "The Thanksgiving Picture" emphasize *The Blind Side*'s central themes.

The Blind Side © 2009 Alcon Film Fund, LLC

Frames 31a, 31b. A key scene in *The Blind Side* violates conventional framing to signify a closeness between the main characters.

The next morning, Michael contacts Leigh Anne, calling her "Mama." They sit on a curb outside a laundromat and have a heart-to-heart talk, clearing the air about the recruitment experience. The way the scene is shot violates conventional rules of framing. Ordinarily, an actor shot in close-up is looking into the lead room (space) in the frame and gesturing in that direction, which leads a viewer's eyes to the action about to be captured. That the lead room lies behind Michael and Leigh Anne suggests that the other person fills that space and signifies a closeness between them (frames 31a, 31b).

The NCAA incident serves to exonerate Leigh Anne and Sean and, dramatically, to create a crisis leading to a climax that finally binds Michael and the Tuohys together. When he meets with the NCAA official again, Michael tells her with complete confidence now that he wants to attend Ole Miss, "Because that's where my family goes to school. It's where they've always gone to school." His declaration signifies that the narrative goal has been achieved: Michael is now a full-fledged member of the Tuohy family.

When the Tuohys are dropping him off at Ole Miss, Michael looks with interest at co-eds walking past (as do Sean and S.J.). No longer a child, Michael is one of the Tuohy family men. As an added touch, it's Michael who initiates a "proper hug" in saying goodbye to Leigh Anne, completing a pattern established earlier at his graduation ceremony. The movie ends with a sequence of graphics updating the (real) lives of the characters, documentary footage showing Michael becoming the Baltimore Ravens' 2009 first-round draft pick, and photos of Michael, Miss Sue, and the Tuohys. And everyone lives happily ever after.

Racial Color Blindness

The film's title is a double entendre, using football parlance to make a point about *racial color blindness*, displayed in both the Tuohy family's attitude toward Michael and the film's overarching narrational perspective. Race doesn't matter, at least not for the central characters, and by implication, it should not matter, which is evidently the film's intended moral lesson. "From my standpoint," Hancock said, "Leigh Anne didn't stop the car and put Michael in the back seat because he was black. She did it because he was cold."[68]

The notion of racial color blindness is associated with a *post-racial society*, one that at least theoretically is free of racial prejudice, discrimination, and inequality. The world of *The Blind Side*, however, represents what scholars Michael O. Emerson and Christian Smith define as a *racialized society* where "race matters profoundly for differences in life experiences, life opportunities, and social relationships." They explain, furthermore, that "racism is not mere individual, overt prejudice or the free-floating driver of race problems, but the collective misuse of power that results in diminished life opportunities for some racial groups."[69] Racism is a complex system affecting not only individual attitudes and actions but also public policies and institutional practices such as redlining, gerrymandering, and voting restrictions. Consequently, confronting racial injustice involves reforming institutional and long-term structural problems embedded in American life and society.

In one sense, the film's narration displays an awareness of the story's racialized setting. For example, the film's setting and design aptly portray the racial divisions and socioeconomic inequalities that affect real-life Memphis. The film pits the squalor, poverty, crime, drug abuse, and violence of Hurt Village against the ordered, manicured, and rich suburban world surrounding Wingate Christian School. And Leigh Anne's fierce warning to Alton discloses a shared understanding of the sharp class and racial divisions in Memphis. "You so much as cross into downtown, you will be sorry," she lets him know. "I'm in a prayer group with the DA, I'm a member of the NRA, and I am always packing." It's a declaration of white, upper-class privilege that affirms the status quo—it's also an entertaining scene to watch.

Michael's size and skin color make him stand out at Wingate Christian School. A shot of him sitting uncomfortably, squeezed into a small school desk, looks a bit comical. It also makes him seem completely out of place, surrounded by a room full of white classmates, and it highlights racial difference. He expresses his deep unease in the "White Walls" essay he submits to Briarcrest teacher Mrs. Boswell. Michael writes: "I look and I see white everywhere: white walls, white floors, and a lot of white people."

We also get hints that social inequities might be alleviated with something more than individual acts of kindness. Driving to a restaurant, Michael asks Sean, "What do y'all do with the leftover food? At the restaurant?" What's been cooked is thrown away. "That's too bad," Michael says. Sean says he would prefer to sell it, with S.J. interjecting, "Seems like you could give it away or something? You should check into that, Daddy." In another scene, Leigh Anne has an idea that she and Sean might "start a charity. For kids like him [Michael]. . . . Maybe fund a program at Wingate."

In another sense, however, the movie treats not just race but other identifiers as having no more than a surface bearing on the story and characterizations. Cousin Bobby's reaction to seeing Michael in the Tuohy's annual Christmas family photo plays for some light humor: "Listen, I've had about five cold ones so I'm just gonna go ahead and ask. Y'all know there's a colored boy in your Christmas card?" Leigh Anne's luncheon friends joke about it too until they realize she's serious about legally adopting Michael. "Honey, you're changing that boy's life," Beth tells her. Leigh Anne responds, "No. He's changing mine." But while finding Leigh Anne's altruism admirable, Elaine makes a racist insinuation about Michael and Collins. "He's a boy, a large black boy, sleeping under the same roof." Clearly irritated, Leigh Anne replies, "Shame on you." Here and throughout, the film only addresses racism directly as personal prejudice.

The same goes for politics and religion. Even though she is a talented educator, Miss Sue "wasn't religious enough" to teach at Wingate Christian School. Before Leigh Anne hires her to be Michael's tutor, Miss Sue feels obligated to let her know that she's a Democrat. Later Sean says, "Who'd a thought we'd have a black son before we knew a Democrat." It's a funny line of dialogue. To even things out perhaps, one scene makes a slight joke at the expense of President George W. Bush. "I've been waiting for over an hour and I look around and all I see is people shooting the bull and drinking coffee," Leigh Anne complains to an African American woman at Child Protection Services. "Who runs this place anyway?" The civil servant gestures toward a portrait of the Republican president on the wall behind her. "Well," the plain-speaking Leigh Anne says, backing off a bit. "I'd have it in shape in two days, I can tell you that."

These illustrations show how the film treats social identifiers as if they don't really matter, at least not for the central characters, thus implying that they should not matter, apparently the movie's intended moral. It is an admirable theme—representing unmistakably the idea of love of neighbor in a life-affirming way. That said, these are inescapable dynamics, the crucible out of which this story of ascent emerges. For that reason, exploring the effects of these realities on characters plays a critical part in examining the film's *complexity*, the way it comes together on multiple levels to deepen and enrich the movie's overall meaning.

Race and socioeconomic difference, features of the film's landscape, being underplayed, serve merely as a backdrop to the unfolding drama. In effect it lifts the fictional characters out of the very conditions that make this such an inspiring real-life story in the first place. This narrative design gives the movie version enough of a mythical quality that A. O. Scott goes so far as to describe it as "a live-action, reality-based version of a Disney cartoon."[70]

All things considered, it's understandable that some critics might categorize this as a white savior film, or as Scott puts it, that "the best hope for a poor black child in America is to have rich white parents."[71] In his memoir, Oher insists, "I would have found my way out of the ghetto one way or another. Failure was not an option for me,"[72] even if that meant working multiple jobs, including taking orders at one of the fast-food franchises Sean Tuohy owns.[73] Maybe so, but the movie itself makes it hard to imagine he would have made it to Ole Miss, let alone the NFL, apart from the Tuohy's personal intervention, wealth, and generosity.

All in all, the film's resolution suggests nothing about addressing—by confronting the failure of programs, institutions, and public policies—the harmful and oppressive conditions in which Oher's story takes shape. Instead, it shows a fortunate individual, through hardly any initiative of his own, being afforded the benefits of white privilege. (It can be read as an instance of outside magical assistance attributed directly here to God's intervention.) That the movie is based on a true story legitimizes this view, but not without creating interpretive difficulties. "It would all seem a bit patronizing if it wasn't true," a reviewer for the *Christian Science Monitor* points out, while still noting, "The filmmakers pay lip service to the story's racial undertones without ever really rocking the leaky boat."[74]

In the end, *The Blind Side* holds up an individual act of Christian charity as the solution to the racial and socioeconomic inequalities that the movie reveals to be the real source of the problem. As we've seen, this aligns with mainstream Hollywood movies that favor individual achievement over collective or systemic action. In *The Blind Side*, no matter how much it portrays a legacy of racism and socioeconomic disadvantage as reasons limiting Michael Oher's opportunities, these systemic conditions merely provide a backdrop for this American success tale, one laced with religious sentiment.

Overarching Viewpoint

The Blind Side's directorial viewpoint displays a genuineness in representing the outlook of Leigh Anne and Sean Tuohy as conservative evangelical Christians. "We'd like to take the credit. But there's no way we can," Sean Tuohy said in an interview about Oher's extraordinary success. Adopting Michael "just let him become who he was supposed to be. We really believe that Michael was sent to us—by God."[75] From this angle, the study of race and white evangelical cultural engagement by Emerson and Smith offers an interesting and insightful way of thinking about the movie's narrational outlook. Using the metaphor of a cultural "tool kit," these sociologists show how three core values influence the way white evangelicals approach the problem of race relations in America: accountable freewill individualism, relationalism, and antistructuralism. These beliefs and assumptions hang together by stressing individual responsibility. Making the right personal choices and having strong relationships like family, friends, and church community are enough for anyone to succeed, independent of social structures and institutions. This view, however, skews evangelicals' understanding of racial dynamics, Emerson and Smith argue, by limiting "their ability either to recognize institutional problems or to acknowledge them as important."[76] This evangelical mindset is consistent in many ways with the American individualist culture that, as we've seen, is the dominant view in mainstream Hollywood cinema.

Two key scenes explicitly express this viewpoint. During lunch with her snooty and prejudiced girlfriends, Leigh Anne mentions Alabama Street and Hurt Village "on the other side of town." Beth's patronizing remark—"I'm actually from there, but didn't mind hard work and look where I am now"—implies that others have only themselves to blame for their failure. The story reinforces this perspective with characterizations that fit recognizable stereotypes: Hurt Village gangster Alton, Michael's crack-addicted mother, and especially his friend David.

The film's final scene serves as a dramatic bookend recalling the prologue. We hear Leigh Anne's voice-over again over shots now of newspaper accounts of young men killed by gang violence in the housing projects. One of them is Michael's friend David, who hung out with Alton, and whose unfortunate and premature death serves to mark Michael's life as exceptional. "That could have been anyone. It could have been my son, Michael," Leigh Anne realizes. "But it wasn't. And I suppose I have God to thank for that. God and Lawrence Taylor." What's left unsaid, having already been demonstrated in the narrative, is that Michael made different choices and had a personal relationship with the Tuohys, without whose aid he might well have suffered the same fate as David. Leigh Anne's internal monologue echoes and answers John Lee Hancock's pivotal question: "How did the stars align so brightly around this one kid from the projects?"

While racial color blindness might emphasize our shared humanity, the idea puts the onus on the individual to succeed regardless of race or other factors. Seeing things this way can make it hard for whites to recognize—or admit, perhaps—the benefits, advantages, and power incurred simply because of their skin color. It allows people, however well meaning, to overlook racially biased patterns of segregation and practices that oppress and disadvantage racial minorities in jobs, housing, education, health care, and voting. "Moving away from colorblindness can actually serve as a pathway towards antiracism," sociologist Adia Harvey Wingfield explains. She highlights studies showing that "as whites came to understand themselves as members of a racial group which enjoyed unearned privileges and benefits, this compelled them to forge a different sense of white identity built on antiracism rather than simply supporting the status quo."[77]

A key line of critique of American individualist culture throughout this book has been the realization that social arrangements deeply shape people's lives. As we considered earlier, Christian faithfulness has as much to do with social, cultural, and institutional practices as with personal life. The Bible confronts us with a more complex understanding of class than the popular beliefs of the American individualist culture might allow. Poverty might result from laziness (Prov. 10:4) or from unfairness: "An unplowed field produces food for the poor, but injustice sweeps it away" (Prov. 13:23). And those who oppress the poor show contempt for God (Prov. 14:31). Whether rich or poor, everyone is accountable to God; neither poverty nor wealth necessarily results in virtue or vice. As a former colleague and political theorist Simona Goi succinctly puts it, "If some people fall in poverty because they are irresponsible, lazy, untrustworthy, self-indulgent, promiscuous, and given to theft and deception, it is also the case that people can become or stay wealthy because they are greedy, selfish, arrogant, deceitful, uncompassionate, and blind to the suffering of others."[78] To be fair, *The Blind Side* is not really interested in these sorts of dynamics, however much the story's theme, characterizations, and drama depend on them. The story is nonetheless moving and inspiring even as it affirms an individualistic solution to the problems of racism that are deeply embedded in the fabric of American life and society.

This is par for the course in mainstream Hollywood cinema, which thrives on stories about "beating the odds" that express the mythic ideals of an individualist culture. As we've seen, the tendency of countless American movies is to affirm the status quo and conceal whatever contradictions might exist in American life and society. At some point, however, this plethora of films ought to make us wonder more about the real-life majority whose statistical presence makes the heroic rise from rags to riches so exceptional. In a country that prides itself on being the land of opportunity, you would think a measure of greatness would be the extent to which all its citizens have equal access to opportunities and can become who they are "supposed to be."

Epilogue

The original *Shrek* (2001) has a humorous bit of dialogue with Shrek, who feels that everyone wrongly prejudges him, trying to explain to Donkey that ogres are more emotionally complex than people think. He uses a metaphor, comparing ogres to onions. Donkey doesn't get it. Is that because they stink? Make you cry? "No," Shrek yells in frustration. "Layers. Onions have layers. Ogres have layers. We both have layers." Donkey persists without realizing he's only affirming the very misperception Shrek detests. If it's about layers, he suggests that parfait would make a better analogy since people like it more than onions: "Parfaits may be the most delicious thing on the whole damn planet!"

Choose your metaphor—ogres, onions, parfait—or come up with your own. Film viewing has layers. Movies fulfill a legitimate human need for pleasure, entertainment, and contemplation, and can be enjoyed in many ways and appreciated at different levels.

A well-crafted film has a compelling story and believable characters. It lends us some insight into ourselves, others, and the world, and perhaps even conveys something of the mystery of life. These movies are worthwhile viewing—regardless of your viewpoint on the subject. Ann Hornaday writes, "Anything that seeks to honor or nourish or at least acknowledge our fumbling, feeble, quietly heroic attempts to help get each other through the heartbreak and suffering of life will always earn at least a nod of gratitude from me."[1]

As stated in the preface, the aim of this book is to heighten our enjoyment and aesthetic appreciation of movies with a deeper understanding of the ways they express meaning and, in doing so, communicate life perspectives. In addition, illustrations enhance awareness of the way mainstream Hollywood movies convey dominant beliefs and values. Just as important is being able to tease out differences, whether explicit or subtle, between "movies Christians think are Christian" and those that resonate with a biblical outlook and so deepen our awareness of the ways that humans bear God's image and flourish through acts of love, forgiveness, and generosity. Does this approach open up possibilities for the production and criticism of movies? Does it serve as a workable approach and achieve worthwhile results? That is my aim and hope.

Notes

Chapter 1: Why a Christian Approach?

1. Allen Barra, "The Best Baseball Movie Ever? *Bull Durham*," *Atlantic*, June 25, 2013, http://www.theatlantic.com/entertainment/archive/2013/06/the-best-baseball-movie-ever-i-bull-durham-i/277191.

2. Brooks Barnes, "Hollywood's Summer of Extremes: Megahits, Superflops and Little Else," *New York Times*, September 4, 2016, http://www.nytimes.com/2016/09/05/business/media/hollywoods-summer-of-extremes-megahits-superflops-and-little-else.html.

3. Scott Bowles, "Hollywood Turns to Divine Inspiration," *USA Today*, April 14, 2006, http://usatoday30.usatoday.com/life/movies/news/2006-04-13-religion-based-movies_x.htm.

4. Richard Corliss, "The Gospel according to Spider-Man," *Time*, August 9, 2004, http://content.time.com/time/magazine/article/0,9171,678640,00.html. Jonathan Bock of Grace Hill Media is the Christian promoter quoted. Corliss dubbed the phenomenon "the gospel of cinevangelism."

5. Joseph Helfgot, quoted in Sharon Waxman, "The Passion of the Marketers," *New York Times*, July 18, 2005, http://www.nytimes.com/2005/07/18/business/media/the-passion-of-the-marketers.html.

6. Barna Group, "Superheroes, Presidents, a Girl on Fire," *Barna*, Research Releases in Culture & Media, April 10, 2013, https://www.barna.com/research/superheroes-presidents-a-girl-on-fire; Barna Group, "Birdman vs. Mockingjay: The Movies Americans Watched in 2014," *Barna*, Research Releases in Culture & Media, February 25, 2015, https://www.barna.org/barna-update/culture/710-birdman-vs-mockingjay-the-movies-americans-watched-in-2014; Barna Group, "La La Land to Living Rooms: A Year in Movies," *Barna*, Research Releases in Culture & Media, February 21, 2017, https://www.barna.com/research/la-la-land-living-rooms-year-movies.

7. Barna Group, "Superheroes, Presidents, a Girl on Fire."

8. David G. Myers, *The American Paradox: Spiritual Hunger in an Age of Plenty* (New Haven: Yale University Press, 2000), 206.

9. Quoted in Steve Erickson, "Interview with Manohla Dargis," *Sense of the Cinema*, December 2002, http://sensesofcinema.com/2002/feature-articles/dargis. For most moviegoers, perhaps, a summary of story, themes, and overall valuation is generally enough to give them a sense of whether seeing a film is worth their time. But for those interested in extended analysis, there is no shortage of commentators, Dargis included, who talk about movies in terms of design, themes, cinematic tradition, and cultural and historical contexts.

10. Manohla Dargis, "Review: 'Dunkirk' Is a Tour de Force War Movie, Both Sweeping and Intimate," *New York Times*, July 20, 2017, https://www.nytimes.com/2017/07/20/movies/dunkirk-review-christopher-nolan.html.

11. Quoted in Jesse Carey, "Horror's Most Influential Filmmaker Is a Committed Christian," *Relevant*, November 13, 2015, https://relevantmagazine.com/culture/horrors-most-influential-filmmaker-committed-christian. Derrickson calls horror "the genre of non-denial. I like the fact that it's a genre about confronting evil, confronting what's frightening in the world." Quoted in Steven D. Greydanus, "Interview: Filmmaker Scott Derrickson on Horror, Faith, Chesterton and His New Movie," *National Catholic Register*, July 1, 2014, http://www.ncregister.com/daily-news/interview-scott-derrickson.

12. The way we find our "direction both within and by way of culture" is what philosopher Lambert Zuidervaart calls a *cultural orientation*. Lambert Zuidervaart, *Artistic Truth: Aesthetics, Discourse, and Imagination Disclosure* (Cambridge: Cambridge University Press, 2004), 66.

13. Jeremy Douglass, "Command Lines: Aesthetics and Technique in Interactive Fiction and New Media" (PhD diss., University of California Santa Barbara, 2007), 284–85.

14. Roger Ebert, "Groundhog Day," *RogerEbert.com*, January 30, 2005, https://www.rogerebert.com/reviews/great-movie-groundhog-day-1993.

15. Alex Kuczynski, "Groundhog Almighty," *New York Times*, December 7, 2003, http://www.nytimes.com/2003/12/07/style/groundhog-almighty.html.

16. "Librarian of Congress Adds Home Movie, Silent Films and Hollywood Classics to Film Preservation List," *Library of Congress*, December 27, 2006, http://www.loc.gov/today/pr/2006/06-234.html.

17. James Parker, "Reliving *Groundhog Day*," *Atlantic*, March 2013, http://www.theatlantic.com/magazine/archive/2013/03/reliving-groundhog-day/309223.

18. Andrew Buncombe, "Groundhog Day: The Greatest Story Ever Told?," *Independent*, February 2, 2016, originally published February 2, 2004, http://www.independent.co.uk/arts-entertainment/films/features/the-greatest-story-ever-told-67132.html.

19. Michael P. Foley, "Phil's Shadow," *Touchstone*, April 2004, quoted in Jonah Goldberg, "A Movie for All Time," *National Review*, February 2, 2006, http://www.nationalreview.com/article/216686/movie-all-time-jonah-goldberg.

20. Charlene King, quoted in Kuczynski, "Groundhog Almighty."

21. "I Am Danny Rubin, and I Wrote the Movie 'Groundhog Day,'" post on Reddit.com, March 4, 2012, https://www.reddit.com/r/IAmA/comments/qhkyh/i_am_danny_rubin_and_i_wrote_the_movie_groundhog.

22. Quoted in Buncombe, "Groundhog Day."

23. Quoted in Mike Sacks, "In the Beginning: 'Year One' Writer-Director Harold Ramis Looks Back on His Early Days," *Tablet*, June 19, 2009, http://www.tabletmag.com/jewish-arts-and-culture/6796/before-%E2%80%98year-one%E2%80%99.

Chapter 2: Culture Communicates

1. Cindy Sher, "The Oscars: What Makes a Film 'Jewish?,'" *Charisma News*, February 23, 2015, http://www.charismanews.com/opinion/standing-with-israel/48418-the-oscars-what-makes-a-film-jewish-academy.

2. Maxine Springer, "What Makes a Film Jewish?," *Moment Magazine*, October 27, 2011, http://www.momentmag.com/great-jewish-films.

3. William Park, "The 50 Best Catholic Movies of All Time," *Crisis*, November 1997, 82–91, http://www.catholicculture.org/culture/library/view.cfm?recnum=395.

4. Dave Christiano, quoted in "About Us," *ChristianFilms.com*, http://christianfilms.com/about-us.php.

5. See Richard John Neuhaus, "Living between the Now and the Not Yet," *First Things*, August 8, 2008, https://www.firstthings.com/web-exclusives/2008/08/living-between-the-now-and-the.

6. Terry Eagleton, *The Idea of Culture* (Oxford: Blackwell, 2000), 2.

7. James K. A. Smith, "Editorial: We Believe in Institutions," *Comment*, Fall 2013, https://www.cardus.ca/comment/article/4039/editorial-we-believe-in-institutions.

8. George Lakoff and Mark Johnson, *Metaphors We Live By* (Chicago: University of Chicago Press, 1980), 57.

9. See Clifford Geertz, *The Interpretation of Cultures* (New York: Basic Books, 1973), 89.

10. Lakoff and Johnson, *Metaphors We Live By*, 196.

11. Robert McKee, *Story: Substance, Structure, Style, and the Principles of Screenwriting* (New York: Itbooks, 1997), 25 (emphasis original).

12. McKee, *Story*, 110–11.

13. I am drawing on philosopher Calvin Seerveld's crisp description of perspective as "the simply lived-out, expressed, or carefully articulated hanging-togetherness of a sane person's thought, word, and deed." Calvin Seerveld, "What Makes a College Christian?," in *In the Fields of the Lord: A Seerveld Reader*, ed. Craig Bartholomew (Toronto: Toronto Tuppence Press; Carlisle, UK: Piquant, 2000), 122.

14. Jennifer Van Sijll, *Cinematic Storytelling: The 100 Most Powerful Film Conventions Every Filmmaker Must Know* (Studio City, CA: Michael Wiese Productions, 2005), x.

15. Richard Allen Greene, "Religious Belief Is Human Nature, Huge New Study Claims," *CNN Belief Blog*, May 12, 2011, http://religion.blogs.cnn.com/2011/05/12/religious-belief-is-human-nature-huge-new-study-claims. The Cognition, Religion and Theology Project is a three-year study based at the University of Oxford.

16. Paul Tillich, *Theology of Culture* (New York: Oxford University Press, 1959), 8. Tillich's other famous maxim, "religion is the substance of culture, culture is the form of religion," stresses the inseparability of religion and culture (42).

17. Calvin Seerveld, *A Christian Critique of Art and Literature*, rev. ed. (Sioux Center, IA: Dordt College Press, 1995), 21.

18. Bono, "Psalm Like It Hot," *Guardian*, October 30, 1999, http://www.theguardian.com/theobserver/1999/oct/31/featuresreview.review2.

19. S. Brent Plate does something similar, arguing that "religion and film are *like* each other, and that their similarities exist on a formal level." See *Religion and Film: Cinema and the Re-Creation of the World* (London: Wallflower, 2008), vii.

20. McKee, *Story*, 113.

21. Theologians distinguish "common grace" from "saving" or "special" grace, which has to do with personal salvation: "For it is by grace you have been saved, through faith—and this is not from yourselves, it is the gift of God—not by works, so that no one can boast" (Eph. 2:8–9).

22. A. O. Scott, *Better Living through Criticism: How to Think about Art, Pleasure, Beauty, and Truth* (New York: Penguin, 2016), 8–9.

23. See George Gerbner, Larry Gross, Michael Morgan, and Nancy Signorielli, "Growing Up with Television: The Cultivation Perspective," in *Media Effects: Advances in Theory and Research*, ed. Jennings Bryant and Dolf Zillmann (Hillsdale, NJ: Lawrence Erlbaum, 1994), 17–41; Brandon S. Centerwall, "Television and Violence: The Scale of the Problem and Where to Go from Here," *Journal of the American Medical Association* 267, no. 22 (June 10, 1992): 3059–63.

24. Olan Farnall and Kim A. Smith, "Reactions to People with Disabilities: Personal Contact Versus Viewing of Specific Media Portrayals," *Journalism and Mass Communication Quarterly* 76, no. 4 (1999): 659–60.

25. Yuki Fujioka, "Television Portrayals and African-American Stereotypes: Examination of Television Effects When Direct Contact Is Lacking," *Journalism and Mass Communication Quarterly* 76, no. 1 (1999): 52–75.

26. Ken Fong, "Justin Chang," December 6, 2016, in *Asian America: The Ken Fong Podcast*, podcast audio, 1:54:11, http://asianamerica.libsyn.com/justin-chang.

27. Ann Hornaday, "Essay: Confessions of a Christian Film Critic," *Washington Post*, April 12, 2014, https://www.washingtonpost.com/lifestyle/style/essay-confessions-of-a-christian-film-critic/2014/04/10/0208f5b0-be6f-11e3-bcec-b71ee10e9bc3_story.html.

28. Ann Hornaday, "Sleek, Sophisticated and Thoughtful 'Arrival' Joins a Mini Golden Age of Sci-Fi Films," *Washington Post*, November 10, 2016, https://www.washingtonpost.com/goingoutguide/movies/sleek-sophisticated-and-thoughtful-arrival-joins-a-mini-golden-age-of-sci-fi-films/2016/11/09/d2d5b31c-a5c2-11e6-8fc0-7be8f848c492_story.html.

29. Quoted in Carolyn Giardina, "How 'Arrival's' Editor Handled a Movie 'Free of Narrative,'" *Hollywood Reporter*, December 18, 2016, http://www.hollywoodreporter.com/behind-screen/how-arrivals-editor-handled-a-movie-free-narrative-956219.

Chapter 3: Moviemaking Magic

1. Roger Ebert, "Hugo," *RogerEbert.com*, November 21, 2011, http://www.rogerebert.com/reviews/hugo-2011.

2. Philip French, "Hugo—Review," *Guardian*, December 3, 2011, https://www.theguardian.com/film/2011/dec/04/hugo-review-martin-scorsese-kingsley.

3. Rod Dreher, "What Was 'Star Wars' Like in 1977?," *American Conservative*, May 25, 2017, http://www.theamericanconservative.com/dreher/what-was-star-wars-like-in-1977.

4. Susan Sontag, "The Decay of Cinema," *New York Times on the Web*, February 25, 1996, https://www.nytimes.com/books/00/03/12/specials/sontag-cinema.html.

5. Samuel Taylor Coleridge, *Biographia Literaria: Or, Biographical Sketches of My Literary Life and Opinions* (New York: American Book Exchange, 1881), 442.

6. Anthony J. Ferri, *Willing Suspension of Disbelief: Poetic Faith in Film* (Lanham, MD: Lexington, 2007), xiii.

7. Thomas Elsaesser and Malte Hagener, *Film Theory: An Introduction through the Senses* (New York: Routledge, 2010), 37–38. See also Stanley Cavell, *The World Viewed: Reflections on the Ontology of Film* (New York: Viking, 1971).

8. Sam Adams, "Everything You Wanted to Know about 'Inception,'" *Salon*, July 19, 2010, http://www.salon.com/2010/07/19/inception_explainer.

9. Robert McKee, *Story: Substance, Structure, Style, and the Principles of Screenwriting* (New York: Itbooks, 1997), 111 (emphasis original).

10. Carl Plantinga, *Moving Viewers: American Film and the Spectator's Experience* (Berkeley: University of California Press, 2009), 72–73. Plantinga also considers four other types of emotions: global, local, fiction, and artifact (69).

11. Nöel Carroll, *Philosophy of Mass Art* (New York: Oxford, 1998), 309–10.

12. See Murray Smith, "Engaging Characters," in *The Philosophy of Film*, ed. Thomas E. Wartenberg and Angela Curran (London: Blackwell, 2005), 160–69.

13. Carroll, *Philosophy of Mass Art*, 340, 326.

14. John G. Cawelti, *Adventure, Mystery, and Romance: Formula Stories as Art and Popular Culture* (Chicago and London: University of Chicago Press, 1976), 27.

15. J. R. R. Tolkien, *Tree and Leaf* (Boston: Houghton Mifflin, 1964), 36–37.

16. Robert Scholes, James Phelan, and Robert Kellogg, *The Nature of Narrative*, 40th anniv. ed. (New York: Oxford, 2006), 82.

17. Philip K. Dick, quoted in Stephen Dalton, "Blade Runner: Anatomy of a Classic," British Film Institute, October 26, 2016, https://www.bfi.org.uk/news-opinion/news-bfi/features/blade-runner.

18. See "Blade Runner Riddle Solved," *BBC News*, July 9, 2000, http://news.bbc.co.uk/2/hi/entertainment/825641.stm.

19. Ted Greenwald, "Q&A: Ridley Scott Has Finally Created the Blade Runner He Always Imagined," *Wired*, September 26, 2007, http://www.wired.com/2007/09/ff-bladerunner.

20. Kevin Jagernauth, "Ridley Scott Explains Why Deckard Is a Replicant, Says 'Alien' Franchise Is Still Financially Viable," *Playlist*, October 17, 2017, https://theplaylist.net/ridley-scott-deckard-alien-20171017.

21. Michael Carlisle, "A Blood-Soaked Calculus and Cyanide Apples: *The Imitation Game*," *Tor.com*, December 1, 2014, http://www.tor.com/2014/12/01/the-imitation-game-film-review-benedict-cumberbatch-keira-knightley.

Chapter 4: Creating an Illusion of Reality

1. Lindsay Zoladz, "True Confessions of a Female Director," *Ringer*, February 16, 2017, https://theringer.com/amy-heckerling-fast-times-at-ridgemont-high-clueless-female-directors-ee9568144c24.

2. A. O. Scott, "A President Engaged in a Great Civil War," *New York Times*, November 8, 2012, http://www.nytimes.com/2012/11/09/movies/lincoln-by-steven-spielberg-stars-daniel-day-lewis.html.

3. Charles McGrath, "Abe Lincoln as You've Never Heard Him," *New York Times*, October 31, 2012, http://www.nytimes.com/2012/11/04/movies/daniel-day-lewis-on-playing-abraham-lincoln.html.

4. See Stephen Prince, *Movies and Meaning: An Introduction to Film*, 5th ed. (Boston: Allyn & Bacon, 2010), 41–46, here 45.

5. Ed Sikov, *Film Studies: An Introduction* (New York: Columbia University Press, 2010), 25.

6. Maya Deren, "Cinematography: The Creative Use of Reality," *Daedalus* 89, no. 1 (1960): 152, 159, 153, respectively.

7. Deren, "Cinematography," 156–57.

8. John Berger, *Ways of Seeing* (London: BBC and Penguin, 1972), 7.

9. Blain Brown, *Cinematography: Theory and Practice*, 2nd ed. (New York: Focal Press, 2012), 12, 15.

10. Todd McCarthy, "Review: 'The Da Vinci Code,'" *Variety*, May 16, 2006, http://variety.com/2006/film/awards/the-da-vinci-code-2-1200516217.

11. McCarthy, "Review."

12. Emily Rome, "How *Arrival* Turned Linguistics into One of the Most Gripping Dramas of the Year," *Gizmodo*, November 15, 2016, http://io9.gizmodo.com/how-arrival-turned-linguistics-into-one-of-the-most-gri-1789009881.

13. Marks calls this the "transformational arc," which is a way of disclosing how "a person [character] succeeds or fails to grow and change [arc] within the context of the conflict that is unfolding [plot] from the writer's point of view [theme]." Dara Marks, *Inside Story: The Power of the Transformational Arc* (Studio City, CA: Three Mountain Press, 2007), 29.

14. Rome, "How *Arrival* Turned Linguistics."

15. Quoted in Molly Creeden, "Dressing *The Hunger Games*: Costume Designer Judianna Makovsky," *Vogue*, March 19, 2012, http://www.vogue.com/873551/dressing-the-hunger-games-costume-designer-judianna-makovsky.

16. Brown, *Cinematography*, 14 (emphasis original).

17. David Bordwell, Kristin Thompson, and Jeff Smith, *Film Art: An Introduction*, 11th ed. (New York: McGraw-Hill Education, 2017), 52.

18. Quoted in Erin McCarthy, "Inside the New Harry Potter Movie's VFX Tech," *Popular Mechanics*, September 30, 2009, http://www.popularmechanics.com/technology/gadgets/a4370/4324866.

19. Paul Gaita, "Scene Dissection: 'Up' Director Pete Docter on the Film's Emotional Opening Montage," *Los Angeles Times*, February 25, 2010, http://articles.latimes.com/2010/feb/25/entertainment/la-etw-pete-docter25-2010feb25.

20. Quoted in Bill Desowitz, "Immersed in Movies: Cinematographer Emmanuel Lubezki Climbs 'The Tree of Life,'" *IndieWire*, February 10, 2012, http://www.indiewire.com

/2012/02/immersed-in-movies-cinematographer-emmanuel-lubezki-climbs-the-tree-of-life
-182992.

21. Peter Bradshaw, quoted in Ben Child, "You Review: Up," *Guardian*, October 12, 2009, https://www.theguardian.com/film/filmblog/2009/oct/12/you-review-up; Sukhdev Sandhu, "Up Review: 'A Very Special Gift,'" *Telegraph*, August 10, 2009, http://www.telegraph.co.uk/film /up/review.

22. Quoted in Gaita, "Scene Dissection."

23. Child, "You Review: Up."

24. Joseph Baxter, "Why Pixar Almost Cut the Best, Saddest Scene of Up," *Cinema Blend*, June 17, 2015, http://www.cinemablend.com/new/Why-Pixar-Almost-Cut-Best-Saddest-Scene -Up-72089.html.

25. Quoted in Gaita, "Scene Dissection."

26. McGrath, "Abe Lincoln as You've Never Heard Him."

27. Forrest Wickman, "Does Daniel Day-Lewis Sound Like Lincoln?," *Slate*, September 18, 2012, http://www.slate.com/blogs/browbeat/2012/09/18/lincoln_s_voice_was_it_as_whiny _as_daniel_day_lewis_s_in_the_lincoln_trailer_.html.

28. "Daniel Day-Lewis' 'Lincoln' Voice Historically Accurate?," *CBS News*, November 9, 2012, http://www.cbsnews.com/news/daniel-day-lewis-lincoln-voice-historically-accurate.

29. Bill Desowitz, "Immersed in Movies: Production Designer Rick Carter Goes Inside Out with 'Lincoln,'" *IndieWire*, December 10, 2012, http://blogs.indiewire.com/thompsononholly wood/immersed-in-movies-production-designer-rick-carter-goes-inside-out-with-lincoln. See also Diane Haithman, "Oscars: 'Lincoln' Production Design," *Deadline*, February 16, 2013, http://deadline.com/2013/02/oscars-lincoln-production-design-431982.

30. Quoted in Ann Oldenburg, "'Lincoln' Screenwriter Fires Back at Conn. Congressman," *USA Today*, February 8, 2013, http://www.usatoday.com/story/life/people/2013/02/08/lincoln -screenwriter-tony-kushner-defends-accuracy/1901351. Kushner's entire statement can be found in Melena Ryzik, "Mr. Spielberg, Connecticut Objects!," *New York Times*, February 7, 2013, http://carpetbagger.blogs.nytimes.com/2013/02/07/mr-spielberg-connecticut-objects.

31. Harold Holzer, "What's True and False in 'Lincoln' Movie," *Daily Beast*, November 22, 2012, http://www.thedailybeast.com/articles/2012/11/22/what-s-true-and-false-in-lincoln -movie.html.

32. Joshua Zeitz, "Fact-Checking 'Lincoln': Lincoln's Mostly Realistic; His Advisers Aren't," *Atlantic*, November 12, 2012, https://www.theatlantic.com/entertainment/archive/2012/11/fact -checking-lincoln-lincolns-mostly-realistic-his-advisers-arent/265073.

33. Quoted in Walter W. Woodward, "What 'Lincoln' Gets Right—and Wrong—about Connecticut," *Wall Street Journal*, February 11, 2013, http://blogs.wsj.com/speakeasy/2013/02/11 /what-lincoln-gets-right-and-wrong-about-connecticut.

34. Woodward, "What 'Lincoln' Gets Right—and Wrong."

35. Quoted in McGrath, "Abe Lincoln as You've Never Heard Him."

Chapter 5: Connecting the Dots

1. Peter Travers, "Natural Born Killers," *Rolling Stone*, August 26, 1994, http://www.rolling stone.com/movies/reviews/natural-born-killers-19940826.

2. Janet Maslin, "Film Festival Review: Pulp Fiction; Quentin Tarantino's Wild Ride on Life's Dangerous Road," *New York Times*, September 23, 1994, https://www.nytimes.com/1994/09/23 /movies/film-festival-review-pulp-fiction-quentin-tarantino-s-wild-ride-life-s-dangerous.html.

3. John D. Hagen Jr., Richard Alleva, and Frank McConnell, "It's Time to Take Sides: Catholicism, Yes; Popular Culture, No," *Commonweal*, September 22, 1995, 20.

4. Hagen, Alleva, and McConnell, "It's Time to Take Sides," 22–23.

5. Richard Barsam and Dave Monahan, *Looking at Movies: An Introduction to Film*, 5th ed. (New York: Norton, 2012), 36 (emphasis original).

6. Scott Tobias, "Pinning Down Kathryn Bigelow's Fascinating, Elusive Filmography," A. V. Club, January 17, 2013, http://www.avclub.com/article/pinning-down-kathryn-bigelows-fascinating-elusive--91227.

7. Kevin B. Lee, quoted in Melena Ryzik, "Staring in Awe? It's 'the Spielberg Face,'" Carpetbagger: The Awards Season Blog of The New York Times, December 19, 2011, http://carpetbagger.blogs.nytimes.com/2011/12/19/staring-in-awe-its-the-spielberg-face.

8. Roger Ebert, Scorsese by Ebert (Chicago: University of Chicago Press, 2008), 3.

9. See Tony Zhou, "David Fincher—And the Other Way Is Wrong," Vimeo, October 1, 2014, https://vimeo.com/107779620#at=4.

10. Sam Adams, "Everything You Wanted to Know about 'Inception,'" Salon, July 19, 2010, http://www.salon.com/2010/07/19/inception_explainer.

11. Quoted in Ashley Lee, "Christopher Nolan Talks 'Inception' Ending, Batman and 'Chasing Reality' in Princeton Grad Speech," Hollywood Reporter, June 1, 2015, http://www.hollywoodreporter.com/news/christopher-nolan-princeton-graduation-speech-799121.

12. Quoted in Bob Carlton, "Chadwick Boseman Says Playing Jackie Robinson in '42' Had Him 'Vibrating with Excitement' Every Day," AL.com, April 11, 2103, http://www.al.com/entertainment/index.ssf/2013/04/chadwick_boseman_says_playing.html.

13. Roger Copeland, "When Films 'Quote' Films, They Create a New Mythology," New York Times, September 25, 1977, http://www.nytimes.com/1977/09/25/archives/when-films-quote-films-they-create-a-new-mythology-when-films-quote.html.

14. George Lucas, A New Hope: Star Wars: Episode IV (New York: Random House, Del Rey Book, 1976), 118.

15. Stephen Prince, Movies and Meaning: An Introduction to Film, 5th ed. (Boston: Allyn & Bacon, 2010), 238.

16. Brooks Barnes, "Secular Hollywood Quietly Courts the Faithful," New York Times, December 24, 2016, http://www.nytimes.com/2016/12/24/business/media/hollywood-movies-christian-outreach.html.

17. See Zack Sharf, "'Star Wars: The Last Jedi' Divides Fans: An 'A' Cinemascore, and a Negative Rotten Tomatoes User Grade," IndieWire, December 16, 2017, http://www.indiewire.com/2017/12/star-wars-last-jedi-divides-fans-cinemascore-rotten-tomatoes-user-score-1201908384/; Angela Watercutter, "Star Wars: The Last Jedi Will Bother Some People. Good," Wired, December 15, 2017, https://www.wired.com/story/star-wars-last-jedi-inclusion.

18. John Coffey, "Engaging with Cinema," Cambridge Papers 8, no. 1 (March 1999): 3.

19. Roger Ebert, "Schindler's List," RogerEbert.com, December 15, 1993, https://www.rogerebert.com/reviews/schindlers-list-1993.

20. Les White, "Schindler's List: My Father Is a Schindler Jew," Jump Cut 39, June 1994, 4, https://www.ejumpcut.org/archive/onlinessays/JC39folder/schindlersList.html.

21. These categories, posited by cultural theorist Stuart Hall, are found in Robert Stam, Film Theory: An Introduction (Malden, MA: Blackwell, 2000), 230–31.

22. Jonathan Bock, quoted in Barnes, "Secular Hollywood Quietly Courts the Faithful."

23. Quoted in Naomi Pfefferman, "'The King's Speech' Cinematographer, Danny Cohen," Jewish Journal, February 24, 2011, http://jewishjournal.com/culture/arts/89508.

24. Mark Kermode, "Eye in the Sky Review—A Morality Tale of Modern Warfare," Guardian, April 17, 2016, https://www.theguardian.com/film/2016/apr/17/eye-in-the-sky-review-helen-mirren.

25. Ann Hornaday, "'Eye in the Sky' Is a 'Fail Safe' for the Drone Generation," Washington Post, March 17, 2016, https://www.washingtonpost.com/goingoutguide/movies/eye-in-the-sky-is-a-fail-safe-for-the-drone-generation/2016/03/17/16257aa6-ead1-11e5-a6f3-21ccdbc5f74e_story.html.

26. "Eye in the Sky," Rotten Tomatoes, accessed November 26, 2018, https://www.rottentomatoes.com/m/eye_in_the_sky.

27. James Berardinelli, "Eye in the Sky (United Kingdom, 2015)," *Reel Views*, March 25, 2016, http://www.reelviews.net/reelviews/eye-in-the-sky.

28. Stephen Holden, "Review: 'Eye in the Sky,' Drone Precision vs. Human Failings," *New York Times*, March 10, 2016, https://www.nytimes.com/2016/03/11/movies/review-eye-in-the-sky-drone-precision-vs-human-failings.html.

29. Hornaday, "'Eye in the Sky.'"

30. Hornaday, "'Eye in the Sky.'"

31. Rand Richards Cooper, "'Eye in the Sky': Grim Reaper, Reporting for Duty," *Commonweal*, April 28, 2016, https://www.commonwealmagazine.org/eye-sky.

32. Godfrey Cheshire, "Eye in the Sky," *RogerEbert.com*, March 11, 2016, http://www.rogerebert.com/reviews/eye-in-the-sky-2016.

33. Quoted in Kevin McFarland, "*Eye in the Sky* Is the Quintessential Modern War Film," *Wired*, April 1, 2016, https://www.wired.com/2016/04/eye-in-the-sky-modern-war-film.

34. Joe Leydon, "Toronto Film Review: 'Eye in the Sky,'" *Variety*, September 11, 2015, http://variety.com/2015/film/festivals/toronto-film-review-helen-mirren-in-eye-in-the-sky-1201591280.

35. David Sterritt, *The Films of Alfred Hitchcock* (Cambridge: Cambridge University Press, 1993), 20–21.

36. Sterritt, *Films of Alfred Hitchcock*, 19.

37. See David Bordwell, Kristin Thompson, and Jeff Smith, *Film Art: An Introduction*, 11th ed. (New York: McGraw-Hill Education, 2017), 61–62.

38. Robin Wood, *Hitchcock's Films Revisited*, rev. ed. (New York: Columbia University Press, 2002), 103.

39. Wood, *Hitchcock's Films Revisited*, 103.

40. Marilyn Fabe, *Closely Watched Films: An Introduction to the Art of Narrative Film Technique* (Berkeley: University of California Press, 2004), 135.

41. Quoted in Richard A. Blake, *Afterimage: The Indelible Catholic Imagination of Six American Filmmakers* (Chicago: Loyola Press, 2000), 49–50.

42. Blake, *Afterimage*, xiv, 11–12.

43. Sterritt, *Films of Alfred Hitchcock*, 1, 7.

44. Roger Ebert, "Rear Window," *RogerEbert.com*, February 20, 2000, http://www.rogerebert.com/reviews/great-movie-rear-window-1954.

45. Roger Ebert, "Rear Window," *RogerEbert.com*, October 7, 1983, http://www.rogerebert.com/reviews/rear-window-1954.

46. Wood, *Hitchcock's Films Revisited*, 100–101.

47. Blake, *Afterimage*, 74.

Chapter 6: Redemption American-Style

1. David Ansen, "Our Titanic Love Affair," *Newsweek*, February 23, 1998, 60. Previous Hollywood blockbusters like *Star Wars*, *Jurassic Park*, *Independence Day*, and *Raiders of the Lost Ark* were action films aimed at males.

2. David Sterritt, "*Titanic* Surfaces with Hefty Tab and Big Heart," *Christian Science Monitor*, December 19, 1997, 12A.

3. Todd McCarthy, "Titanic," *Variety*, November 2, 1997, http://variety.com/1997/film/reviews/titanic-5-1117339997 (emphasis added).

4. Film scholar Linda Williams uses "melodramatic mode" as "a more general aesthetic term that describes aspects of a wide range of media." She argues, "Melodrama can be viewed, then, not as a genre, an excess or an aberration, but as what most often typifies popular American narrative in literature, stage, film, and television when it seeks to engage with moral questions." Linda Williams, *Playing the Race Card: Melodramas of Black and White from Uncle Tom to O. J. Simpson* (Princeton: Princeton University Press, 2001), 313n7, 17, respectively.

5. Andrew Horn, "Ideology and the Melodramatic Vision: Popular Theatre in Black South Africa and Nineteenth-Century America," *English in Africa* 12, no. 1 (1985): 1. Horn shows that black South African theatrical plays depict "social ills of which everyone in the segregated black audiences are fully aware" but, as is characteristic of American melodrama, propose remedies that "concentrate upon pulling one's self up by one's own frayed bootstraps" (5).

6. Ben Singer, *Melodrama and Modernity: Early Sensational Cinema and Its Contexts* (New York: Columbia University Press, 2001), 136.

7. Singer proposes thinking of melodrama as a "cluster concept." A movie exhibiting a combination of any two or more of five basic features might be designated as melodrama: strong pathos, heightened emotionality, moral polarization, nonclassical narrative mechanics, and spectacular effects. Singer, *Melodrama and Modernity*, 7.

8. Stephen Holden, "Off to Save America with Cape and Mask," *New York Times*, October 28, 2005, http://movies2.nytimes.com/2005/10/28/movies/28zorr.html.

9. Williams, *Playing the Race Card*, 19, 25. Williams draws on Peter Brooks's influential *The Melodramatic Imagination: Balzac, James and the Mode of Excess* (New Haven: Yale University Press, 1995).

10. Singer, *Melodrama and Modernity*, 133. See also David Grimsted, "Melodrama as Echo of the Historically Voiceless," in *Anonymous Americans: Explorations in Nineteenth-Century Social History*, ed. Tamara K. Hareven (Englewood Cliffs, NJ: Prentice-Hall, 1971), 83.

11. Alan Trachtenberg, *The Incorporation of America: Culture and Society in the Gilded Age* (New York: Hill and Wang, 1982), 81. The phrase is used in reference to the "enormous role of luck" in nineteenth-century author Horatio Alger's influential young-adult, rags-to-riches novels.

12. George Barna, *Index of Leading Spiritual Indicators* (Dallas: Word, 1996), 80.

13. Bill McKibben, "The Christian Paradox: How a Faithful Nation Gets Jesus Wrong," *Harper's Magazine*, August 2005, 31.

14. George Gao, "How Do Americans Stand Out from the Rest of the World?," *Pew Research Center*, March 12, 2015, http://www.pewresearch.org/fact-tank/2015/03/12/how-do-americans -stand-out-from-the-rest-of-the-world.

15. Jeffrey D. Mason, *Melodrama and the Myth of America* (Bloomington: Indiana University Press, 1993), 12.

16. Grimsted, "Melodrama as Echo of the Historically Voiceless," 88–89.

17. Grimsted explains that the villain acts against feeling and is driven instead by "its opposite, passion, which, by melodramatic definition, meant amoral and antisocial feelings." Grimsted, "Melodrama as Echo of the Historically Voiceless," 88–89.

18. Carl Plantinga, *Moving Viewers: American Film and the Spectator's Experience* (Berkeley: University of California Press, 2009), 194.

19. Dara Marks, *Inside Story: The Power of the Transformational Arc* (Studio City, CA: Three Mountain Press, 2007), 3.

20. Eric Bentley, *The Life of the Drama* (New York: Atheneum, 1964), 216.

21. Quoted in Maureen Dowd, "Hollywood's Most Decent Fella on Weinstein, Trump and History," *New York Times*, October 11, 2017, https://www.nytimes.com/2017/10/11/style/tom -hanks-uncommon-type-harvey-weinstein-donald-trump.html.

22. Horn, "Ideology and the Melodramatic Vision," 1.

23. Quoted in Jon D. Witmer, "Force Perspective," *American Cinematographer* 97, no. 2 (February 2016): 76.

24. Joseph G. Kickasola, *The Films of Krzysztof Kieślowski* (New York: Continuum, 2004), 34.

25. See "Chance, Coincidence, Miracles, Pseudonyms, and God," *Quote Investigator*, April 20, 2015, https://quoteinvestigator.com/2015/04/20/coincidence.

26. Quoted in Pete Krämer, "Women First: Titanic, Action-Adventure Films, and Hollywood's Female Audience," in *Titanic: Anatomy of a Blockbuster*, ed. Kevin S. Sandler and Gaylyn Studlar (New Brunswick, NJ: Rutgers University Press, 1999), 116.

27. James Cameron, "Foreword," *James Cameron's Titanic* (New York: HarperPerennial, 1997), vi.

28. Quoted in Robert D. Ballard with Jean-Louis Michel, "How We Found Titanic," *National Geographic*, December 1985, 718.

29. Stanley Kauffmann, "TNR Film Classics: 'Titanic' (January 5 and 12, 1998)," *New Republic*, January 4, 1998, https://newrepublic.com/article/102445/tnr-film-classics-titanic-january-5-12-1998.

30. Janet Maslin, "Film Review: A Spectacle as Sweeping as the Sea," *New York Times*, December 19, 1997, https://www.nytimes.com/1997/12/19/movies/film-review-a-spectacle-as-sweeping-as-the-sea.html.

31. Laurie Ouellette, "Ship of Dreams: Cross-Class Romance and the Cultural Fantasy of *Titanic*," in Sandler and Studlar, *Titanic*, 183.

32. Ansen, "Our Titanic Love Affair," 62–63; David Ansen, "Rough Waters," *Newsweek*, December 14, 1997, http://www.newsweek.com/rough-waters-170336.

33. Ouellette, "Ship of Dreams," 169.

34. Quoted in Krämer, "Women First," 119.

35. Katha Pollitt, "Women and Children First," *Nation*, March 30, 1998, 9.

36. Adrienne Munich and Maura Spiegel, "Heart of the Ocean: Diamonds and Democratic Desire in *Titanic*," in Sandler and Studlar, *Titanic*, 166.

37. Ansen, "Rough Waters."

Chapter 7: The Yellow Brick Road to Self-Realization

1. Manohla Dargis and A. O. Scott, "One Nation under a Movie Theater? It's a Myth," *New York Times*, September 7, 2017, https://www.nytimes.com/2017/09/07/movies/movies-politics-conservatives-liberals.html.

2. George Gerbner, Larry Gross, Michael Morgan, and Nancy Signorielli, "Growing Up with Television: The Cultivation Perspective," in *Media Effects: Advances in Theory and Research*, ed. Jennings Bryant and Dolf Zillmann (Hillsdale, NJ: Lawrence Erlbaum, 1994), 25–28.

3. Andrew Higson, *Waving the Flag: Constructing a National Cinema in Britain* (Oxford: Clarendon, 1995), 6, 1, 4, respectively. Higson draws on Benedict Anderson, *Imagined Communities: Reflections on the Origin and Spread of Nationalism* (London: Verso, 1991). A set of basic American values includes equality, liberty, opportunity, democracy, individualism, competition, and materialism. See L. Robert Kohls, "The Values Americans Live By," April 1984, http://www1.cmc.edu/pages/faculty/alee/extra/American_values.html.

4. See David Bordwell, Janet Staiger, and Kristin Thompson, *The Classical Hollywood Cinema: Film Style and Mode of Production to 1960* (New York: Columbia University Press, 1985).

5. Gary Althen, *American Ways: A Guide for Foreigners in the United States* (Yarmouth, ME: Intercultural Press, 1988), 34.

6. Geoff King, *New Hollywood Cinema: An Introduction* (New York: Columbia University Press, 2002), 39. British film scholar Andrew Higson similarly observes, "The rhetoric of democracy and populism is built into the formal organization of the American film, with its classically strong and dynamic narrative drive towards individual achievement—although this also points to the limitations of the rhetoric, since problems and their resolutions are invariably articulated only in relation to the *individual* within a substantially unchanged capitalist patriarchy." Andrew Higson, "The Concept of National Cinema," in *European Cinema Reader*, ed. Catherine Fowler (New York: Routledge, 2002), 135 (emphasis original).

7. Dara Marks, *Inside Story: The Power of the Transformational Arc* (Studio City, CA: Three Mountain Press, 2007), 304 (emphasis original).

8. Quoted in Steve Chagollan, "One for All," *Variety* (Supplement), March 5–11, 2001, 4.

9. David G. Myers, *The American Paradox: Spiritual Hunger in an Age of Plenty* (New Haven: Yale University Press, 2000), 7.

10. Dargis and Scott, "One Nation under a Movie Theater?"

11. Dave Zirin, "A Review of '42': Jackie Robinson's Bitter Pill," *Nation*, April 17, 2013, http://www.thenation.com/article/review-42-jackie-robinsons-bitter-pill.

12. Zirin, "A Review of '42.'"

13. Quoted in "The Sounds, Space and Spirit of 'Selma': A Director's Take," *NPR: Fresh Air*, January 8, 2015, http://www.npr.org/2015/01/08/375756377/the-sounds-space-and-spirit -of-selma-a-director-s-take.

14. Ann Hornaday, "'Selma' Movie Review: Humanizing Rev. Martin Luther King Jr.," *Washington Post*, December 23, 2014, https://www.washingtonpost.com/goingoutguide/movies /selma-movie-review-humanizing-rev-martin-luther-king-jr/2014/12/23/eb2ec2e4-8aaa-11e4-a 085-34e9b9f09a58_story.html.

15. Odie Henderson, "Selma," *RogerEbert.com*, December 24, 2014, http://www.rogerebert .com/reviews/selma-2014.

16. Paul Krugman, "'The Big Short,' Housing Bubbles and Retold Lies," *New York Times*, December 18, 2015, http://www.nytimes.com/2015/12/18/opinion/the-big-short-housing-bubbles -and-retold-lies.html.

17. Jim Slotek, "'The Big Short' Review: Star-Studded Cast Makes Sense of the '08 Financial Crisis," *Toronto Sun*, December 23, 2015, http://www.torontosun.com/2015/12/23/the-big-short -review-star-studded-cast-makes-sense-of-the-08-financial-crisis.

18. "The Impact of the September 2008 Economic Collapse," *Pew Charitable Trusts*, April 28, 2010, http://www.pewtrusts.org/en/research-and-analysis/reports/2010/04/28/the-impact-of -the-september-2008-economic-collapse.

19. Jesse Eisinger, "The Rise of Corporate Impunity," *ProPublica*, April 30, 2014, https:// www.propublica.org/article/the-rise-of-corporate-impunity; Gretchen Morgenson and Louise Story, "In Financial Crisis, No Prosecutions of Top Figures," *New York Times*, April 14, 2011, http://www.nytimes.com/2011/04/14/business/14prosecute.html.

20. Robert Benne and Philip Hefner, *Defining America: A Christian Critique of the American Dream* (Philadelphia: Fortress, 1974), 8.

21. Ben Singer, *Melodrama and Modernity: Early Sensational Cinema and Its Contexts* (New York: Columbia University Press, 2001), 136–37.

22. Michael Ryan and Douglas Kellner, *Camera Politica: The Politics and Ideology of Contemporary Film* (Bloomington: Indiana University Press, 1988), 112.

23. Quoted in David Sterritt, "The Man Behind *Rocky*," *Christian Science Monitor*, January 13, 1977, 12. For a full treatment, see Daniel J. Leab, "The Blue Collar Ethnic in Bicentennial America: *Rocky*," in *American History/American Film: Interpreting the Hollywood Image*, ed. John E. O'Connor and Martin A. Jackson (New York: Unger, 1979), 257–72.

24. Joel W. Martin, "Redeeming America: *Rocky* as Ritual Racial Drama," in *Screening the Sacred: Religion, Myth, and Ideology in Popular American Film*, ed. Joel W. Martin and Conrad E. Ostwalt Jr. (Boulder, CO: Westview, 1995), 125–33.

25. Richard Brody, "'Creed' Is a Knockout," *New Yorker*, online edition, November 24, 2015, https://www.newyorker.com/culture/richard-brody/creed-is-a-knockout.

26. David Edelstein, "*Creed* Forges an Exciting New Path While Staying True to Its *Rocky* Lineage," *Vulture*, November 25, 2015, http://www.vulture.com/2015/11/review-creed-rocky .html.

27. The reference is to *Boyz N the Hood* (1991), but applies just as well here. Michael Eric Dyson, "Between Apocalypse and Redemption: John Singleton's 'Boyz N the Hood,'" *Cultural Critique* 21 (1992): 135–36. For a full analysis of *Do the Right Thing*, see Sharon Willis, "Do the Right Thing (1989), Spike Lee," *Film Analysis: A Norton Reader*, ed. Jeffrey Geiger and R. L. Rutsky (New York: Norton, 2005), 776–93.

28. The scene reworks a similar love/hate dichotomy speech by a murdering phony preacher who has "love" and "hate" tattooed on the fingers of each hand in *The Night of the Hunter*

(1954). See Lee Weston Sabo, "Radio Raheem Is a Broken Record: Lessons from *Do the Right Thing* on Its 25th Anniversary," *Bright Lights Film Journal*, December 12, 2014, http://bright lightsfilm.com/radio-raheem-is-a-broken-record-lessons-from-do-the-right-thing.

29. Quoted in Doctor RJ, "'Do the Right Thing' Is So Relevant Now, 25 Years On," *Daily Kos*, August 18, 2014, http://www.dailykos.com/story/2014/8/18/1322499/--Do-the-Right-Thing-is-so-relevant-now-25-years-on.

30. Roger Ebert, "Do the Right Thing," *RogerEbert.com*, June 30, 1989, http://www.roger ebert.com/reviews/do-the-right-thing-1989.

31. Sabo, "Radio Raheem Is a Broken Record."

32. Michael Eric Dyson, "Death in Black and White," *New York Times*, July 7, 2016, http://www.nytimes.com/2016/07/10/opinion/sunday/what-white-america-fails-to-see.html.

Chapter 8: A Man's Gotta Do What a Man's Gotta Do

1. Don D'Ammassa, introduction to *Encyclopedia of Adventure Fiction*, ed. Don D'Ammassa (New York: Facts On File, Infobase Publishing, 2009), vii.

2. Thomas Schatz, *Hollywood Genres: Formulas, Filmmaking, and the Studio System* (Philadelphia: Temple University Press, 1981), 46.

3. John Cawelti, *The Six-Gun Mystique* (Bowling Green, OH: BGSU Popular Press, 1970), 39.

4. Robert Jewett and John Shelton Lawrence, *The Myth of the American Superhero* (Grand Rapids: Eerdmans, 2002), 6. See Richard Slotkin, *Regeneration through Violence: The Mythology of the American Frontier, 1600–1860* (Middletown, CT: Wesleyan University Press, 1973).

5. Jewett and Lawrence, *Myth of the American Superhero*, 6–7.

6. Cawelti, *Six-Gun Mystique*, 39.

7. See Conrad E. Ostwalt Jr., "Hollywood and Armageddon: Apocalyptic Themes in Recent Cinematic Presentation," in *Screening the Sacred: Religion, Myth, and Ideology in Popular American Film*, ed. Joel W. Martin and Conrad E. Ostwalt Jr. (Boulder, CO: Westview, 1995), 55–63.

8. A. O. Scott, "Review: 'Wonder Woman' Is a Blockbuster That Lets Itself Have Fun," *New York Times*, May 31, 2017, https://www.nytimes.com/2017/05/31/movies/wonder-woman-review-gal-gadot.html.

9. A. O. Scott, "Superheroes, Super Battles, Super Egos," *New York Times*, May 3, 2012. See also Natalie Finn and Baker Machado, "*Avengers* Attack! *New York Times* Critic A. O. Scott Responds to Samuel L. Jackson's Fury over Review," *E News*, May 3, 2012, http://www.eon line.com/news/313695/avengers-attack-new-york-times-critic-a-o-scott-responds-to-samuel-l-jackson-s-fury-over-review.

10. Manohla Dargis and A. O. Scott, "One Nation under a Movie Theater? It's a Myth," *New York Times*, September 7, 2017, https://www.nytimes.com/2017/09/07/movies/movies-politics-conservatives-liberals.html. Dargis's remark is in direct reference to *Batman* (1989), which helped launch the superhero trend.

11. Andrew Romano, "Hollywood Declares 2014 the Year of the Bible," *Daily Beast*, January 19, 2014, http://www.thedailybeast.com/articles/2014/01/09/hollywood-declares-2014-the-year-of-the-bible.html.

12. "In Biblical Blockbuster, Aronofsky Rocks Noah's Boat," *NPR: All Things Considered*, March 29, 2014, http://www.npr.org/2014/03/29/295926640/in-biblical-blockbuster-aronofsky-rocks-noahs-boat.

13. Quotes taken from Philip Sherwell, "Noah Epic Awash in Flood of Controversy for Green Agenda and Taking Liberties with Bible," *Telegraph*, March 23, 2014, http://www.telegraph .co.uk/culture/film/film-news/10717724/Noah-epic-awash-in-flood-of-controversy-for-green-agenda-and-taking-liberties-with-Bible.html.

14. Tim Newcomb, "The Strange Battle over Darren Aronofsky's *Noah*," *Time*, October 17, 2013, http://entertainment.time.com/2013/10/17/the-strange-battle-over-darren-aronofskys-noah.

15. NRB president and CEO Jerry A. Johnson said his "intent in reaching out to Paramount with this request was to make sure everyone who sees this impactful film knows this is an imaginative interpretation of Scripture, and not literal." See "National Religious Broadcasters and Paramount Pictures Jointly Announce Explanatory Message for *Noah* Movie," *NRB*, February 27, 2014, http://nrb.org/news-room/press_center/national-religious-broadcasters -paramount-noah-disclaimer.

16. Quoted in Kim Masters, "Rough Seas on 'Noah': Darren Aronofsky Opens Up on the Biblical Battle to Woo Christians (and Everyone Else)," *Hollywood Reporter*, February 12, 2014, http://www.hollywoodreporter.com/news/rough-seas-noah-darren-aronofsky-679315.

17. Romano, "Hollywood Declares 2014 the Year of the Bible"; Claudia Puig, "'Son of God' Goes by the Book," *USA Today*, February 27, 2014, http://www.usatoday.com/story/life/ movies/2014/02/27/son-of-god-review/4990053.

18. Quoted in Erica Orden, "Hollywood's New Bible Stories," *Wall Street Journal*, September 27, 2012, http://online.wsj.com/article/SB10000872396390444180004578016711320291332.html.

19. Masters, "Rough Seas on 'Noah.'"

20. "In Biblical Blockbuster."

21. Masters, "Rough Seas on 'Noah.'"

22. Masters, "Rough Seas on 'Noah.'"

23. Matt Zoller Seitz, "Noah," *RogerEbert.com*, March 28, 2014, http://www.rogerebert .com/reviews/noah-2014.

24. Steven D. Greydanus, "The 'Noah' Movie Controversies: Questions and Answers," *National Catholic Register*, March 27, 2014, http://www.ncregister.com/daily-news/noah -controversy.

25. Since I'm making superhero connections, it's worth noting that Noah is orphaned as a child after witnessing his father's brutal and senseless murder by Tubal-Cain. The same happens to Bruce Wayne/Batman, who as a young boy sees his parents gunned down by a common criminal, Jack Napier, who becomes his future nemesis, the Joker. Coincidence? Who knows?

26. Quoted in Tyler Huckabee, "Noah's Co-Writer Explains the Film's Controversial Theology," *Relevant*, April 4, 2014, https://relevantmagazine.com/culture/noah%E2%80%99s-co-writer -explains-film%E2%80%99s-controversial-theology.

27. Richard Alleva, "Deluge and Delusion: Darren Aronofsky's 'Noah,'" *Commonweal*, April 19, 2014, https://www.commonwealmagazine.org/deluge-delusion.

28. Richard Corliss, "Review: Darren Aronofsky's *Noah* Movie: Better Than the Book," *Time*, March 27, 2014, http://time.com/38365/noah-movie-darren-aronofsky-russell-crowe.

29. Aronofsky, quoted in Sherwell, "Noah Epic Awash in Flood."

30. Adele Reinhartz, *Bible and Cinema: An Introduction* (New York: Routledge, 2013), 43.

31. Quotes taken from Sarah Pulliam Bailey, "Q&A: 'Noah' Director Darren Aronofsky on Justice vs. Mercy," *Christian Century*, March 25, 2014, https://www.christiancentury.org/article /2014-03/qa-noah-director-darren-aronofsky-justice-vs-mercy; "In Biblical Blockbuster."

32. Justin Chang, "Why 'Noah' Is the Biblical Epic That Christians Deserve," *Variety*, March 31, 2014, http://variety.com/2014/film/news/noah-is-the-biblical-epic-that-christians -deserve-1201150333.

Chapter 9: Stop Taking My Hand!

1. Alex Abad-Santos, "Review: Wonder Woman Is a Gorgeous, Joyful Triumph of a Superhero Film," *Vox*, June 2, 2017, https://www.vox.com/culture/2017/5/30/15709572/wonder -woman-review-gadot; Rob Moran, "Wonder Woman Breaks 'Superhero Glass Ceiling' with Record $300 Million Opening," *Sydney Morning Herald*, June 5, 2017, http://www.smh.com .au/entertainment/movies/wonder-woman-breaks-superhero-glass-ceiling-with-record-300 -million-opening-20170604-gwkd2b.html.

2. Justin Chang, "The Stirring 'Wonder Woman' Comes to the Rescue of the DC Comics Universe," *Los Angeles Times*, May 31, 2017, http://www.latimes.com/entertainment/movies/la-et-mn-wonder-woman-review-20170531-story.html.

3. Chang, "The Stirring 'Wonder Woman.'"

4. Alex Abad-Santos, "Wonder Woman's 'No Man's Land' Scene Was the Best Superhero Moment of 2017," *Vox*, December 15, 2017, https://www.vox.com/2017-in-review/2017/12/15/16767902/wonder-womans-no-mans-land-scene.

5. Meredith Woerner, "Why I Cried through the Fight Scenes in 'Wonder Woman,'" *Los Angeles Times*, June 5, 2017, http://www.latimes.com/entertainment/herocomplex/la-et-hc-wonder-woman-crying-20170605-htmlstory.html.

6. Angelica Jade Bastien, "Wonder Woman," *RogerEbert.com*, June 2, 2017, https://www.rogerebert.com/reviews/wonder-woman-2017.

7. Abad-Santos, "Review: Wonder Woman Is a Gorgeous, Joyful Triumph."

8. Robin Wood, "Ideology, Genre and Auteur," *Film Comment* 13, no. 1 (January–February 1977): 47.

9. Wood, "Ideology, Genre and Auteur."

10. Stephen Holden, "From the Heat of Royal Passion, Poof! It's Permafrost," *New York Times*, November 26, 2013, http://www.nytimes.com/2013/11/27/movies/disneys-frozen-a-makeover-of-the-snow-queen.html.

11. Jackson Cuidon, "Star Wars: The Force Awakens," *Christianity Today*, December 16, 2015, http://www.christianitytoday.com/ct/2015/december-web-only/star-wars-force-awakens.html.

12. Kenneth Turan, "Review: 'The Hunger Games' a Winning Story of Sacrifice and Survival," *Los Angeles Times*, March 21, 2012, http://articles.latimes.com/2012/mar/21/entertainment/la-et-hunger-games-20120322.

13. Linda J. Cowgill, *Writing Short Films: Structure and Content for Screenwriters* (Los Angeles: Lone Eagle, 2005), 38–39.

14. Scholars describe Katniss as "a 'male-identified' female character." Ellyn Lem and Holly Hassel, "'Killer' Katniss and 'Lover Boy' Peeta: Suzanne Collins's Defiance of Gender-Genred Reading," in *Of Bread, Blood and "The Hunger Games": Critical Essays on the Suzanne Collins Trilogy*, ed. Mary F. Pharr and Leisa A. Clark (Jefferson, NC: McFarland, 2012), 118–27.

15. Jeffrey Overstreet, "Million Dollar Baby," *Christianity Today*, December 15, 2004, http://www.christianitytoday.com/ct/2004/decemberweb-only/milliondollarbaby.html.

16. Todd McCarthy, "Review: 'Million Dollar Baby,'" *Variety*, December 4, 2005, http://variety.com/2004/film/awards/million-dollar-baby-3-1200529218. Critics faulted the film's excessive, even "cartoonishly awful" depictions of supporting cast members. See Rob Mackie, "Million Dollar Baby," *Guardian*, June 30, 2005; Ann Hornaday, "'Million Dollar Baby': A One-Two Punch to the Emotions," *Washington Post*, January 7, 2005, http://www.washingtonpost.com/wp-dyn/articles/A55030-2005Jan6.html.

17. Roger Ebert, "Million Dollar Baby," *RogerEbert.com*, December 14, 2005, http://www.rogerebert.com/reviews/million-dollar-baby-2005.

18. Ebert, "Million Dollar Baby."

19. A. O. Scott, "3 People Seduced by the Bloody Allure of the Ring," *New York Times*, December 15, 2004, http://www.nytimes.com/2004/12/15/movies/3-people-seduced-by-the-bloody-allure-of-the-ring.html.

20. Katherine Frumin, "Million Dollar Baby," *Media Fix*, December 26, 2010, http://themediafix.com/blog/2010/12/26/million-dollar-baby. Frumin points out that this is a noticeable pattern in Stern's work with director Sam Mendes on *American Beauty* (1999) and *Road to Perdition* (2002) and Eastwood's *Mystic River* (2003).

21. Christopher Lyon, "Million Dollar Baby," *PluggedIn*, accessed April 5, 2018, http://www.pluggedin.com/movie-reviews/milliondollarbaby.

22. Roger Ebert, "Critics Have No Right to Play Spoiler," *RogerEbert.com*, January 29, 2005, http://www.rogerebert.com/rogers-journal/critics-have-no-right-to-play-spoiler.

23. Steven D. Greydanus, "Million Dollar Baby (2004)," *Decent Films: SDG Reviews*, accessed August 16, 2018, http://decentfilms.com/reviews/milliondollarbaby.

24. Peter T. Chattaway, "Million Dollar Baby and Unforgiven—Good or Bad, It Doesn't Matter," *Patheos*, March 16, 2005, http://www.patheos.com/blogs/filmchat/2005/03/million-dollar-baby-and-unforgiven-good-or-bad-it-doesnt-matter.html.

25. James Langton, "Disabled Groups Condemn Eastwood Euthanasia Film," *Telegraph*, January 23, 2005, http://www.telegraph.co.uk/news/1481835/Disabled-groups-condemn-Eastwood-euthanasia-film.html. Tim Gilmer, editor of *New Mobility*, the nation's foremost magazine on disability lifestyles, was concerned that the film might "perpetuate a harmful stereotype," but hoped the spirited debate might bring to light the truth that "people with serious disabilities usually embrace life." Quoted in Jeff Shannon, "Eastwood Film Draws Criticism and Support," *Seattle Times*, January 28, 2005, http://www.seattletimes.com/entertainment/eastwood-film-draws-criticism-and-support.

26. Quoted in Shannon, "Eastwood Film Draws Criticism and Support."

27. Sharon Waxman, "'Million Dollar' Storm," *New York Times*, February 2, 2005, http://www.nytimes.com/2005/02/02/arts/million-dollar-storm.html.

28. Frumin, "Million Dollar Baby."

29. Ebert, "Critics Have No Right to Play Spoiler."

30. Ebert, "Critics Have No Right to Play Spoiler."

31. Quoted in Chris Lee, "'Baby' Plot Twist Angers Activists," *Los Angeles Times*, January 27, 2005, http://articles.latimes.com/2005/jan/27/news/wk-mdb27.

32. Lennard J. Davis, "Why 'Million Dollar Baby' Infuriates the Disabled," *Chicago Tribune*, February 2, 2005, http://articles.chicagotribune.com/2005-02-02/features/0502020017_1_mission-ranch-inn-disability-film. For more on *Million Dollar Baby* and filmic depictions of individuals with disabilities, see Rhonda S. Black and Lori Pretes, "Victims and Victors: Representation of Physical Disability on the Silver Screen," *Research and Practice for Persons with Severe Disabilities* 32, no. 1 (2007): 66–83. Studies suggest that media depictions are more likely to influence viewers who have had little or no direct contact with people with disabilities. Olan Farnall and Kim A. Smith, "Reactions to People with Disabilities: Personal Contact Versus Viewing of Specific Media Portrayals," *Journalism and Mass Communication Quarterly* 76, no. 4 (1999): 659–73.

33. Overstreet, "Million Dollar Baby."

34. David DiCerto, quoted in Shannon, "Eastwood Film Draws Criticism and Support."

35. Jeff Shannon, "Frankie, Maggie and Me: Inside the Million Dollar Maelstrom," *New Mobility*, April 1, 2005, http://www.newmobility.com/2005/04/million-dollar-maelstrom.

36. High on the list are MGM musicals like *An American in Paris* and *Singin' in the Rain* and French filmmaker Jacques Demy's *The Umbrellas of Cherbourg* and *The Young Girls of Rochefort*.

37. Syd Field, *The Screenwriter's Workbook*, rev. ed. (New York: Delta, 2006), 49.

38. Peter Bradshaw, "Why La La Land Should Win the Best Picture Oscar," *Guardian*, February 14, 2017, https://www.theguardian.com/film/2017/feb/14/la-la-land-best-picture-oscars-2017-emma-stone-ryan-gosling-damien-chazelle.

39. See David Sims, "*La La Land*'s Double-Edged Nostalgia," *Atlantic*, January 9, 2017, https://www.theatlantic.com/entertainment/archive/2017/01/la-la-lands-double-edged-nostalgia/512351.

40. Quoted in Clarisse Loughrey, "La La Land Interview: Damien Chazelle on the Death and Rebirth of the Screen Musical," *Independent*, January 11, 2017, http://www.independent.co.uk/arts-entertainment/films/features/damien-chazelle-interview-la-la-land-oscars-2017-ryan-gosling-emma-stone-a7522311.html.

41. Jennifer Vineyard, "Damien Chazelle Reveals the Movie That Influenced *La La Land*'s Ending," *Vulture*, January 5, 2017, http://www.vulture.com/2017/01/movie-that-inspired-la -la-lands-ending.html.

42. Bradshaw, "Why La La Land Should Win."

43. Quoted in Sandra Gonzalez, "'La La Land' Director on Love, Romance and That Ending," *CNN*, February 17, 2017, http://www.cnn.com/2017/02/05/entertainment/la-la-land-ending-damien-chazelle/index.html.

44. Owen Gleiberman, "A Second Look at 'La La Land': Why It's Not Just Good, but Great," *Variety*, January 1, 2017, http://variety.com/2017/film/columns/la-la-land-emma-stone -ryan-gosling-1201950715.

45. Quoted in Vineyard, "Damien Chazelle Reveals the Movie."

46. Quoted in Sims, "*La La Land*'s Double-Edged Nostalgia."

47. Quoted in Andrea Mandell, "Is 'La La Land's Ending Happy or Sad? We're Still Debating," *USA Today*, February 21, 2017, https://www.usatoday.com/story/life/movies/2017/02/21 /spoilers-la-la-land-dream-sequence-ending-meaning/98164730.

48. Vineyard, "Damien Chazelle Reveals the Movie."

49. Lexy Perez, "'La La Land' Producer, Director Defend Ending as an Alternative to the Hollywood Fairy Tale," *Hollywood Reporter*, February 23, 2017, https://www.hollywoodreporter .com/news/la-la-land-ending-meaning-explained-978105.

50. Sims, "*La La Land*'s Double-Edged Nostalgia."

51. Hunter Harris, "*La La Land*'s Ending Reveals the Movie's True Romance," *Vulture*, December 22, 2016, http://www.vulture.com/2016/12/la-la-land-ending-isnt-that-sad.html.

52. Michael Oher with Don Yaeger, *I Beat the Odds: From Homelessness to "The Blind Side" and Beyond* (New York: Gotham, 2011), xvi.

53. Michael Lewis, *The Blind Side: Evolution of a Game* (New York: Norton, 2006), 41.

54. J. R. Jones, "The Blind Side," *Chicago Reader*, February 19, 2010, http://www.chicago reader.com/chicago/the-blind-side/Film?oid=1007605.

55. Claudia Puig, "Strong Acting Can't Outrun Shallow Tale in 'The Blind Side,'" *USA Today*, November 11, 2009, http://usatoday30.usatoday.com/life/movies/reviews/2009-11-20 -blindside20_ST_N.htm.

56. Melissa Anderson, "Saintly White People Do the Saving in *The Blind Side*," *Village Voice*, November 17, 2009, http://www.villagevoice.com/film/saintly-white-people-do-the -saving-in-the-blind-side-6393795.

57. Brandon Fibbs, "The Blind Side," *Christianity Today*, November 20, 2009, http://www .christianitytoday.com/ct/2009/novemberweb-only/blindside.html. What follows in this Movie Musing is a movie analysis and not to be taken as a commentary on the lives of Michael Oher and the Tuohy family.

58. Quoted in Patrick Goldstein, "'Blind Side' Director John Lee Hancock Is Out of Movie Jail," *Los Angeles Times*, November 24, 2009, http://articles.latimes.com/2009/nov/24 /entertainment/la-et-bigpicture24-2009nov24.

59. Quoted in Michelle A. Vu, "Interview: 'The Blind Side' Director John Lee Hancock," *Christian Post*, March 19, 2010, http://www.christianpost.com/news/interview-the-blind-side -director-john-lee-hancock-44354.

60. Quoted in Megan Basham, "The Blinded Side," *World*, November 21, 2009, https:// world.wng.org/2009/11/the_blinded_side.

61. Quoted in Josh Levin, "The Other Blind Sides," *Slate*, October 14, 2010, http://www .slate.com/articles/sports/sports_nut/2010/10/the_other_blind_sides.single.html.

62. Quoted in Goldstein, "'Blind Side' Director."

63. Quoted in Michel Martin, "New Movie 'Blind Side' and the Great White Hope," *NPR: Tell Me More*, December 11, 2009, http://www.npr.org/templates/story/story.php?storyId=12 1335966.

64. Steven D. Greydanus, "The Blind Side (2009)," *Decent Films: SDG Reviews*, accessed August 16, 2018, http://decentfilms.com/reviews/blindside.

65. Martin, "New Movie 'Blind Side.'"

66. Oher, *I Beat the Odds*, 205–6, 150, respectively.

67. Thaddeus Russell, "Is Sandra Bullock's New Movie Racist?," *Daily Beast*, December 3, 2009, http://www.thedailybeast.com/articles/2009/12/03/the-return-of-the-black-saint.html.

68. Quoted in Goldstein, "'Blind Side' Director."

69. Michael O. Emerson and Christian Smith, *Divided by Faith: Evangelical Religion and the Problem of Race in America* (New York: Oxford University Press, 2000), 7, 9.

70. A. O. Scott, "Steamrolling over Life's Obstacles with Family as Cheerleaders," *New York Times*, November 19, 2009, http://www.nytimes.com/2009/11/20/movies/20blindside.html.

71. A. O. Scott, "Two Films, Two Routes from Poverty," *New York Times*, November 18, 2009, http://www.nytimes.com/2009/11/22/movies/22scott.html.

72. Oher, *I Beat the Odds*, xvii.

73. Quoted in Deirdre Donahue, "Ravens' Michael Oher Tells His Side in Memoir," *USA Today*, February 8, 2011, http://usatoday30.usatoday.com/life/books/news/2011-02-08-oher08 _CV_N.htm.

74. Peter Rainer, "'The Blind Side'—Movie Review," *Christian Science Monitor*, November 20, 2009, https://www.csmonitor.com/The-Culture/Movies/2009/1120/p17s06-almo.html.

75. Quoted in Donahue, "Ravens' Michael Oher Tells His Side."

76. Emerson and Smith, *Divided by Faith*, 76, 79–80.

77. Adia Harvey Wingfield, "Color-Blindness Is Counterproductive," *Atlantic*, September 13, 2015, http://www.theatlantic.com/politics/archive/2015/09/color-blindness-is-counter productive/405037.

78. Simona Goi, "Christian Politics: Between or Beyond Red and Blue?" *Perspectives: A Journal of Reformed Thought*, June/July 2005, 21.

Epilogue

1. Ann Hornaday, "Essay: Confessions of a Christian Film Critic," *Washington Post*, April 12, 2014, https://www.washingtonpost.com/lifestyle/style/essay-confessions-of-a-christian-film -critic/2014/04/10/0208f5b0-be6f-11e3-bcec-b71ee10e9bc3_story.html.

Film Index

General Index

action-adventure film, 10, 106, 137–47, 151–53,
   155, 158, 206n1
  epic moment, 69, 141–42, 151–52
  film patterns, 140–43
  hero/heroine, 38, 89, 143, 146, 148–50, 155,
   158, 161
aesthetics, 2, 6–8, 68, 76, 197
  aesthetic emotion, 36–37
  criteria for assessing art/film, x, 90–91, 170
  disinterested contemplation, 7
  framework of expectations, 8
  melodrama, 96–97, 116, 138, 206n4
afterimage, 92
Alleva, Richard (critic), 67–68, 151
American Film Institute's 100 Greatest Movies
  of All Time, 1, 87, 106
American
  American Dream, 106, 110–13, 126–31
  cinema, ix–x, 3, 10, 16, 25, 115–16, 122,
   157–58, 195
    dominant beliefs in, 9, 158, 193, 197
  culture, 19, 21, 96, 99, 115, 146
  individualism, 98–101, 103–6, 116–17, 208n3
   evangelical mindset and, 193–95
   movies and, 122–26, 128, 131, 139, 143–47,
    165, 183–84
   radical, 120–21
  monomyth, 141–43, 147. *See also* action-
   adventure film; westerns

mythology, 22, 73–74, 128, 130–32, 184
  rags-to-riches theme, 38, 73, 121, 128, 184,
   195, 207n11
society, 4
  and melodramatic vision, 99–101, 103–4
  racialized, 191, 195. *See also* race
  values, 103–4, 115–16, 168, 208n3
Ansen, David (critic), 96, 110, 113
Aronofsky, Darren (writer/director), 148–52
art, 20, 22–23, 48, 67–68
  as imagined reality, 34–36, 49–50
  and perspective, 10
  criteria for assessing, x, 90–91, 170

Barna survey, 5–6, 98–99
Bible, 16–17, 21, 24, 99, 194
  and *Noah*, 148–53, 211n15
biblical, 22, 24, 99, 102, 106
  blockbuster, 147–48, 150–53
  narrative, 76, 99
  perspective, 16, 21, 102–4, 198
Bond, James, 74, 100, 138, 140, 142–43, 158
Brown, Blain (cinematographer), 47, 50, 53, 60

Cameron, James (writer/director), 95–97, 107,
  109–10
Campbell, Joseph (author), 75
Carroll, Nöel (scholar), 38
Carter, Rick (production designer), 64, 105